Pinhole Photography

Second Edition

Pinhole Photography
Rediscovering a Historic Technique

Second Edition

Eric Renner

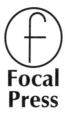

Focal Press

Boston   Oxford   Auckland   Johannesburg   Melbourne   New Delhi

Library of Congress Cataloging-in-Publication Data
Renner, Eric.
  Pinhole photography : rediscovering a historic technique / Eric
Renner. — 2nd ed.
     p.   cm.
  Includes bibliographical references and index.
  ISBN 0-240-80350-7 (alk. paper)
  1. Photography, Pinhole. I. Title.
TR268.R46   1999   99-25672
771—dc21   CIP

British Library Cataloguing-in-Publication Data
A catalogue record for this book is available from the British Library.

The publisher offers special discounts on bulk orders of this book.
For information, please contact:
Manager of Special Sales
Butterworth-Heinemann
225 Wildwood Avenue
Woburn, MA 01801-2041
Tel: 781-904-2500
Fax: 781-904-2620

For information on all Focal Press publications available, contact our
World Wide Web home page at: http://www.focalpress.com

10 9 8 7 6 5 4 3
Printed in the United States of America

In memory
of my parents
Josie and Richie Renner

*Another and more remarkable property of light is that when rays
come from different, or even opposite, directions each produces its
effect without disturbances from the other. Thus several observers are
able, all at the same time, to look at different objects through one
single opening, and two individuals can look into each other's eyes at
the same instant.*

CHRISTIAAN HUYGENS
Traite de la Lumière, 1690

and of my grandmother

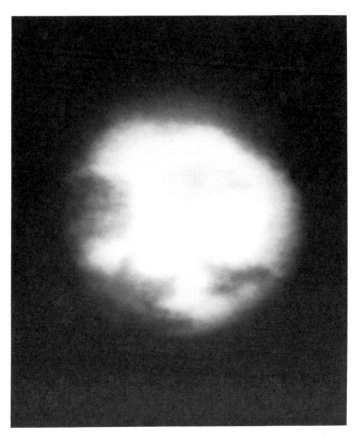

© *Eric Renner,* Grandma Becomes the Moon. *16" x 20" pinhole
photograph, 1976.*

Contents

Preface

The first edition of this book appeared in 1995. Its success was due in large part to the huge interest that has evolved in pinhole photography. In just a few years' time new material in both historic and contemporary terms and changed photographic techniques resulted in this updated edition. It baffles me that the pinhole aperture's contribution to the history of art and science has remained so unrecognized. That is the reason for this book.

Everything we see is composed of a myriad of light rays. Light rays are reflecting from everything in all possible directions. We cannot see the light rays individually, so what we see is a sophisticated, complete picture of all of them, at least the millions in front of our eyes. Any of these same millions of light rays, if they happen to be directed toward a pinhole, go into that pinhole to either be destroyed on entering or to produce a minuscule part of an image; in total, they produce a complete picture. In our eyes those same millions of light rays are focused on our retina and transformed into a complete, upright picture by our brain after traveling along our visual pathway.

The pinhole image we see as a photograph is different from a lens image in that everything being photographed, at any distance from the pinhole, whether it be one-quarter inch away or forty feet away, is in the same relative sharpness. Just try seeing something with your eye one-quarter inch away from it; it certainly will be blurry. It is not, however, if you are looking through a pinhole.

A pinhole's degree of sharpness is its identifying mark, its DNA so to speak; no amount of manipulation of a lens will give a pinhole image. A pinhole image is always less sharp than a focused lens-camera image.

Thirty-one years ago I started making pinhole photographs not knowing that anyone else in the world might also be doing the same thing. Nor did I know the pinhole was a *primary* instrument or a tool like a mirror or a wheel. The contents of this book explain the importance of pinhole in the history of art and science.

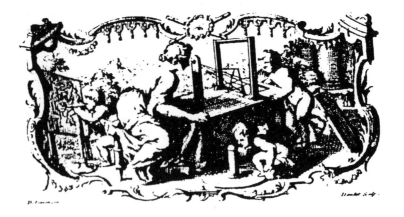

Figure P.1 *Etching on the title page of Isaac Newton's* Opticks, *1740 Latin edition. In the etching, the seated person is viewing through a pinhole in a pinhole perspective device.*

Brunelleschi, da Vinci, Dürer, Raphael, Kepler, Newton (Figure P.1), Descartes—all used the pinhole as the starting point for some of their theories.

After a few years of making pinhole photographs, I began meeting other people also using pinhole. One, Phil Pocock, head of the Canadian Parliament's Science Policy Committee, showed me his stop-action pinhole images (Figure P.2a) and camera (Figure P.2b)—invented and produced in one afternoon! His camera was a 35mm film canister with a piece of 35mm Tri-X film placed inside. A revolving second canister became the shutter. With a flick of his wrist, Pocock could make a nonblurred image of his daughter Joanna jumping from a chair. At that moment, amazed at his camera and photographs, I knew someone should be collecting this exceptional yet relatively obscure material.

In 1984, I founded Pinhole Resource, a nonprofit photographic archive. Within the first year of receiving photographs, I decided to publish *Pinhole Journal*. The first issue appeared in December 1985.

Through the existence of *Pinhole Journal*, more pinhole photographers around the world discovered Pinhole Resource. Since that first issue, almost three thousand photographs have been contributed to Pinhole Resource. It is an honor to open the mail and see images and enthusiastic letters, such as the following beautiful letter with literary allusions from Peeter Laurits of Estonia.

Figure P.2a *Philip Pocock,* Joanna Jumping, *1975, 8" x 10" pinhole photograph, from 35mm Tri-X film placed in an aluminum film container. From the collection of the photographer.*

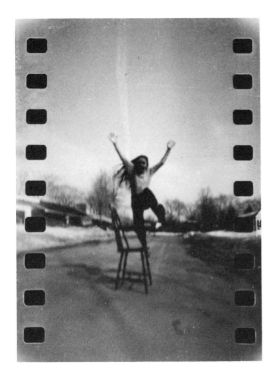

Tallinn, July 31, 1988

A photograph is always invisible; it is not it that we see.
ROLAND BARTHES

Usually, a photograph is considered a document, a miniature copy of "reality." To my mind, the photograph's relation to "reality" is strange. They look so much like a piece of the world our senses can grasp, but they have none of its qualities other than visibility. Flat, motionless objects without sound and smell form the world from their own similar dreams. They have mainly an associative bond, a loose rhyme with our "reality." As far as a photograph is invisible for us and we try to look through it at the objects and events depicted, we can never get quite close to that spectral world.

Taking pinhole pictures can draw us very near to the photograph's essence. The phantasmal quality of these images can be felt more easily. Anything can serve as a camera, anything can serve as a pinhole. If we took the pain to reflect, we would easily notice that the world around us is full of "pinhole cameras." At least symbolically, it is made up of them. Thus moth holes in a worn-out coat, tiny apertures in foliage. Keyholes are windows between different worlds: light and dark (remember the mirrors in Vonnegut's *Breakfast of Champions*). We live in a labyrinth of shadows and projections, between mirrors. Our every act and expression has a myriad of doubles and every one of them has a life of its own. The world looks like an enormous compound eye, looking at us, through us, over us. What is seen? Nobody knows that. Nobody has ever asked.

Quite an awkward way of getting the answer is to put sensitive sheets behind tiny holes. I have enjoyed myself in such a way for a whole week. I have made use of such everyday vessels as an old bag [Figure P.3a], a drawer and a candy box, trying not to move them from their usual places. As a result I have got a series of silver mummies of the ever-changing atmospheres and moods in my room [Figure P.3b]. On the seventh day I started to feel like an intruder. Our kingdom is not of these worlds. I felt dizzy thinking about these countless visions without the seer, this kaleidoscope of projections we live in, the visions of the visions of the visions. But the thing that struck me most was the realization that

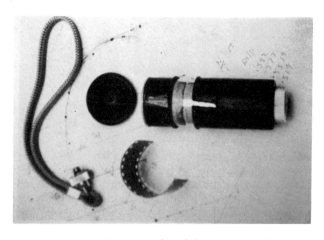

Figure P.2b *Philip Pocock*, Pinhole Stop-action Camera, *1975, lens photo from the collection of the photographer.*

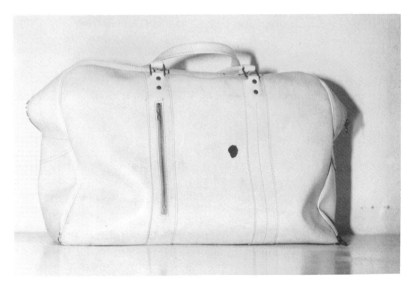

Figure P.3a © *Peeter Laurits*, Worn Out Bag Pinhole Camera, *1988. A lens photo from the collection at Pinhole Resource.*

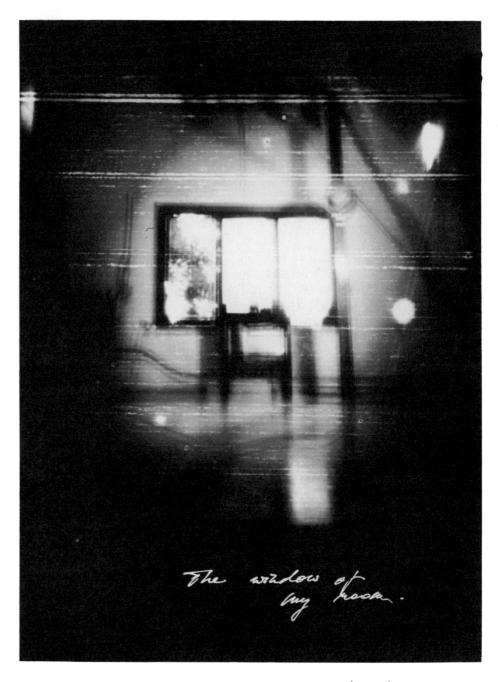

Figure P.3b © *Peeter Laurits,* Window of My Room, *1988. An $8\frac{1}{2}$" x $11\frac{1}{2}$" pinhole photograph made with a bag camera. From the collection at Pinhole Resource.*

every photographic image in itself is a pinhole pricked in time, a window between past and present, exposing our minds to the ghosts of lost moments, mixing memory and desire, breeding lilacs out of dead land, stirring dull roots with spring rain.

I must confess that I have not yet thrown away my camera and get paid as a photographer still. Do not mind the illiteracy of my letter, please, my clumsiness in linguistic thickets is in direct accordance with my awe of the labyrinth of light and time.[1]

Or consider this letter from Steven Pippin of London, England, describing his "archival" pinhole technique (conservators are going to love this):

25/9/91
London

The slides enclosed show a commercial washing machine (a Wasco-mat Senior) fitted with a push-on aluminum shutter device. This contains a leaf shutter mechanism, operated with a cable attachment, behind which is the pinhole. There is also a micro switch which operates the flash attachment. The exposure time was 30 minutes. The film used was Kodak Ektapan 4162, 11" x 14". After the exposure was complete, the developer was introduced into the machine via the soapsuds compartment and the machine was turned on. The machine's "warm wash" cycle was the closest to the film's normal developing temperature. On completion of the wash cycle the machine was left to make one rinse and then the fixer was added. The machine's final rinse made sure that the film was free of any chemicals and then spun dry the film. The resulting image (which is a contact print from the original) is very badly damaged. This is due to the machine's very vigorous wash action, and on some occasions it completely destroyed the image.[2]

Why pinhole? For everyone doing pinhole there is a slightly different answer. The variety in pinhole cameras and personal imagery is unlimited. Why not use a small matchbox, as Paul Cimon does for his 35mm exposures? Why not use five- to ten-minute exposures, as Sarah Van Keuren does to make portraits? Why not put Ilfochrome Classic color paper (designed to be used under an enlarger, not in outside light) right in the camera, as Willie Anne Wright does? Why not make images using the holes in saltine crackers as apertures, as Paolo Gioli does?

Why pinhole? Because pinhole is intuitive. Pinhole fits a certain kind of sensibility. A certain kind of feeling exists in every image, more or less. That feeling, I believe, relates directly to the very enigmatic piece of matter (or is it nonmatter?) known as a person's soul. Of course, this is an elusive demand to place upon every pinhole photograph and not something that anyone can obtain simply by using pinhole cameras, yet I do believe somehow this connection exists.

I think most people use a pinhole camera because the image is a more personal, direct, and obtainable link to a universal mental picture of the beyond. Time and living have never been particularly easy concepts for me to understand, yet constructing pinhole cameras and creating pinhole photographs somehow makes these concepts more accessible. I've always been excited to see just what my pinhole camera will do, with a certain amount of help from sources beyond my conscious faculties, for I never fully know what's going to be in the image—there's the surprise I look forward to! It seems I am somehow closer to my own person by allowing the image to be something over which I don't have full control.

NOTES

1. Peeter Laurits, "Letter to the Editor," *Pinhole Journal* 5(2):2. Literary allusions: "Lilacs out of the dead land," "stirring dull roots with spring rain," from T. S. Eliot's *The Waste Land*, 1922. "I must confess I have not thrown away . . . ," from Henry David Thoreau, *Walden*, 1854.
2. Steven Pippin, personal communication with the author, 25 September 1991.

Acknowledgments

There are probably two thousand artists working with pinhole throughout the world and an equal number of scientists using pinhole in high-energy studies. I am hesitant to try to list all of those artists and scientists who have generously shared their photographs for this book or who have also given images to Pinhole Resource, for I am sure to leave too many people unmentioned. The photographs and text in the following chapters name some of these people. Suffice it to say, a most sincere thanks to everyone who has contributed photographs and articles to Pinhole Resource. Their contributions have been the inspiration for this book.

A debt of gratitude goes to the following nine people. Sharing their work has been invaluable to Pinhole Resource and to this book. To the late Maurice Pirenne, who understood that the pinhole was a perspective imaging device used throughout the last six centuries in art; to Ken Connors, for his efforts to communicate scientific information about pinhole and zone plates; to Stan Page, who collected all of the published articles on pinhole (since 1850); to pinhole photographers Paolo Gioli, Dominique Stroobant, and Larry Bullis; to slit photographer Marnie Cardozo; and to Richard Vallon and Russ Young, who supplied much of the information in Chapter 6 on zone plates.

I would also like to sincerely thank Father Joseph Metzler of *Archivio Segreto Vaticano*, who led Nancy Spencer and me to see the pinhole in the Tower of Winds at the Vatican; Margaret Drower of England, who helped with the information on Flinders Petrie in Chapter 2; Jan-Erik Lundström of Sweden, who translated August Strindberg's writings on pinhole that appear in Chapter 2; Gary Urton, who supplied information on Kogi temple pinholes for Chapter 4 (Sheila Pinkel of Pomona College told me of these temples); James Hugunin of Chicago, who wrote passages on contemporary pinhole photographers in "Notes Toward a Stenopaesthetic," published by the Center for Contemporary Arts of Santa Fe in its

International Pinhole Photography Exhibition Catalogue (1989) and partially reprinted in Chapter 4; and Marie Lee, my editor at Focal Press.

Most of all, I thank Nancy Spencer for her immense help. Without Nancy, this book would not exist. She cowrote Chapter 5, "The How-to of Pinhole Photography." Nancy and I both direct Pinhole Resource and edit *Pinhole Journal.*

I have made extensive use of quotes and written material from artists and scientists who have used the pinhole. Quoting their own words seemed to be the most direct way to communicate their ideas.

Pinhole's History in Science

HOLED STONES

An aperture is an opening—a place of transformation, symbolically feminine. Many ancient cultures have similar emergence legends designating a hole in the earth or a hole in the sky as the sacred place of origin where their forebears first appeared. A long, large stone placed vertically appeared visually like a structure rooted deeply in Mother Earth. This same large stone, with a hole in it (Figures 1.1a, 1.1b), was used ritualistically to reenact the transformation of birth. A baby who passed through the hole received regenerated birth energy. The East Indian definition for a holed stone was "gate of deliverance."

EARLY PINHOLE OPTICS—ECLIPSES, TELLING TIME, AND OPTICAL PHENOMENA

Pinhole images are everywhere. Without a doubt, early humans were able to see pinhole images of the eclipsed sun on the ground under tree canopy—the sun is seen as a crescent. Every eclipse seen in the accompanying lens photograph (Figure 1.2) is actually a pinhole image of the sun. Pinholes are created naturally by chinks in overlapped leaves (Figure 1.3). Hardwoods, such as maples, have leaves that work best. When there is not an eclipse, the leaves cast pinhole images of the full solar disc as circular spots onto the ground. Present-day soil physicists study these pinhole images to determine amounts of sunshine hitting the earth.

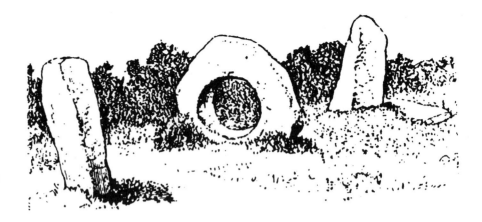

Figure 1.1a Men-an-tol Stones in West Cornwall, *drawn by John Thomas Blight, 1856.*

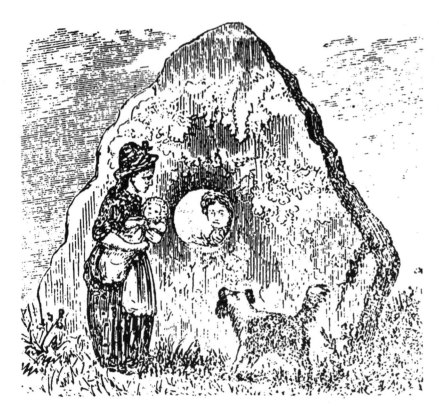

Figure 1.1b The Tolvan Stone of Constantine in Cornwall *depicts one of the last places where the pre-Christian rites of baptism survived. Babies were passed nine times through the hole in the stone and then laid to sleep on a grassy knoll. The stone is about nine feet tall. Drawn by Joseph Blight, 1873.*

Many myths have been retold of ancient peoples' seeing pinhole images inside tents, darkened rooms, and the like; so it would seem that a living knowledge of pinhole images has occurred for tens of thousands of years. An interesting primitive example comes from *Life above the Jungle Floor* by Donald Perry. Perry describes his descent into the cavernous recesses of a fifty-foot-tall hollow tree in the rain forest of Costa Rica. His ageless experience could have happened at any point in human history. Perry wrote:

I climbed a few feet above the floor and turned off the light, again hoping to draw additional animals to the hollow. After several moments I became aware of slight changes in the natural light level within the cavern. For a moment I thought it was my eyes adjusting to the darkness, but I soon realized the phenomenon was due to an opening in the opposite wall. Very weak and wavering light came through a small, cone-shaped hole three feet above the floor. In effect, the hole and near pitch-black cavern constituted a crude optical device. The hole acted as a lens to cast a fuzzy image of the outside world onto a wall. . . . A weak upside-down image of Doyly was projected onto the opposite wall. . . . I looked at my watch: five hours had passed, longer than it had seemed. . . . I screamed through the hole as loudly as possible to get Doyly's attention, but my cries were totally muted by the cavern. It was then that the extent of my isolation from the outside world became very real. The rope, my only connection to civilization rose to a very distant tiny exit, and I wondered what would happen if somehow it became untied. [1]

People have always needed to tell time. A straight stick known as a *gnomon* placed vertically in the ground will cast a shadow from the sun. Because the shadow is longer in winter and shorter in summer, the top of the shadow cast from the tip of the stick becomes a very basic solar clock. Ancient cities such as Rome had gnomons in public places (Figure 1.4). Adding a metal disc pierced with a pinhole at the top of the stick gives a more precise measure, because a bright point is created on the ground above the shadow. This bright point is a pinhole image of the sun. The metal disc with a pinhole is known as a *shadow definer* and the entire instrument as a *pierced gnomon* (Figure 1.5). Since prehistory, some primitive tribes have used this early type of sundial, even into the beginning of the twentieth century. Researchers delving into the history

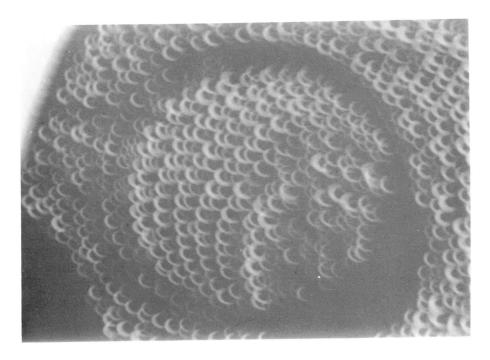

Figure 1.2 © *Nancy Spencer and Eric Renner,* Pinhole Images of the Solar Eclipse May 10, 1994, *lens photograph. Pinhole images of the solar eclipse have been projected through holes in a straw hat. From the collection at Pinhole Resource.*

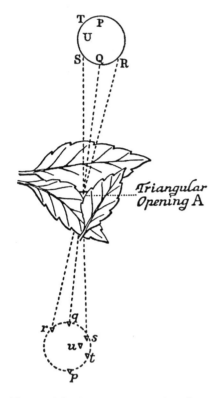

Figure 1.3 Sun's Image Projected through Chinks in Leaves. *The upper circle represents the sun and the lower circle its image on the ground; even though the pinhole is triangular, the image is round. Drawing by Sir William Bragg,* The Universe of Light, *1933.*

of sundials, astrolabes, and any precise instrument that requires a point source of light uncover many ancient to present-day uses of pinholes.

Most likely the earliest recorded description of pinhole optics, although very cryptic in nature, comes from Mo Ti in China, circa 4000 B.C., which is translated as follows:

> CANON: The turning over of the shadow is because the crisscross has a point from which it is prolonged with the shadow.

> EXPLANATION: The light's entry into the curve is like the shooting of arrows from a bow. The entry of that which comes from below is upward, the entry of that which comes from high up is downward. The legs cover the light from below, and therefore form a shadow above; the head covers the light from above, and therefore forms a shadow below. This is because at a certain distance there is a point which coincides with the light; therefore the revolution of the shadow is on the inside. [2]

In the west, the first recorded description of the pinhole comes much later, from Aristotle, circa 330 B.C., in *Problems XV:*

> #6: Why is it when the sun passes through quadrilaterals, as for instance in wicker work, it does not produce figures rectangular in shape but circular?

Here, too, is the first recorded description of viewing an eclipse using a pinhole:

> #11: Why is it that in an eclipse of the sun, if one looks at it through a sieve or through leaves, such as a plane tree or other broad-leaved tree, or if one joins the fingers of one hand over the fingers of the other [Figure 1.6], the rays are crescent shaped when they reach the earth? Is it for the same reason as that when light shines through a rectangular peep-hole, it appears circular in the form of a cone? [3]

Aristotle's question in #6 became known in optics as *Aristotle's problem.* The problem was first solved by Franciscus Maurolycus (1494–1575) in *Photosmi de lumine et umbra* (1521).

An appreciation for the high degree of sophistication in understanding pinhole optics can be gained by studying Figure 1.7, a rarely published light-ray diagram constructed by Anthemius of Tralles in A.D. 555.

Anthemius wrote:

Similarly, by the same construction on the straight line ΔB, we shall show that the summer ray BΞ which falls on the plane mirror on MΞO will be reflected to A along the straight line ΞA. If then we suppose a hole placed symmetrically about the point B as

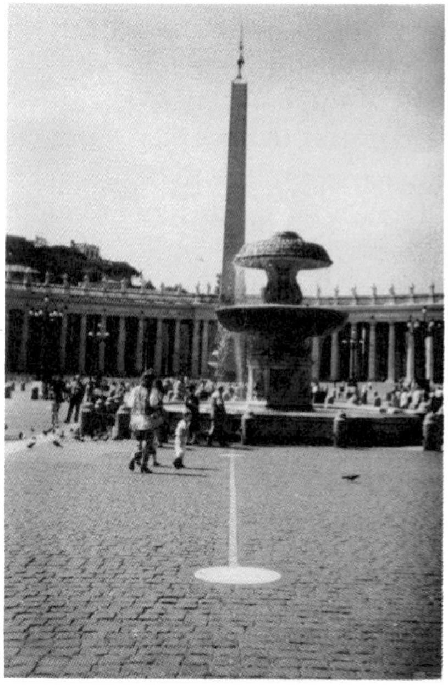

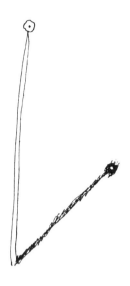

Figure 1.5 Pierced Gnomon, *drawing by author after Rene R. J. Rohr in Sundials, 1965.*

Figure 1.4 © Gnomon at St. Peter's, Rome, *lens photograph by the author. The "noon line" is directed toward the winter solstice disc in the foreground. Originally erected by Emperor Augustus of Alexandria.*

centre, all the rays falling through the hole, that is through the point B, upon the continuous mirrors already described will be reflected to A.[4]

One of the greatest optical scientists of all time, Ibn al-Haitham (A.D. 965–1039) of Egypt, known in the west as Alhazen, showed the pinhole to be an *instrument*—one that could be placed in the shutter of a darkened laboratory for use in examining solitary light rays. Alhazen's book, *Kitab al-Manazir* (Optical Thesaurus), was published around A.D. 1020. Alhazen wrote in Theorum 29:

> Light and colour penetrate transparent bodies separately: That lights and colours are not mixed in the air or in transparent bodies is shown by the following. When in one place several candles are put at various different points, all opposite an opening leading into a dark place (*locus obscuras*), with a wall or an opaque body opposite the opening, the lights (*luces*) of these candles appear on the body or that wall separately and corresponding in number to the candles. Each one of them appears opposite one candle on a line passing through the opening.[5]

In centuries to follow, optical scientists were inspired by Alhazen's use of the pinhole. For these scientists also the pinhole became a starting point—*a primary tool for studying sunlight projected through a small aperture.* For instance, the scientists Theodoric of Freiberg (1250–1311) and Kamal al-Din al-Farisi of Persia (d. 1320) analyzed sunlight coming through a small pinhole and directed into a water-filled glass globe to explain the rainbow's complicated color principles (Figure 1.8a). Both scientists, although thousands of miles apart, worked simultaneously; both admired Alhazen's pinhole ideas. Some centuries later, this same experiment was rediscovered and reinvestigated independently by Antonio de Dominis (1564–1624), René Descartes (1596–1650) (Figure 1.8b), and Johannes Kepler (1571–1630) (Figure 1.8c).

Medieval attitudes seemed to influence the scientist-monk Roger Bacon (1219–1292) in his drawing (Figure 1.9) of a three-tiered pinhole *camera obscura* that demonstrates an integration of religious dogma and science. Bacon shows a *camera obscura* as a darkened place wherein the devil can magically teleport—through the pinhole. When the three pinhole images are reversed inside the *camera obscura*, Satan is still the upper image; however, as reversed, Satan ends up below the crosses representing Christianity. Human intelligence, shown as numbers, reverses to be above the crosses. The point Bacon subliminally makes is that a pinhole *camera obscura* in its magical reproduction of an image is a place of evil magic, a place where proof of the devil exists.

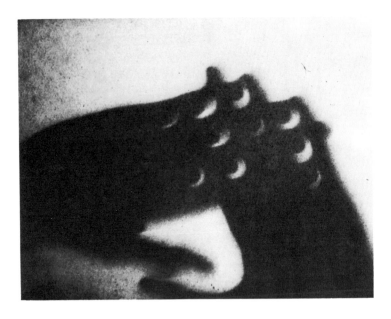

Figure 1.6 © *David Stork,* Pinhole Images of Partially Eclipsed Sun. *Hands are held on top of one another, so that pinholes occur between overlapping fingers; hands shown are actually a shadow on the ground. From the collection at Pinhole Resource.*

Figure 1.7 *Anthemius of Tralles,* Ray Diagram.

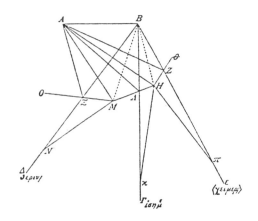

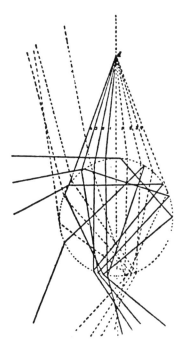

1.8a

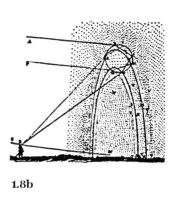

1.8b

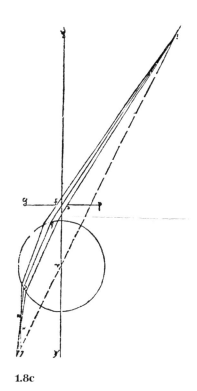

1.8c

Religiously clouded indoctrination toward *camera obscura* imagery, even with a lens, was placed deeper into the public mind-set. Typical of this is a drawing in Johann Arndt's mid-1600s Bible *Wahren Christenthum*. Evil, guilt, and fear were proved to the parishioner reading the caption under the seemingly ordinary drawing of a *camera obscura* (Figure 1.10). Translated from old German this reads as follows:

Darkened and Backwards

This person stands before a camera obscura which is a chamber that has been darkened except for a little hole, and a prepared glass is held before it. Then it happens that the people who are walking past in the alley and can be seen in the chamber, but indeed upside down. Through this it is indicated that man because of his dark fall from grace in his heart and in his mind, unfortunately is lost! Totally dark, even backwards, and upside down. This is transforming an image of God into an image of Satan.

Fortunately, there were intellectual writings about the *camera obscura* in opposition to Johann Arndt's extremist views, yet undoubtedly these musings were not as available to the public as a Bible. The English philosopher John Locke (1632-1704) offered an insight into *camera obscura* imagery with a generously thoughtful overview. Theorizing, although somewhat cryptically, on the human condition in "An Essay Concerning Human Understanding," Locke stated:

Figure 1.8a *Kamal al-Din al-Farisi*, Ray Diagram. *Sunlight refracted into a water-filled glass globe, which acts like a raindrop, and internally reflected back to the eye of the viewer.* Tanquh al-Manazir, *1310.*

Figure 1.8b *René Descartes*, Diagram *showing the formation of the rainbow.* Les Meteores, *1637.*

Figure 1.8c *Johannes Kepler*, Diagram *showing light from the pin-hole entering a glass globe filled with water.* Ad Vitellionem Paralipomena, *1604.*

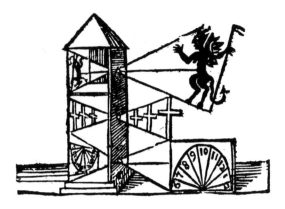

Figure 1.9 *Roger Bacon, thirteenth-century drawing of a three-tiered pinhole camera obscura, from Von Der Camera Obscura zum Film, Werner Nekes, 1992.*

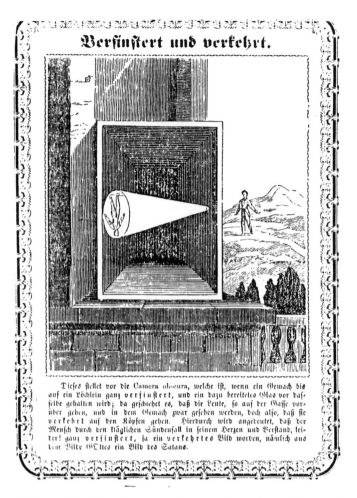

Figure 1.10 Lens Camera Obscura, *etching from Johan Arndt Waahren Christenthum, mid 1600s.*

External and internal sensations are the only passages that I can find of knowledge to the understanding. These alone, as far as I can discover, are the windows by which light is let into this dark room. For, methinks, the understanding is not much unlike a closet wholly shut from light, with only some little opening left . . . to let in external visible resemblances, or some idea of things without; would the pictures coming into such a dark room but stay there and lie so orderly as to be found upon occasion it would very much resemble the understanding of a man.[6]

NOON-MARKS IN ITALIAN RENAISSANCE CATHEDRALS

Because a cathedral is a very large darkened room when a pinhole is made in its ceiling, the cathedral becomes an ideal *camera obscura* and produces a pinhole image of the sun that transits the floor. In 1475, at the age of 78, the great Renaissance mathematician and astronomer Paolo Toscanelli placed a bronze plate with an aperture (Figure 1.11a) at the junction of Filippo Brunelleschi's dome and lantern in the Duomo in Florence, Italy. On the marble floor he placed a round disc that designates noon at the summer solstice, June 21st. A solar image is projected through this large pinhole on sunny days and is visible more than 300 feet below on the cathedral floor. It was Toscanelli who suggested to Christopher Columbus that he sail west to find the east.

In 1756 a brass meridian line (Figure 1.11b) was meticulously inset into the floor of the Duomo, aimed and perfectly leveled in a true north-south direction. This line is known as a noon-mark. At noon, as the sun traverses the sky, a solar image bisects this meridian line. Technologically, the noon-mark in a darkened cathedral is an advance over the open-air pierced gnomon—a more precise solar image can be studied. Time could be better calculated. Toscanelli's pinhole can also be used architecturally to see if the building has shifted.

The ceiling of the Basilica di San Petronio in Bologna contains a beautifully figured pinhole one hundred twenty feet above the marbled floor (Figure 1.12a). It projects an image of the sun twelve inches in diameter onto the floor (Figure 1.12b). That pinhole solar image crosses a ninety-foot-long noon-mark meridian line. Both the pinhole and the noon-mark were designed by the brilliant Renaissance mathematician Ignatio Danti (1536–1586) in 1576. Because the sun is higher in the sky in the summer and lower in the winter, ecclesiastical holidays, shown as inscriptions along the meridian line, are lit by the solar disc on the correct day.

William Livingston, a solar astronomer from Kitt Peak Observatory, Tucson, AZ, studied the Basilica di San Petronio pinhole solar image transiting the floor. He calculated that the solar image moves its own diameter in one hundred twenty seconds, or one tenth of an inch per second. It is actually feasible to set your watch—or back then, your water clock—to one-second accuracy.[7]

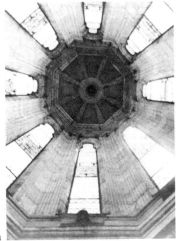

1.11a

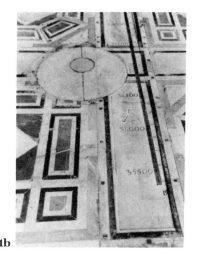

1.11b

Figure 1.11a View Upward into the Lantern, *Cathedral of Florence. The bronze ring with pinhole is the rounded shape at bottom of photograph in front of window. Lens photograph © Pinky Bass, from the collection at Pinhole Resource.*

Figure 1.11b Detail of Noon-mark on the Floor, *Cathedral of Florence. Lens photograph © Pinky Bass, from the collection at Pinhole Resource.*

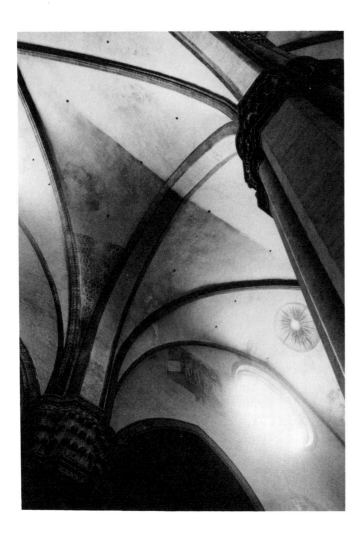

Figure 1.12a View Upward, *Basilica di San Petronio, Bologna. Pinhole in ray figure, center right. Lens photograph © W. Livingston, courtesy of the National Optical Astronomy Observatories, Tucson.*

Figure 1.12b Projected Solar Image, *Basilica di San Petronio, Bologna. Solar image is crossing the noon-mark on marbled floor; some distortion results from the camera angle. Lens photograph © W. Livingston, courtesy of the National Optical Astronomy Observatories, Tucson.*

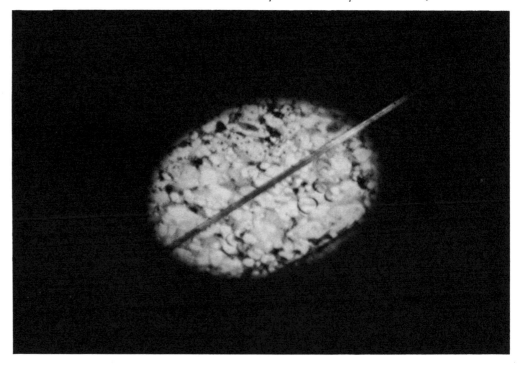

Since the 1500s, other large Italian cathedrals had noon-marks and pinholes placed in them. Probably the most beautiful is in Michelangelo's S. Maria degli Angeli in Rome, a brief walk from the central train terminal. This cathedral has two pinholes, one in the south wall for a solar image that crosses the noon-mark and another in the north wall for aligning the north star with a point on a set of elliptical rings inset into the marble floor. These rings were calculated to determine the position of the North Star over a nine-hundred-year period. To verify this alignment, an ancient telescope is used to connect the pinhole, the North Star, and a point on the elliptical ring. Pinholes, meridian line, and the North Star verification ellipses all were designed in 1702 by Francesco Bianchini (1662–1729). S. Maria degli Angeli is also fortunate to have intricately colored marble astrologic signs along the lengthy meridian line. The scorpion sign (October 21st to November 21st) is a small, triangular, hidden inset that abuts an adjoining column.

The most important pinhole historically is in Rome—in the Tower of Winds at the Vatican (Color Plate 1.13). The pinhole is clearly visible as a hole in the mouth of the God of the South Wind, painted almost at the top of *La Tempesta Sedata* on the south wall. This pinhole casts a solar image onto the floor of the tower, and the image crosses a meridian-line noon-mark. In 1580, using this pinhole image of the sun, Ignazio Danti and his papal astronomers showed Pope Gregory XIII that the spring equinox fell on March 11 rather than March 21. This was because in the Julian calendar a year had $365\frac{1}{4}$ days, which is 11 minutes 14 seconds longer than the true solar year. This difference had led to a gradual change in the calendar date of the equinox, so that by 1580 the calendar date was ten days earlier than the equinox. By 1582, after careful consideration, Gregory corrected the Julian calendar by ten days, thus creating his new Gregorian calendar. The Pope decreed that October 5 in the outmoded Julian calendar would become October 15 in the new Gregorian calendar, so the March equinox of 1583 fell on the correct day, March 21. Under the Julian calendar, a single day was gained in about 400 years. To correct this discrepancy, the Gregorian calendar omits the additional day in February in century years not divisible by 400. Thus 1600 was a leap year, but 1700, 1800, and 1900 were common years. The year 2000 is a leap year.

Noon-marks with pinholes exist in other buildings throughout Europe. The St. Sulpice Cathedral in Paris has one, although the meridian line is not displayed well. Outside Madrid, in El Escorial, in Philip II's private apartments, there are two pinholes and noon-marks, each in adjoining rooms, designed by Joan Werlingen (1715–1790) in 1755. These rooms are open to the public.

The astronomer Gemma Frisius (1508–1555) used the pinhole in his darkened room to study the solar eclipse of 1544 (Figure 1.14). Room and eclipse are figured in *De Radio Astronomica et Geometrico* (1545); this is apparently the first published illustration of a pinhole *camera obscura*. The term *camera obscura* was coined by Johannes Kepler (1571–1630)—camera meaning room and *obscura* meaning dark. After about 1570, a *camera obscura* referred to a box, tent, or room with a lens aperture used by artists to draw the landscape. A lens made the image brighter than a pinhole and focused it to a specific distance from the lens. Many fascinating *camera obscuras* are shown in John Hammond's *The Camera Obscura: A Chronicle* (1981, Adam Hilger Ltd.).

Gemma Frisius also used his *camera obscura* to study sunspots, small, dark areas that appear from time to time on the sun. That Frisius could observe these sunspots by viewing the projected pinhole solar image (Figure 1.15) was proved by the twentieth-century solar astronomer Ronald Giovanelli from Australia, who duplicated Frisius's apparatus and experiment.[8]

In a 1689 drawing by Cornelius Meyer, it can be seen that pinholes were used in spectacles (Figure 1.16). Each lens was opaque, and a pinhole was placed in the middle, offering the viewer who might have been nearsighted a sharper view. This is explained later.

Evidently the Inuit have known of the advantages of pinhole glasses for many centuries, as illustrated by the following from *A Yellow Raft in Blue Water* by the late Michael Dorris:

> In school I had been warned about snow blindness. I remember learning the Eskimos wore goggles made out of a seal's stomach.

Figure 1.14 *Gemma Frisius,* Observing the Solar Eclipse, 24 January 1544, *apparently the first published illustration of a camera obscura, in* De Radio Astronomica et Geometrico, *1545.*

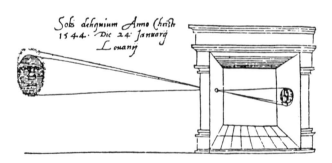

Figure 1.15 © *Ronald Giovanelli,* Pinhole Images of the Sun, *showing a sunspot. From* Secrets of the Sun *(1984) by the late Ronald Giovanelli. Reproduced by permission, Cambridge University Press.*

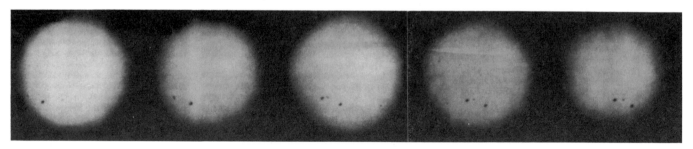

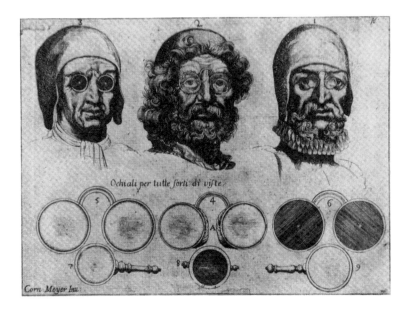

Figure 1.16 *Cornelius Meyer, Spectacles for All Manners of Sight, drawing, 1689. Note that the man on the left is wearing pinhole glasses, shown in a detail in lower right.*

They stretched swatches of it across a frame and used a bone needle to punch pinholes to look through. Without protection people saw strange things, saw too much, too wide.[9]

THE PINHOLE IN THE WAVE THEORY OF LIGHT

Optical scientists investigated optical properties within the cone of light issuing from a pinhole. Over the centuries, these studies were to be paramount for proving the wave theory of light. What follows is a brief chronologic documentation of scientists' experiments with diffraction and interference phenomena inherent in wave theory. Their discoveries are profound.

Diffraction

The first accurate description of diffraction, whereby light bends after grazing an edge (Figure 1.17) came from Francesco Grimaldi (1618–1663) and was published in 1665 in his *Physico-mathesis de lumine, coloribus, et iride*.[10] In Grimaldi's experiment, light from the sun entered his darkened laboratory through a very small pinhole (Figure 1.17, CD). Light from this pinhole had to pass through a second small pinhole (GH) placed in an opaque screen. Light that passed through both pinholes fell on a white screen (IK). If light propagation remained in straight lines after grazing an edge, light would be confined in area N to O. However, Grimaldi observed light in the areas beyond N and O, all the way out to IK. This proved that diffraction occurred. Light is bent slightly after grazing the edge of an obstacle—in this case, two pinholes.

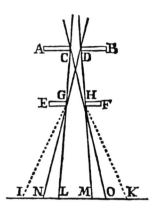

Figure 1.17 *Francesco Grimaldi,*
Diffraction of Light by a Pinhole,
from Physico-mathesis de lumine, coloribus, et iride, aliisque adnexis libri
duo, *1665.*

In another experiment, Grimaldi admitted light into his darkened room through two neighboring pinholes and received this
light on a white screen. Projected onto the screen were two circular pinhole images of the sun, each surrounded by a feebly illuminated ring. By placing the screen a certain distance from the
two pinholes, Grimaldi could overlap the edges of the outer rings,
so that the outer edge of one ring was tangential to the outer edge
of the image on the other ring. Curiously, light in this overlapping
portion was less brilliant than in other areas around the rings.
This phenomenon later would become known as *interference.*

Isaac Newton (1642–1727) in *Opticks* (part I of the third book)
wrote the following:

> Grimaldo [*sic*] has inform'd us, that if a beam of the Sun's Light
> be let into a dark Room through a very small hole, the Shadows
> of things in this Light will be larger than they ought to be if the
> Rays went on by the Bodies in straight lines and that these
> Shadows have three parallel Fringes, Bands or Ranks of color'd
> Light adjacent to them. But if the Hole be enlarged the Fringes
> grow broad and run into one another, so that they cannot be dis-
> tinguish'd. These broad shadows and Fringes have been reckon'd
> by some to proceed from the ordinary refraction of the Air but
> without due examination of the Matter. For the circumstances of
> the Phaenomenon, so far as I have observed them, are as follows.

> Observation: I made in a piece of Lead a small Hole with a Pin,
> whose breadth was the 42d part of an Inch. For 21 of those Pins
> laid together took up the breadth of half an Inch. Through this
> Hole I let into my darken'd Chamber a beam of the Sun's Light,
> and found that the Shadows of Hairs, Thred, Pins, Straws, and
> such like slender Substances placed in this beam of Light, were
> considerably broader than they ought to be, if the Rays of Light
> passed on by these Bodies in right Lines. And particularly a Hair
> of a Man's Head [Figure 1.18], whose breadth was but the 280th
> part of an Inch, being held in this Light, at the distance of about
> twelve Feet from the Hole, did cast a Shadow which at the dis-
> tance of four Inches from the Hair was the sixtieth part of an
> Inch broad, that is, above four times broader than the Hair.[11]

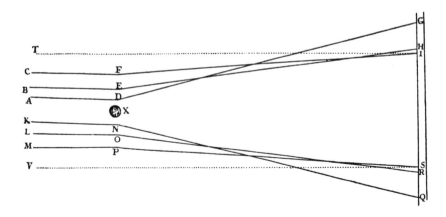

Figure 1.18 *Isaac Newton,* Circle X
Represents the Middle of the Hair,
Opticks, *part 1, book 3, 1730.*

Interference

More than a century after Newton's work, Thomas Young (1773–1839) modified Grimaldi's experiment and observed true interference of light. Young admitted sunlight through a pinhole then received this diverging cone of sunlight onto two other pinholes placed in an opaque screen beyond the first pinhole (Figure 1.19). Each of these two pinholes also casts a diverging cone of light onto a screen. Where the cones of light overlapped on the screen, Young observed dark and light bands. In this experiment, the two pinholes lie on the wave front of the disturbances coming from the first pinhole; consequently they are in the same phase.[12] Thomas Young stated eloquently:

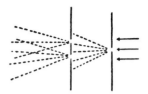

Figure 1.19 *Robert W. Wood*, The work of Thomas Young, sunlight projected through one pinhole onto two pinholes proves interference of light. *From* Physical Optics, *1934.*

It was in May, 1801, that I discovered, by reflecting on the beautiful experiments of Newton, a law which appears to me to account for a greater variety of interesting phenomena than any other optical principle that has yet been made known. I shall endeavor to explain this law by a comparison.

Suppose a number of equal waves of water to move upon the surface of a stagnant lake, with a certain constant velosity [*sic*], and to enter a narrow channel leading out of the lake. Suppose then another similar cause to have excited another equal series of waves, which arrives at the same channel, with the same velosity, and at the same time with the first. Neither series of waves will destroy the other, but their effects will be combined: if they enter the channel in such a manner that the elevations of one series coincide with those of the other, they must together produce a series of greater joint elevations; but if the elevations of one series are so situated as to correspond to the depressions of the other, they must exactly fill up those depressions, and the surface of the water must remain smooth; at least I can discover no alternative, either from theory or experiment.

Now I maintain that similar effects take place whenever two portions of light are thus mixed; and this I call the general law of the interference of light.[13]

The final wave theory comes from Augustin Fresnel (1788–1827), who concluded the following in *Memoire sur de la defraction de la lumière*, 1819:

Let AG be the aperture through which the light passes [Figure 1.20]. I shall at first suppose that it is sufficiently narrow for the dark bands of the first order to fall inside the geometrical shadow of the screen, and at the same time be fairly distant from the edges B and D. Let P be the darkest point in one of these two bands; it is then easily seen that this must correspond to a difference of one whole wavelength between the two extreme rays AP and CR. Let us now imagine another ray, PI, drawn in such a way that its length shall be a mean between the other two. Then, on account of its marked inclination to the arc AIG, the point I

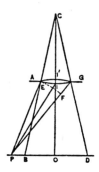

Figure 1.20 *Augustin Fresnel, Aperture through which light passes, Memoire sur la defraction de la lumière, 1819.*

will fall almost exactly in the middle. We now have the arc divided into two parts, whose corresponding elements are almost exactly equal, and send to the point P vibrations in exactly opposite phases, so that these must annul each other.

By the same reasoning it is easily seen that the darkest points in the other dark bands also correspond to differences of an even number of half wave-lengths between the two rays which come from the edges of the aperture; and, in like manner, the brightest points of the bright bands correspond to differences of an uneven number of half wavelengths—that is to say, their positions are exactly reversed as compared with those which are deduced from the interference of the limiting rays on the hypothesis that these alone are concerned in the production of fringes. This is true with the exception of the point at the middle, which, on either hypothesis, must be bright. The inference deduced from the theory that the fringes result from the superposition of all the disturbances from all parts of the arc AG are verified by experiments, which at the same time disprove the theory which looks upon these bands as produced only by rays inflected and reflected at the edges of the diaphragm. These are precisely the phenomena which first led me to recognize the insufficiency of this hypothesis, and suggested the fundamental principle of the theory which I have just explained—namely, the principle of Huygens combined with the principle of interference.[14]

In 1835, F. M. Swerd presented his monumental book on diffraction patterns created by light projected through thousands of pinholes in one plate. The pinholes in each plate were triangular, square, or round. Swerd's book *Die Beugungsercheinungen*, published in Mannheim, Germany, is unfortunately little known; however, his meticulously crafted hand-colored drawings of diffraction patterns have been verified photographically by the contemporary scientist Richard Hoover.

THE PINHOLE IN PHOTOGRAPHY

By 1839, photography had been invented. A lens image from a small, portable *camera obscura* could be chemically preserved. (There is some conjecture that the first photograph by Niépce, an eight-hour exposure made in 1826, might just be pinhole.[15]) However, in 1857, Joseph Petzval was apparently the first to attempt to find, with a mathematical formula, the optimal pinhole diameter for the sharpest definition in a pinhole image. The optimal formula was achieved about thirty years later by the Nobel Prize winner Lord Rayleigh (John William Strutt, 1842–1919). For ten years, Rayleigh worked with pinhole formulas, hoping that pinhole apertures could be appropriately used in telescopes rather than extremely expensive lenses. His formula is used today. Rayleigh spoke of his work in *Nature* (1891):

What, then, is the best size of the aperture? That is the important question in dealing with pin-hole photography. It was first considered by Professor Petzval of Vienna, and he arrived at the result indicated by the formula, $2r^2 = fl$, where $2r$ is the diameter of the aperture, l the wavelength of light, and f the focal length, or, rather simply the distance between the aperture and the screen upon which the image is formed.

His reasoning, however, though ingenious, is not sound, regarded as an attempt at an accurate solution of the question. In fact, it is only lately that the mathematical problem of the diffraction of light by a circular hole has been sufficiently worked out to enable the question to be solved. The mathematician to whom we owe this achievement is Professor Lommel. I have adapted his results to the problem of pinhole photography. The general conclusion is that the hole may advantageously be enlarged beyond that given by Petzval's rule. A suitable radius is $r = \sqrt{fl}$.

I will not detain you further than just to show you one application of pin-hole photography on a different scale from the usual. The definition improves as the aperture increases; but in the absence of a lens the augmented aperture entails a greatly extended focal length. The limits of an ordinary portable camera are thus soon passed. The original of the transparency now to be thrown upon the screen was taken in an ordinary room, carefully darkened. The aperture (in the shutter) was 0.07 inch, and the distance of the 12 x 10 plate from the aperture was 7 feet. The resulting picture of a group of cedars [Figure 1.21] shows nearly as much detail as could be seen direct from the place in question.[16]

In 1889, Lord Rayleigh had shown that the optimal pinhole photographic image could "be at least as well defined as that received upon the retina."[17] This means the optimal pinhole, designed for a specific focal length, projects an image that equals the sharpness produced by the lens in each of our eyes. Even though the biconvex lens in each of our eyes accommodates (changes shape slightly for focusing at different distances), modern-day camera lenses actually focus to a point sharper than our eyes can see. The pinhole photograph in Figure 1.22, by the late mathematician Roy Hines (1929–1981), is probably as sharp a pinhole image as is possible with an optimal pinhole. This surprising sharpness seems similar to 20/20 vision, although all distances are in the same focus. The contrast in lighting helps to make this image appear so sharp. Anyone wishing to make optimally sharp pinhole images should be using the thinnest metal and the cleanest-edged, optimally sized pinhole possible. The metal that edges the pinhole should be sanded with the finest emery paper, to the point where the metal is as absolutely thin as practical. Just having the perfect pinhole is not enough. One should have a thorough knowledge of photography—film, developers, and printing techniques; and most important—a knowledge of light, and how it will respond to the

Figure 1.21 © *Lord Rayleigh, A Group of Cedars. Pinhole photograph, circa 1890. Made by the author from a copy negative of the original print, courtesy of Hon. G. R. Strutt, John William Strutt archive.*

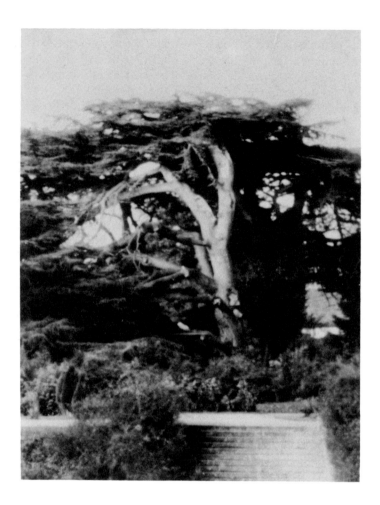

photographic materials you have selected. In making a range of pinhole images from sharp to blurry you will find a slightly different sensibility within each image.

THE PINHOLE AND THE EYE

For decades, ophthalmologists have used an elegant, yet very simple, pinhole instrument known as an *occluder* (Figure 1.23) to determine whether decreased visual acuity can be helped by prescribing eyeglasses for the correction of a refractive error. The occluder is held closely in front of one eye, and an opaque card is held over the other eye. If the patient can see clearly while looking through a pinhole in the occluder, eyeglasses can be prescribed; if not, medical or surgical correction is necessary.

When a person looks through a pinhole in an occluder, the cone of vision is narrowed so that the image enters the viewer's eye only through the center of the lens. Projected onto the retina is a pinhole image. If a person's eyes can be corrected with glasses, then any distance, close or far, is in focus when an occluder is being used.

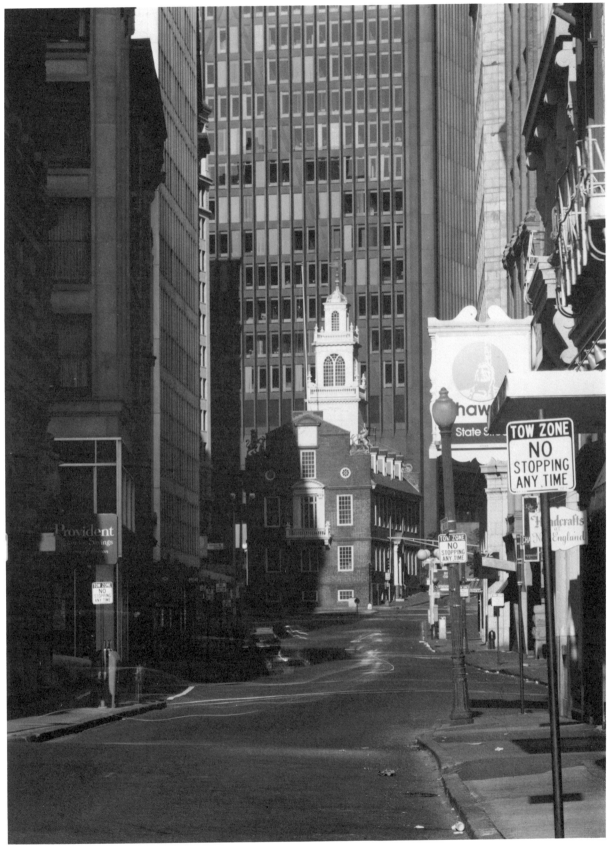

Figure 1.22 © *Roy Hines,* Old State House, Boston, MA, *8" x 10" pinhole photograph made with an 8" x 10" flat-back camera, circa 1977. From the collection at Pinhole Resource.*

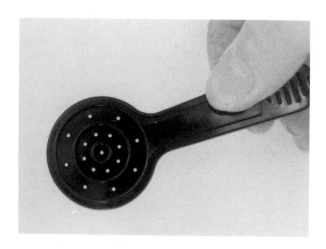

Figure 1.23 A Multiple Pinhole Disc Occluder, *manufactured by Western Optical, reproduced by permission of Western Optical, Seattle.*

To try this, use a large-shafted needle to make a hole in an opaque card. If you wear glasses, take them off. Place your homemade occluder up to your eye, making sure to hold your free hand in front of your other eye. You should be able to see clearly through the pinhole. Because the image you are seeing is a pinhole image, you will be able to see objects at close range. The pinhole can even act as a magnifier. To try this, use the occluder while holding this page very close to your eye. Even if you don't wear glasses, you can magnify the type held at close range while looking through the occluder. After you remove the occluder, you will see you have been viewing an area that is normally blurry.

Many centuries ago, Leonardo da Vinci (1452–1519) made use of this same principle. In *Manuscript D, following 5r,* he wrote:

> If you will make a hole as small as possible in a sheet of paper and then bring it as near as possible to the eye, and if then you look at a star through this hole, you are making use of only a small part of the pupil, which sees this star with a wide space of sky around it and sees it so small that hardly anything could be smaller. And if you make the hole near to the edge of the said paper, you will be able to see the same star with the other eye at the same time, and it will appear to you to be large, and thus in the same time with your two eyes you will see the one star twice, and once it will be very small and the other time very large.[18]

TWENTIETH-CENTURY PINHOLE IMAGING IN HIGH-ENERGY PHYSICS

With the advent of nuclear energy in the 1940s, pinhole cameras began to find their way into nuclear physics to image high-energy particles. It was found that a photographic lens absorbs rather than projects high-energy X rays or gamma rays, whereas a pinhole produces an image. The idea of imaging high-energy X rays and gamma rays from the sun, black holes, and exploding stars with pinhole cameras placed on space vehicles began in the late 1950s. The first soft X-ray pinhole photograph of the sun was achieved on April 19, 1960, when a set of pinhole cameras was flown on an Aerobee-Hi Rocket. Richard Blake, one of the designers of the pinhole cameras (Figure 1.24a) explained the flight, cameras, and resulting photographs (Figure 1.24b) as follows:

> Duration of exposure was 286 seconds. Peak altitude was 220 KM. The camera was kept pointed at the sun within one minute of arc by biaxial pointing control. . . . There were actually eight cameras in the block, four of which survived the flight and impact (the recovery parachute did not function properly). Two of the four

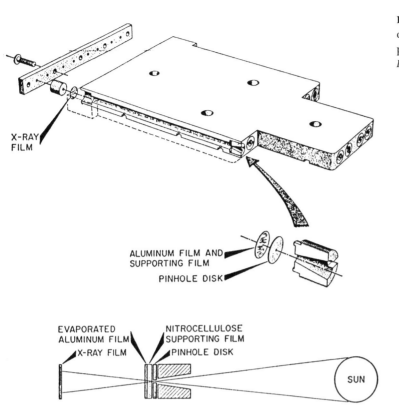

X-RAY
FILM

ALUMINUM FILM AND
SUPPORTING FILM

PINHOLE DISK

EVAPORATED
ALUMINUM FILM

NITROCELLULOSE
SUPPORTING FILM

X-RAY FILM

PINHOLE DISK

SUN

were designed to produce photographs with a resolution of one-fifth solar diameter, the other two with one-tenth solar diameter. The camera producing the best picture utilized a pinhole which was 0.005 inch in diameter and was placed 6 inches from the film.

In order to adapt pinhole photography for use in the x-ray region, it is necessary to prevent visible and ultraviolet light from striking the film. The pinhole was covered with a thin film of Parlodion (a type of nitro-cellulose). The Parlodion, in turn, supported an evaporated film of aluminum.[19]

At the suggestion of R. H. Dicke, scatter-hole X-ray pinhole cameras (Figure 1.25a) were designed in the 1970s. Many pinhole images were allowed to overlap. Blake continues:

> Now the sun is a compact collection of complex sources which can be mapped by scanning collimators with about the same figure of merit as by the scatter-hole camera. . . . [T]wo pictures are taken using complementary aperture plates. One picture has one half of the possible hole positions randomly selected and punched out [Figure 1.25b], the other

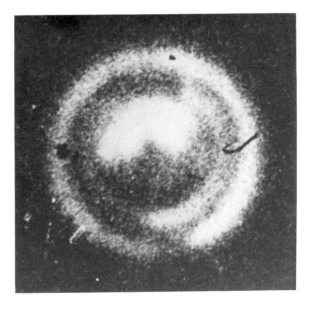

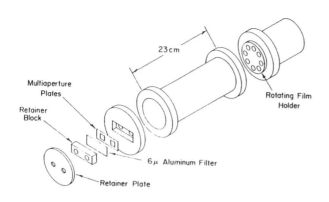

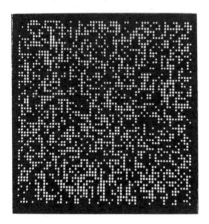

Figure 1.25a © *Richard Blake et al.*
Multiaperture Pinhole Camera *for 30 October 1972 flight camera.*

Figure 1.25b © *Richard Blake et al.*
One of Two Complementary Multiaperture Plates *for 30 October 1972 flight camera.*

plate has the other possible hole positions punched out. The two pictures can be subtracted to form a pseudo picture, which can then be correlated (digitally) with a pseudo aperture formed by subtracting the complementary aperture functions. . . . On 30 October 1972 we flew a camera incorporating two aperture plates to permit implementation of the subtractive postprocessing scheme.[20]

After many years of theoretical groundwork in pinhole astronomy, today's pinhole cameras on space vehicles use multiple-pinhole optics (Figure 1.26) known as *coded-aperture imaging* to photograph high-energy X rays and gamma rays from extreme energy sources such as black holes and exploding stars. One astrophysicist working with pinhole optics, Thomas A. Prince, described the first gamma-ray image of a supernova (exploding star) as follows:

The Caltech imaging gamma-ray telescope was launched from Alice Springs, Northern Territory in Australia on November 18 [1987]. It observed the supernova for approximately two and one-half hours starting at 14 hrs. 30 min. U.T. The telescope used a technique called coded-aperture imaging to produce images in a wavelength where mirrors and lenses are not feasible. A coded-aperture imager functions like a multiple-pinhole camera. In such a camera, multiple holes [Figure 1.27a] cast overlapping images on a position sensitive electronic detector. The individual, overlapping images are unscrambled using a computer and superimposed to yield the final image of a gamma-ray source.

Using the coded-aperture technique, the Caltech telescope produced an accompanying slide image of Supernova 1987A [Color Plate 1.27b]. This is the first such image of the supernova at gamma-ray energies. Indeed, it is one of the first few images at gamma-ray energies (100 keV to 10 MeV) of any astronomical object. The hard x-rays and gamma-rays which make up this image are thought to be direct and scattered photons from the decay of radioactive cobalt 56, newly produced in the explosion of the supernova. The field of view shown in the slide is 12 degrees across and the supernova itself is unresolved. The background in the supernova field is produced by statistical fluctuations in the diffuse hard x-ray and gamma-ray background and does not necessarily represent real structure.[21]

Over the last twenty-five years, the pinhole has also been used widely by nuclear physicists to image high energy in laser plasma. An object is heated by laser beams inside a vacuum chamber to extremely high energies (Figure 1.28a), equal to the sun's nuclear energy reaction heat at 10 million degrees Fahrenheit;

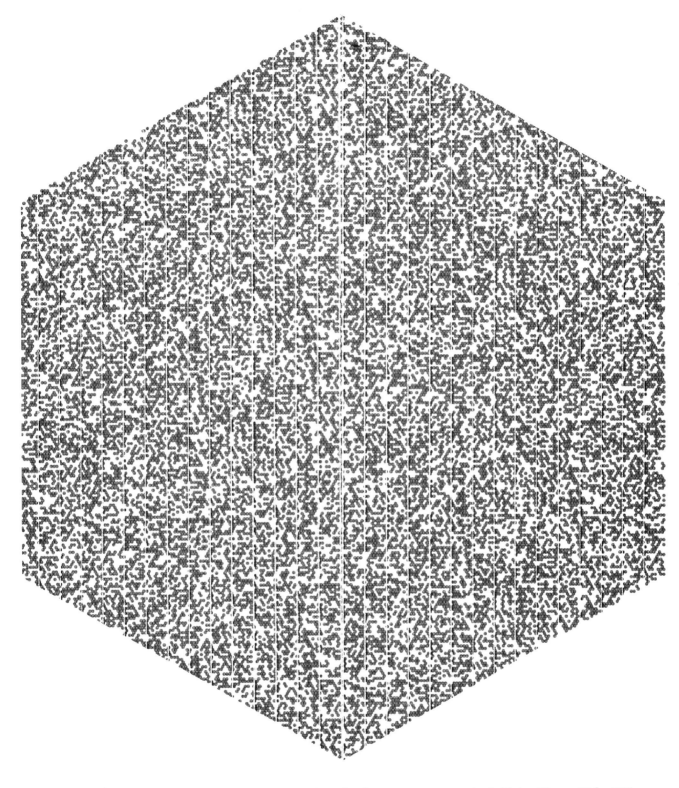

Figure 1.26 © E. E. Fenimore, A 26,232-Pinhole Uniformly Redundant Array Aperture Study Plate, *12" w. x 13" h., 1985, courtesy of the Los Alamos National Laboratories.*

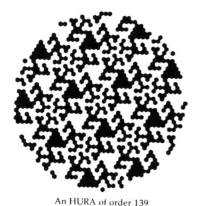

An HURA of order 139

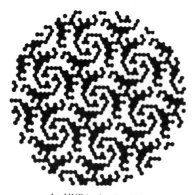

An HURA of order 151

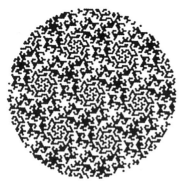

An HURA of order 619

Figure 1.27a © *Thomas A. Prince,* Three Hexagonal, Uniformly Redundant Arrays of Order 139, 151, and 619. *Courtesy of the California Institute of Technology, George W. Downs Laboratory of Physics, Pasadena.*

upon implosion, the object is photographed (Figure 1.28b) with a pinhole camera. This laboratory simulation of the sun's energy allows scientists to study nuclear reactions under somewhat ideal conditions.

NOTES

1. Donald Perry, *Life above the Jungle Floor* (New York: Simon and Schuster, 1988), 46–47.
2. Angus C. Graham, *Later Mohist Logic, Ethics, Science* (London: School of Oriental and African Studies, University of Hong Kong with University of London Press, 1978), 375–79.
3. W. S. Hett, trans., *Aristotle,* Book XV, Chapter 911bl (Cambridge, MA: Loeb Classical Library, Harvard University Press, 1936), 333–35.
4. G. L. Huxley, *Anthemius of Tralles* (Cambridge, MA: Loeb Classical Library, Harvard University Press, 1959), 6–8, 44–46.
5. Ibn al-Haitham, *Opticae Thesaurus* [1572], ed. F. Risnero, Basel, in A. C. Crombie, "The Mechanistic Hypothesis and the Scientific Study of

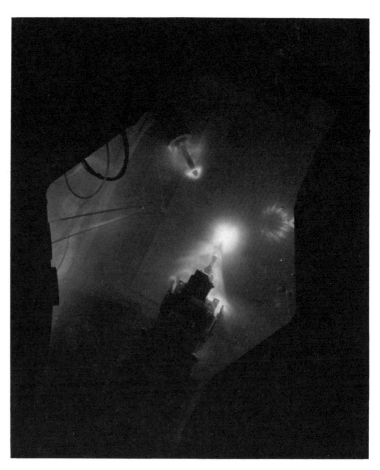

Figure 1.28a © *Allan Hauer,* Inside the Antares Laser Chamber during an Actual Laser Shot, *1985. Pinhole camera is coming down from upper left. Lens photograph provided by Los Alamos National Laboratories.*

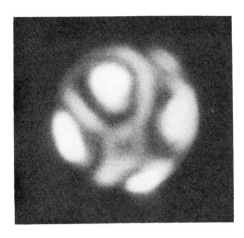

Figure 1.28b © *Allan Hauer,* X-ray Pinhole Photograph of Laser-irradiated Glass Micro Shell, *1985. Laser Plasma Experiments Group, Los Alamos National Laboratory. Laser beams are tightly focused on the surface of the sphere. Four of the focused beams appear as the oval-shaped areas. Tightly focused beams cause very large magnetic fields to be generated. The fields channel some of the blowoff back to the target surface in the "canals" or "channels" between the laser spots. Lens photograph provided by Los Alamos National Laboratories.*

Vision: Some Optical Ideas as a Background to the Invention of the Microscope," in *Historical Aspects of Microscopy,* edited by S. Bradbury and G. L. E. Turner (Cambridge, MA: Heffer and Son, 1967), 108–12.

6. John Locke, *An Essay Concerning Human Understanding* (1690) II, xi, in Jonathan Crary, *Techniques of the Observer—On Vision and Modernity in the Nineteenth Century* (Cambridge, MA: MIT Press, 1990), 17.

7. William Livingston, "Solar Time Standards and the Medieval Church," *Pinhole Journal* 2(1986):2–3.

8. Ronald Giovanelli, *Secrets of the Sun* (New York: Cambridge University Press, 1984), 18.

9. Michael Dorris, *A Yellow Raft in Blue Water* (New York: Warner Books, 1987), 202.

10. Francesco Grimaldi, Physico-mathesis de lumine, coloribus, et iride, aliisque adnexis libri duo, Bononiae, 1665, in M. H. Pirenne, *Optics, Painting and Photography* (New York: Cambridge University Press, 1970), 190.

11. Isaac Newton, *Opticks, Third Book of Optics, Part 1* (London: S. Smith and B. Walford, 1730), 317–18.

12. Robert W. Wood, *Physical Optics* (New York: Macmillan, 1934), 186–87.

13. Henry Crew, *The Rise of Modern Physics* (Baltimore: Williams & Wilkins, 1928), 163–65.

14. Augustin Fresnel, "Memoir on the Diffraction of Light," in *The Wave Theory of Light,* trans. by Henry Crew (New York: American Book Company, 1900), 81, 144.

15. Roy Flukinger, Curator, Harry Ransom Humanities Research Center, Austin, TX, personal communication with author, February 6, 1987.

16. John William Strutt (Lord Rayleigh), "On Photography," *Nature* 44 (16 July 1891): 249–54.

17. Lord Rayleigh, *The Photographic News* 33 (20 September 1889): 611.

18. Leonardo da Vinci, *Manuscript D* following 5r, Institut de France.

19. R. L. Blake, T. Z. Chubb, H. Friedman, and A. E. Unzicker, "Interpretation of X-ray Photograph of the Sun," *The Astrophysical Journal* 137(1963):3–16.

20. R. L. Blake, A. J. Burek, E. E. Fenimore, and R. Puetter, "Solar X-ray Photograph with Multiplex Pin-hole Camera," *Review of Scientific Instruments* 45(1974):513–16.

21. Thomas A. Prince, "Pinhole Telescope: First Gamma-Ray Image of Supernova 1987A," *Pinhole Journal* 4(1988):26–27.

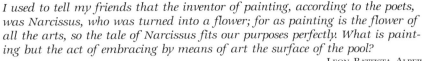

Pinhole's History in Art

BRUNELLESCHI'S PINHOLE PERSPECTIVE DEVICE

Lippo de ser Brunelleschi of Florence founded the procedure of working out this method [of perspective] in which there was truly something ingenious, subtle, and beautiful; by rational procedures he constructed what you see when you look in a mirror.[1]

The western world's concept of space began to change radically at the end of the first quarter of the fifteenth century because of one singular device that had a small aperture (Figure 2.1). Certainly this is not something we were taught in school. We are fortunate to be able to read about it firsthand because Filippo Brunelleschi's small-apertured perspective device was explained to us by his "Anonymous Biographer"—someone who apparently worked with Brunelleschi, yet never has been fully identified (although it is thought to be Antonio Manetti).

In a paper by the Anonymous Biographer, written in approximately 1482, we find the following:

About this matter of perspective, the first thing in which he displayed it was a small panel about half a braccio square on which he made a picture showing the exterior of the church of S. Giovanni in Florence. And he depicted in it all that could be seen in a single view; to paint it he took up a position about three braccia inside the middle door of S. Maria del Fiore. The work was done with such care and accuracy and the colours of the black and white marble were so faithfully reproduced that no miniaturist ever excelled him. In the picture he included everything that the eye could take in, from the Misericordia as far as the corner and the Canto de'Pecori on one side to the column commemorating the miracles of St. Zepotius as far as the Canto alla Paglia and all that could be seen beyond it on the other. And for what he had to show of the sky, that is where the walls in

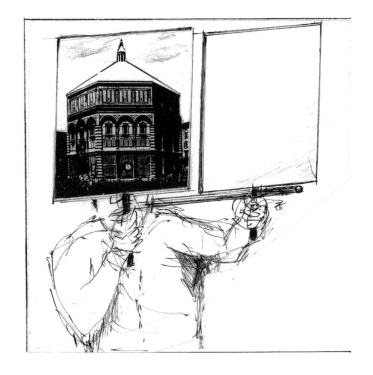

Figure 2.1 Filippo Brunelleschi's Small-apertured Perspective Device. *Brunelleschi stands before the Baptistery in Florence. He uses one eye to look through a lentil-sized hole made through the back of his painting. In his left hand he holds a mirror that reflects the painting. He moves backward or forward to find the correct viewing distance. When the angle of view of the real Baptistery matches the edge of the mirrored image of the painting, Brunelleschi can lower the mirror and have a duplicate of his painting. Circa 1420s. Drawing by the author, 1998.*

the painting stand out against the open air, he used burnished silver so that the actual air and sky would be reflected in it and the clouds also, which were thus seen moving on the silver when the wind blew. Now, the painter had to select a single point from which his picture was to be viewed, a point precisely determined as regards height and depth, sideways extension and distance, in order to obviate any distortion in looking at it (because a change in the observer's position would change what his eye saw). Brunelleschi therefore made a hole in the panel on which the picture was painted; and this hole was in fact exactly at the spot on the painting where the eye would strike on the church of S. Giovanni if one stood inside the middle door of S. Maria del Fiore, in the place where Brunelleschi had stood in order to paint the picture. On the picture side of the panel the hole was as small as a bean, but on the back it was enlarged in a conical shape, like a woman's straw hat, to the diameter of a ducat or slightly more. Now Brunelleschi's intention was that the viewer, holding the panel close to his eye in one hand, should look from the back, where the hole was wider. In the other hand he should hold a flat mirror directly opposite the painting in such a manner as to see the painting reflected in it. The distance between the mirror and the other hand was such that, counting small braccia for real braccia, it was exactly equivalent to the distance between the church of S. Giovanni and the place where Brunelleschi was assumed to be standing when he painted it. Looking at it with all the circumstances exactly as described above—the burnished silver, the representation of the piazza, the precise point of observation—it seemed as though one were seeing the real building. And I have had it in my hand and looked at it many times in my days and can testify to it.[2]

Filippo Brunelleschi (1377?–1446), the brilliant Renaissance architect and engineer, invented the small-apertured perspective device in 1425 when he was about forty-seven years old. The Anonymous Biographer tells us the diameter of the hole was "as small as a bean" (lentil-sized, which is about $\frac{3}{16}$ inch in diameter). (It is interesting to note that the word *lentil* in Latin is lens. A lentil is biconvex, like the lens in our eyes.) The hole enlarged in the back of the painting "to the diameter of a ducat or slightly more" would have been approximately one inch in diameter. Fred Leeman in his book *Hidden Images* simplifies this description as follows:

> This picture had to be observed in a particular way: One had to stand exactly where the artist had stood when he painted his subject, that is, almost six feet inside the entrance of the church. A peephole had been cut in the center of the picture, and the viewer had to look through it from the back of the picture. Gazing through the hole, he would see the cathedral square and the Baptistery just as Brunelleschi had painted them. Then, holding up a mirror, he could look through the peephole and this time see the front of the painting, which coincided exactly with the actual view of the square. In order to enhance the effect, the sky was not painted in on the panel; instead, a layer of silver reflected the real sky. "And so," as Manetti writes, "the clouds that one saw in the silver moved with the wind when it blew." [3]

Brunelleschi used two very basic optical devices—the small aperture and the mirror. He wanted to develop a theory for perspective pertaining to the eye, which sees objects in three dimensions and then places those objects into two dimensions, as in drawings and paintings. In his experiment, Brunelleschi was able to demonstrate that there was a *vanishing point* in three-dimensional space where specific *lines of perspective* converged on a point farthest from the eye (like looking down two railroad tracks, which converge to a point). There also was a vanishing point at one eye where specific *lines of light* converged on the eye. Brunelleschi was able to represent perfectly the reality of three dimensions by looking through the lentil-sized aperture drilled into the two-dimensional painting. The painting was reflected back toward him in the mirror. When he removed the mirror, he had a duplicate of the painting in three dimensions. To accomplish this, he had to be standing exactly at the correct distance in front of the real building, and his eye behind the hole had to remain stationary. This seemingly simple experiment profoundly changed humanity's concept of space. Brunelleschi's theory became known as the "theory of one-point perspective." It was the first scientific proof of how three dimensions could *precisely* become two dimensions.

With Brunelleschi's device, a point and a small aperture (a pinhole) become interchangeable. To thoroughly understand their interchangeability we must be able to comprehend that any point in space can be replaced by a pinhole that will project an image made from a multitude of points of light passing through it. Any point in space consequently can become an image in our eye. These points of light are seen by our eye as a complete three-dimensional picture. Each one of these points forms a straight line of light passing through the aperture. The image in our eye usually is comprehended mentally as a complete image in three dimensions in front of us; it seems difficult for most people to grasp that the image of what is in front of us is really a small retina-sized image in our eye that the brain reverses. This image is similar to a three-dimensional image projected into a *camera obscura* and seen in two dimensions on a flat white sheet held either perpendicular to the pinhole or angled (known later as an *anamorph*). All this works perfectly well in the fifteenth-century view of straight-line geometric optics. Brunelleschi's profound device ushered in the Renaissance.

Brunelleschi's small-apertured device demonstrated the following in one-point perspective:

1. How straight-line geometric optics works in both the eye and the *camera obscura*
2. How to arrive at a "normal" perspective view of a building, in other words, the distance from a building at which the angled perspective feels "normal" to the eye, not too wide angled
3. How a three-dimensional scene, whether it is a building exterior or interior, can be exactly transformed into two dimensions
4. How a vanishing point connects us to distance

Many art historians have written about Brunelleschi's small-apertured perspective device. The historians have failed to realize one crucial element: Brunelleschi's device was operating on the geometric principles of the enlarged pinhole. By failing to recognize this, they fail to realize that Brunelleschi was theoretically demonstrating the workings of a small-apertured *camera obscura*. Historians never mention pinhole optics, and some have even gone so far as to duplicate the experiment by using a lens camera.

ALBERTI'S FIRST DIFFRACTION CAMERA

Brunelleschi's mirror and small aperture had captured three-dimensional space and scientifically placed it into two dimensions. Why couldn't someone capture three-dimensional space and scientifically replace it into *three dimensions*? This can be accomplished by moving the fixed point, where Brunelleschi's eye had been behind the hole in the painting, and placing it as a small aperture in the wall of a darkened room. This produces a *camera obscura.* The projected image can be viewed in two dimensions on a screen, or it can be viewed in three dimensions on the walls, floor, and ceiling.

The early artist, scientist, Renaissance man certainly knew of the "hole in the shutter" optical principle; it was used by researchers in light from Alhazen (A.D. 1020) onward. With an aperture of the correct diameter, the projected image would be well defined on the walls, floor, and ceiling. The only theoretically correct way to see the projected image again was to look through the aperture. Because one's head would naturally block the light coming into the darkened room, the projected image had to be painted. This, of course, preserved the image. When you put your eye at the fixed-point aperture, you could actually see the painted image, precisely as it looked outside. (Of course, the image was painted upside down and light had to be added inside.)

How profound! Theoretically, everything was geometrically correct! The first *diffraction* camera was brilliantly conceived and made by Leon Battista Alberti (1404–1472), a friend of Brunelleschi. An anonymous biography of Alberti published in Muratori's *Rerum Italicarum Scriptores* (xxv296), quoted by Vasari, states:

> Alberti painted wonderful pictures, which were exhibited in some sort of small closed box, viewed through a very small aperture. The pictures showed marvelous verisimilitude; one picture was nocturnal, showing the moon and stars, the other diurnal, showing a day scene. [4]

Undoubtedly, this was a *camera obscura,* because it is stated the paintings were "viewed through a very small aperture." Unfortunately these boxes are lost. A present-day room-sized *camera obscura* is shown in Figures 2.2a through 2.2d.

Alberti probably would have made his day scene a well-known landmark, so that the scene could have been viewed outside the box in its well-known three-dimensional reality or through the aperture in the box in its newly created three-dimensional reality.

How would Alberti have painted this scene? To be theoretically consistent with Brunelleschi, he would have probably made a rectangular or square box with the top removed and a small aperture in one side aimed at the well-known landmark. Alberti could have draped a thick black cloth over himself and the box to exclude all extraneous light from entering the box, except for the image through the small aperture. The image of the landmark would have been upside down on the inside of the box. Alberti could have duplicated the image with paint or in pencil on the entire inside of the box. It would not have been easy to bend over and paint or draw the upside-down image, but if my understanding is right about the milieu of those early Renaissance times, this kind of craziness would have been just perfect.

After the picture was painted, Alberti would have attached a

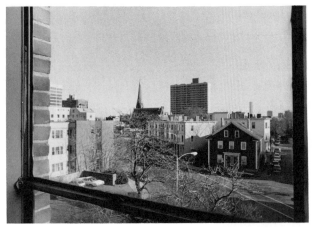

2.2a

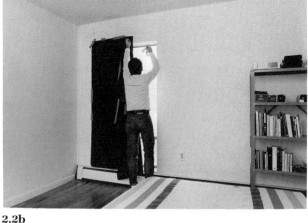

2.2b

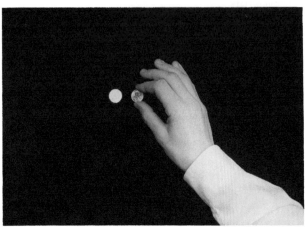

2.2c

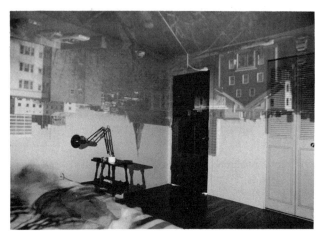

2.2d

Figure 2.2a *To convert an ordinary room into a camera obscura, select a room with a window overlooking a spacious view. To avoid direct sunlight, choose a window facing north, if possible. From* How to Convert an Ordinary Room into a Camera Obscura, © *Bob Rosinsky, 1984.*

Figure 2.2b *With an opaque material block out the selected window and all other windows. Black plastic, available at most hardware stores, is quite effective. Plastic is rather inexpensive and attaches easily with gaffer's tape or pushpins.* © *Bob Rosinsky, 1984.*

Figure 2.2c *Make a hole about the size of a penny in the center of the selected window. A larger hole will render a brighter but fuzzier image and a smaller hole a fainter but sharper image.* © *Bob Rosinsky, 1984.*

Figure 2.2d *Close any door that allows light into the room and turn off all artificial lights. An inverted and reversed image of the outside view appears on the walls and ceiling.* © *Bob Rosinsky, 1984.*

painted top to the box, turned it over so it was right side up, and let people view it through the very small aperture. The painting would not have been lit by the aperture; it could have been lit by an opening in the top or side of the box, or the painting could have been translucent and lit from an opening in the back of the box. The painting in its truthful representation of three-dimensional reality would have seemed miraculous. What a wonderful sense of humor Alberti's boxes must have had!

Are there any other cameras with which you view the image through the aperture? There are. Boxes like Alberti's, with a painting in three dimensions inside viewed through a peephole became known as *peep-show boxes* or *perspective cabinets*. Unfortunately, art historians never refer to them as any type of *camera obscura*. Less than a dozen have survived. The best-preserved peep-show box (Figure 2.3), by Samuel Van Hoogstraten (1627–1678), resides in the National Gallery in London. For light, one of its sides is glass covered. There are two apertures. Each is placed in the side near the glass three fourths of the way up the side. Van Hoogstraten had to invent two different illusionistic pictures for the inside of the box. Each is viewed separately from each pinhole. The larger problem is that each picture had to blend perfectly with the other in the middle of the box—a complex three-dimensional challenge.

Van Hoogstraten was a contemporary of Jan Vermeer. Vermeer's use of optical aids such as the *camera obscura* are well documented. Although partially destroyed, a six-sided peep-show box by Van Hoogstraten is on display at the Detroit Institute of Art. The side containing the small aperture has been removed! Because you don't look at the scene through the aperture, the idea is lost, and the scene simply looks distorted. Several other peep-show boxes are in The Netherlands and Denmark. The peep-show box, a painting in three dimensions, remained only a curiosity—one that was seldom realized by artists over the centuries to follow. A brilliant contemporary use of the peep-show box concept is shown in Gillian Brown's installation (see Color Plates 6.13a, 6.13b).

ALBERTI'S INTERSECTOR

Brunelleschi's small-apertured perspective device was transformed by Alberti in another way. He used it as a device for two-dimensional drawing and painting, known as the *intersector* or the *veil*. This was of great assistance to the artist, particularly in foreshortening, and was widely used over many centuries. In *De Pictura*, Alberti wrote:

> I believe nothing more convenient can be
> found than the veil, which among my friends I
> call the intersection, and whose usage I was
> the first to discover. It is like this: a veil loosely
> woven of fine thread, dyed whatever color you
> please, divided up by thicker threads into as
> many parallel square sections as you like, and
> stretched on a frame. I set this up between the
> eye and the object to be represented, so that
> the visual pyramid passes through the loose
> weave of the veil. This intersection of the veil
> has many advantages, first of all because it

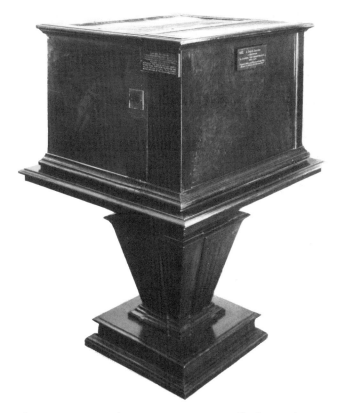

Figure 2.3 *Samuel Van Hoogstraten, Detail of Peep-show Box. Size of interior, $21\frac{1}{2}$" high x $31\frac{1}{2}$" wide x 21" deep. Circa 1660, courtesy of National Gallery, London. The box consists of three sides, a top, and a bottom. The fourth side is clear, covered with glass. About halfway up each side adjoining the glass is a peephole. These two peepholes are approximately $\frac{3}{4}$" in diameter and are near the glass. Viewed in person, the painted interior has a beautiful light and looks real.*

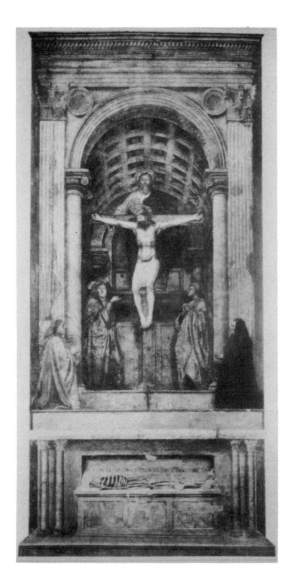

Figure 2.4 *Masaccio,* The Trinity *in S. Maria Novella, Florence. The painting was intended to be viewed at a distance of exactly twenty feet, one inch.*

always presents the same surfaces unchanged, for once you have the fixed positions of the outlines, you can immediately find the apex of the pyramid you started with, which is extremely difficult to do without the intersection. . . . A further advantage is that the position of the outlines and the boundaries of the surfaces can easily be established accurately on the painting panel; for just as you see the forehead in one parallel, the nose in the next, the cheeks in another, the chin in one below, and everything else in its particular place, so you can situate all the features on the panel or wall which you have similarly divided into appropriate parallels. Lastly, this veil affords the greatest assistance in executing your picture, since you can see any object that is round and in relief, represented on the flat surface of the veil.[5]

While the intersector is being used, the artist's eye had to remain stationary at the fixed point; consequently some of the early devices had a small aperture placed at eye level. Many preliminary drawings from the Italian Renaissance show horizontal and vertical grid lines associated with the intersector. Some finished paintings even retain sparse patches of these lines.

Brunelleschi's gifted friend Masaccio (1401–1428) used the intersector for *The Trinity* (Figure 2.4), apparently the first painting in one-point perspective. The woman standing on the left has grid lines across her figure and finer grid lines across her face. It must have been extraordinary to view the superb realism of this painting in 1428. Many consider *The Trinity* to be as powerful a painting in two dimensions as Brunelleschi's dome, several blocks away, is in three dimensions. Another friend of Brunelleschi, Donatello (1386–1466) apparently was the first to use one-point perspective in sculpture. Donatello's *Feast of Herod* sculpted in 1426 can be seen in the cathedral baptistery in Sienna.

The Flemish painter Jan van Eyck (1390–1441) contemporaneously achieved one-point perspective in his masterpiece *The Marriage of Giovanni Arnolfini and Giovanni Cenami,* although his theories and experiments in one-point perspective have not been historically documented. It is known that Flemish painters were in artistic contact with the Italian Renaissance and that van Eyck had even been urged by King Alfonso to emigrate to Naples to decorate his new palace. Flemish artists were known to have painted directly onto the reflection in a mirror to depict interiors, another way of achieving one-point perspective, as long as the painter's eye remained stationary.

LEONARDO DA VINCI

One-point perspective with the intersector as a painting aid was refined to its highest point by Piero della Francesca (1420–1492) in his book *De prospectiva pingendi,* published in 1480. Andrea Mantegna's *Oculus in the Ceiling* (Color Plate 2.5) is a perfect example of a fixed eye point—the viewer has to be standing below the painted ceiling—in combination with an obvious painting in one-point perspective. Leonardo da Vinci (1452–1519) later explained his use of the fixed point (Figure 2.6) as follows:

> You should have a pane of glass as large as a royal half folio, and fix it firmly before your eyes, that is, between your eye and the thing you wish to depict, and then you take up a position with the eye at $\frac{2}{3}$ braccio from the glass, fix your head with some device so you cannot move it, shut or cover one eye, and with the brush or pencil or chalk draw on the glass what you see beyond it, and then polish it down with sandpaper and dust it over good paper and paint it as you wish. [6]

Undoubtedly the best-known painting in one-point perspective is Leonardo's *The Last Supper* (Figure 2.7)—the vanishing point goes to Christ's right eye.

Leonardo mentions the use of a small aperture in at least twenty places in his manuscripts.[7] Some of his more notable quotations on the subject are as follows:

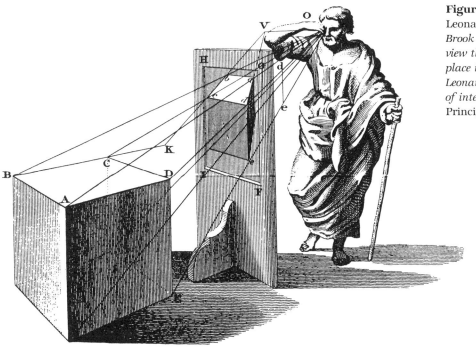

Figure 2.6 The Principle of the Leonardo Window *as illustrated by Brook Taylor. One eye is being used to view the top of the cube, ABCD, and place it in projection, abcd, within the Leonardo window, which is the surface of intersection FGHI. From* New Principles of Linear Perspective, *1811.*

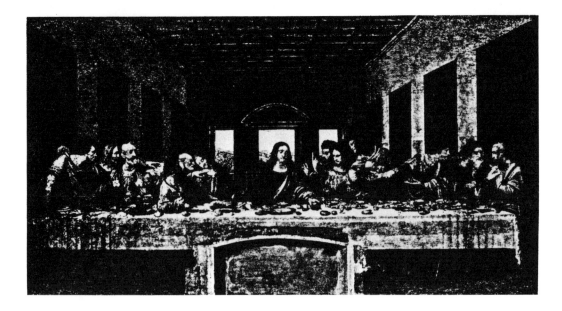

Figure 2.7 *Leonardo da Vinci,* The Last Supper, *circa 1496. In Santa Maria delle Grazie, Milan. The vanishing point goes to Christ's right eye.*

If you transmit the rays of the sun through a hole in the shape of a star you will see a beautiful effect of perspective in the spot where the sun's rays pass.

LEONARDO [C.7a (9b)]

Only one line of the image, of all those that reach the visual power, has no intersection; and this has no sensible dimensions because it is a mathematical line which originates from a mathematical point, which has no dimensions. According to my adversary, necessity requires that the central line of every image that enters by small and narrow openings into a dark chamber shall be turned upside down, together with the images of the bodies that surround it.

LEONARDO [W. 19152a]

That I must first show the distance of the sun from the earth; and, by means of a ray passing through a small hole into a dark chamber, detect its real size; and besides this, by means of the aqueous sphere calculate the size of the globe.

LEONARDO [Leic. Ia]

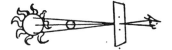

A method of seeing the sun eclipsed without pain to the eye. Take a piece of paper and pierce holes in it with a needle, and look at the sun through these holes.

LEONARDO [Trib. 6b]

The edges of a color transmitted through a small hole are more conspicuous than the central portions.

LEONARDO [C.A. 190a]

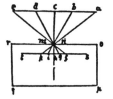

An experiment, showing how objects transmit their images or picture, intersecting within the eye in the crystalline humour. This is shown when the images of illuminated objects penetrate into a very dark chamber by some small round hole. Then, you will receive these images on a white paper placed within this dark room and rather near to the hole, and you will see all the objects on this paper in their proper forms and colors, but much smaller. . . . And let the little perforation be made in a very thin plate of iron.

LEONARDO [D. 80]

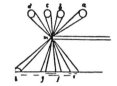

What difference is there in the way in which images pass through narrow openings and through large openings, or in those which pass by the sides of shaded bodies? By moving the edges of the opening through which the images are admitted, the images of immovable objects are made to move.

LEONARDO [W. 19149a]

Leonardo's well-known and frequently published statement on the pinhole *camera obscura* reads as follows:

I say that the front of a building—or any open piazza or field— which is illuminated by the sun has a dwelling opposite to it, and if, in the front which does not face the sun, you make a small round hole, all the illuminated objects will project their images through that hole and be visible inside the dwelling on the oppo- site wall which should be made white; and there, in fact, they will be upside down, and if you make similar openings in several places in the same wall you will have the same result from each. Hence the images of the illuminated objects are all everywhere on this wall and all in each minutest part of it. The reason, as we clearly know, is that this hole must admit some light to the said dwelling, and the light admitted by it is derived from one or many luminous bodies. If these bodies are of various colors and shapes the rays forming the images are of various colors and shapes, and so will the representations be on the wall.

LEONARDO [C.A. 135b]

Two drawings by Leonardo (Figure 2.8) without written expla- nation show light rays entering a human eye and light rays enter- ing a glass globe placed behind the aperture of a small *camera obscura.* These drawings would award Leonardo priority for the first refractive camera (containing a lens); however, historians of science overlook these drawings, choosing instead to credit Daniele Barbaro (1513–1570). Leon Battista Alberti's diffraction camera is not even in the running. Science historians must think a camera has to have a conventional lens. As soon as a lens was placed in a *camera obscura,* artists no longer needed to use the pinhole *cam- era obscura.* When the lens *camera obscura* became portable, by about the late seventeenth century, it made Alberti's intersector somewhat obsolete. This would have happened around the time of Vermeer (1632–1675). For a scholarly discussion on the lens *cam- era obscura,* see M. S. Hammond, *The Camera Obscura: A Chapter in the Pre-history of Photography.* Dissertation Abs. Int. 47(10) (doc- toral dissertation, Ohio State University, 1987).

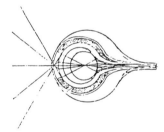

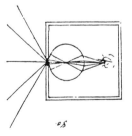

Figure 2.8 *Leonardo da Vinci,* Light rays entering the eye and light rays entering the glass globe placed inside a small *camera obscura.* Codex Atlanticus *fol. 337 r., circa 1500.*

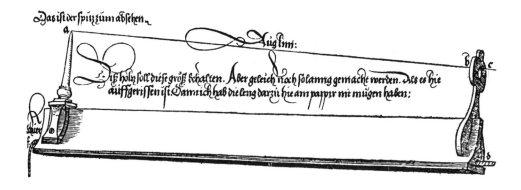

Figure 2.9a *Albrecht Dürer,* Perspective Instrument, *from* Book of Measurements. *Artist views scene through small aperture in upright, sighting past top of pointed column, circa 1525.*

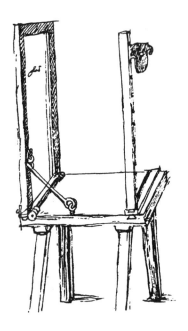

Figure 2.9b *Albrecht Dürer,* Perspective Apparatus, *from* Book of Measurements, *circa 1525.*

Albrecht Dürer (1471–1528) was responsible for transporting concepts of the Italian Renaissance to Germany. He learned the use of one-point perspective, the intersector, the small aperture, and the fixed eye point while traveling in Italy. Dürer, the great draftsman, had gone there specifically "to learn the secrets of the art of perspective from a man who is willing to teach me." [8] It is thought that Dürer learned perspective through personal instruction from Leonardo or from Luca Pacioli (1450?–1520?), the author of *The Divine Proportion.* It is known that Dürer read Piero della Francesca's *De prospectiva pingendi,* published in 1480, because in 1525, Dürer wrote della Francesca's five rules of perspective in his own *Book of Measurements:*

> perspective is a Latin word meaning "Seeing-Through" [seeing through the small aperture]. To this same "seeing through" belongs five things.
>
> 1. The first is the eye that sees.
> 2. The second is the object seen.
> 3. The third is the distance between (eye and object).
> 4. The fourth; one sees everything by means of straight lines, that is to say the shortest lines.
> 5. The fifth is the dividing from one another of the things seen. [9]

Included in Dürer's *Book of Measurements* were drawings (Figures 2.9a through 2.9d) of many tools for the artist to use in creating one-point perspective by using the fixed point. Two books thoroughly describe perspective mathematics and tools: *The Science of Art,* Martin Kemp (Yale University Press, 1990) and *The Invention of Infinity,* J. V. Field (Oxford University Press, 1997). Agnes Merlet's French film *Artemisia* (1997) has scenes in which the artist is using pinhole perspective devices.

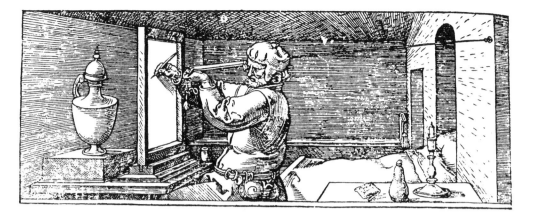

Figure 2.9c *Albrecht Dürer,* Perspective Instrument, *from* Book of Measurements. *Artist is viewing through a tube, which is attached to the back wall, circa 1525.*

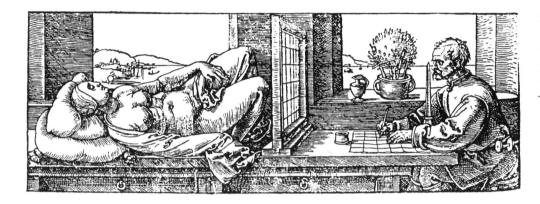

Figure 2.9d *Albrecht Dürer,* Perspective Apparatus, *from* Book of Measurements, *circa 1525. Note the small-aperture fixed eye point.*

ANAMORPHOSIS—THE DECEPTION OF THE EYE

By the sixteenth and seventeenth centuries, many artists had become aware of a kind of superrealism that could be obtained by using the fixed point for casting a picture. To achieve this heightened realism, the finished picture had to be viewed from the same fixed eye point. A new school of art, known as *trompe l'oeil,* which translates "to deceive the eye," evolved around this concept. Possibly the highest achievement of *trompe l'oeil* is to be found in the curved vault at St. Ignazio in Rome in the painting *Entrance of Saint Ignatius into Paradise* (Figure 2.10a) by Fra Andrea Pozzo (1642–1709). To show the viewer the position of the fixed eye point, Pozzo placed a marble disc on the floor below the curved vault. When viewers stand on that disc and look upward, their eyes match the fixed point, and the entire painting snaps into place. The multitude of painted figures on the vault look as if they are truly floating in space above the viewer. No two-dimensional reproduction of this painting can reproduce the beauty of the three-dimensional illusion. It has to be seen in person.

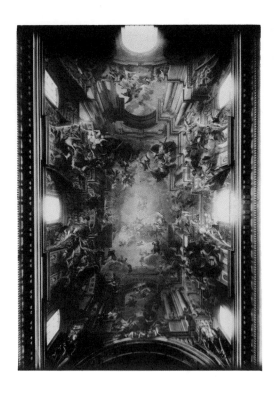

Figure 2.10a *Fra Andrea Pozzo,* Entrance of St. Ignatius into Paradise, *Church of San Ignnazio Di Loyola, Rome, circa 1685–1694. Everything above the brightly lit windows is painted onto a curved vault. Even the columns seem to be projecting upward into deep space.*

To create the painting, Pozzo placed grid lines across the surface of his flat preliminary drawing. Next he placed a giant net (Figure 2.10b) enlarged in scale from the same grid horizontally across the bottom of the vault. Pozzo then ran a set of strings from the fixed point, which was at eye level above the marble disc, through each intersection in the net. He then marked where each string held taut touched the vaulted ceiling. This showed him how to place the original grid onto the curved ceiling, thereby enabling the flat painting to be reproduced onto the curved surface.

Pozzo's painting is an anamorphosis, directly descended from Brunelleschi's small-apertured perspective device, Alberti's intersector, and Leonardo's anamorphic pinhole projections. In an anamorphosis, an image is projected and then drawn onto a surface that is angled away from the fixed point. Examples are Pozzo's painted curved vault and

Figure 2.10b *Fra Andrea Pozzo,* The method of drawing the net or lattice work on vaults *(the 100th Figure) from* "Perspectiva Pictorum et Architectorum," *1693. The eye point is shown as o in the elevation drawings. Angled dotted lines are stretched through the net intersections onto the vault.*

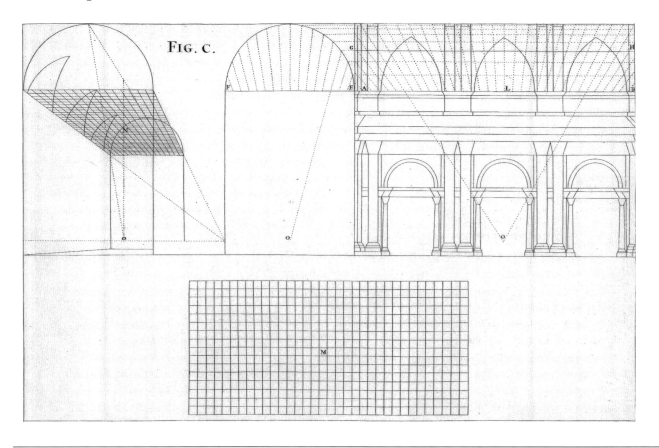

the side walls, ceiling, and floor of Van Hoogstraten's peep-show box (see Figure 2.3). Leonardo wrote the following about creating anamorphic projection:

> If you want to represent a figure on a wall, the wall being foreshortened, while the figure is to appear in its proper form, and as standing free from the wall, you must proceed thus: have a thin plate of iron and make a small hole in the center; this hole must be round. Set a light close to it in such a position that it shines through the central hole, then place any object or figure you please so close to the wall that it touches it and draw the outline of the shadow on the wall; then fill in the shade and add the lights; place the person who is to see it so that he looks through that same hole where at first the light was; and you will never be able to persuade yourself that the image is not detached from the wall.
>
> LEONARDO [A. 42b]

Leonardo's drawing of a child's face is the first known anamorphic drawing (Figure 2.11). Viewed frontally, the child's face is very wide and almost unrecognizable; viewed on edge, the face becomes recognizable. It is best to view Leonardo's drawing by holding one hand over one eye and viewing the drawing from the right edge. In the same drawing is another anamorph, an eye, also to be viewed from the right edge.

The anamorphic pinhole, which da Vinci is credited with discovering, results in two views:

1. A distorted view of reality (what a person sees when viewing the anamorph from the conventional frontal position).
2. An undistorted view of reality (the true picture). This view can be found only if you know where the pinhole or small aperture was situated to make the painting or drawing. Usually, the pinhole was on one side. A number of historic anamorphs are shown in *Perspective,* by Pierre Descargues (Harry N. Abrams, 1977), and *Hidden Images,* by Fred Leeman (Harry N. Abrams, 1976).

The only large anamorph still in existence that dates from the Italian Renaissance is *St. Francis of Paolo* by Emmanuel Maignan in the Monastery at Church of Trinità dei Monte in Rome, painted in 1642–1646. This remarkable sixty foot long painting (Figure 2.12) lines a hallway. Entering from the far end of the hallway, one sees St. Francis in prayer kneeling on his cloak under a tree and floating over the Straits of Messina—one of his miraculous deeds. Standing directly in front of the painting, one sees the robes become a lake with several boats and small villages dotting a mountainous terrain. Maignan, a monk in the Order of the Minims, made this anamorph using a tubular, fixed eye point and a hinged, two-dimensional, miniature gridded painting. Strings

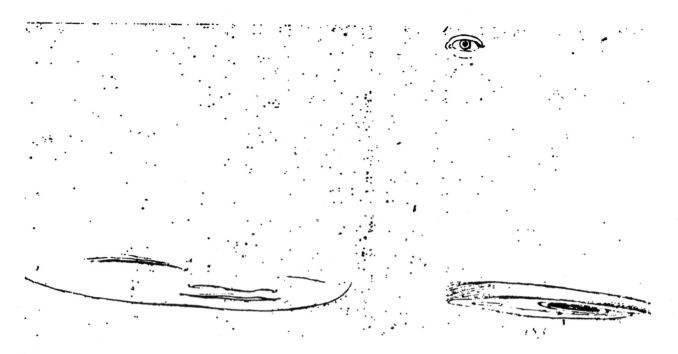

Figure 2.11 *Leonardo da Vinci,* Child's Face and an Eye. *Anamorphic drawing in Codex Atlanticus, fol. 35, versa a, circa 1485.*

were stretched from the eye point through the hinged miniature to arrive at distant placement points on the long wall. The creation of this anamorphic technique can be credited to Jean-Françoise Niceron (1613–1646), also of the Order of Minims, who while living at the same monastery wrote the influential book *Thaumaturgus Opticus* published posthumously in 1648. The book's title refers to St. Francis as a "performer of optical miracles." Both Maignan and Niceron were friends with well-known Renaissance scientist-philosopher Rene Descartes, who lived nearby. Niceron made many circular anamorphs that could be viewed with a mirrored tube. A history of anamorphs is found in *Anamorfosi* by Jurgis Baltrusaitis (Adelphi Edizioni, Milano, 1990).

Even more deceptive is a painting that looks completely real from the front but may contain an area within it that is an anamorph. The best-known example of an anamorph within a realistic painting is *The Ambassadors* by Holbein the Younger (1497?–1543). The anamorph is located in the center foreground. When viewed from the front, the anamorph looks like a diagonal blur; when viewed from the above right it is seen as a skull.

THE FIRST PINHOLE PHOTOGRAPHS

Except for a few peep-show boxes and a limited number of anamorphs, the pinhole technique lay relatively dormant from about 1653 to 1850. This was changed by the invention of photography. Sir David Brewster, the well-known English scientist, was one of the first to make pinhole photographs. In his 1856 book, *The*

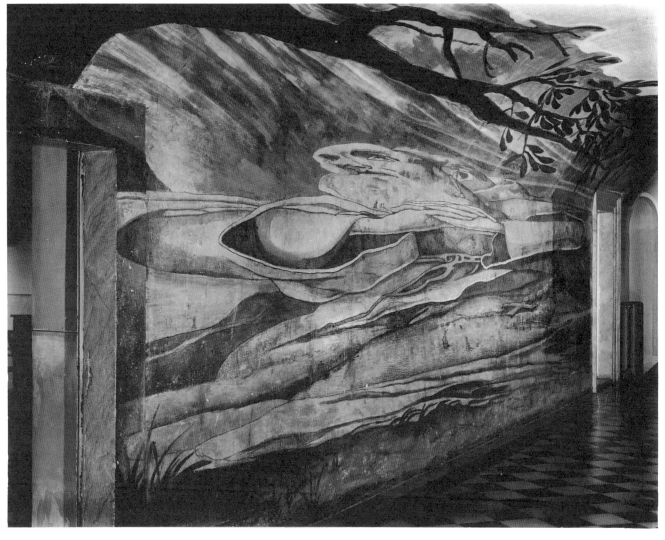

Figure 2.12 *Emmanuel Maignan,* St. Francis of Paola, *anamorphic painting in the Monastery of Church of Trinità dei Monte, Rome, circa 1646.*

Stereoscope, Brewster coined the word *pin-hole,* and it stuck. Other names have been suggested or even urged as a replacement. The following are examples:

- *Natural camera,* Joseph Petzval, 1859
- *Stenopaic photography,* Dehors and Deslandres, the late 1880s
- *Natural camera,* George Davison, 1889
- *Lensless,* Alfred Maskell, 1890
- *Rectographic,* J. B. Thomson, 1901
- *Needle-hole,* Edward Gray, 1907[10]

As inappropriate as it might seem because the pinhole is almost always made with a needle or drill, the term *pinhole* has its own particular charm and historical appropriateness. Here is Brewster's observation as he coined *pin-hole*:

> Pictures thus taken are accurate representations of the object, whether it be lineal, superficial, or solid, as seen from or through the hole; and if we throw sufficient light upon the object, or make the material which receives the image very sensitive, we should require no other camera for giving us photographs of all sizes. The only source of error which we can conceive, is that which may arise from the inflexion of light, but we believe that it would exercise a small influence, if any, and it is only by experiment that its effect can be ascertained.

> The Rev. Mr. Egerton and I have obtained photographs of a bust, in the course of ten minutes, with a very faint sun, and through an aperture less than a hundredth of an inch; and I have no doubt that when chemistry has furnished us with a material more sensitive to light, a camera without lenses, and with only a pin-hole, will be the favorite instrument of the photographer. At present, no sitter could preserve his composure and expression during the number of minutes which are required to complete the picture.[11]

Sir William Crookes (1832–1919), John Spiller, and William de Wiveleslie Abney, all from England, were also some of the first photographers to try pinhole. Probably the earliest extant group of pinhole photographs were made by the English Flinders Petrie (1853–1942), the "father of archaeology," during his excavations in Egypt (Figures 2.13a and 2.13b). His first pinhole photographs were taken in 1881 at Giza during his second expedition to Egypt. Petrie's biscuit tin camera is described by Margaret Drower in a 1985 biography titled *Flinders Petrie*. She wrote:

> . . . never having owned or used a camera in his life, he set to work to design one. It was essentially a box of japanned tin about the size and shape of a biscuit tin; the lens had two apertures, drilled in a sheet of tin, and the drop-shutter was also of tin, strengthened by a slip of wood; there was a sleeve of opaque material into which he could insert his hand to remove and replace successive plates, exposed and unexposed plates being separated by a slip of cardboard.[12]

Petrie's pinhole camera is lost. However, from Drower's description and from Petrie's suggestions in *Methods and Aims in Archaeology* (1904), it is possible to reconstruct his camera. It had a simple lens, stopped down with two pinholes, one at f/100 and the other at f/200. If one of these pinholes had been of optimum diameter, Petrie's camera would have produced true pinhole images while that pinhole was in use. (Maurice Pirenne in *Optics, Painting, and Photography* states: "Indeed for a pinhole of the optimum size it is not possible to improve the accuracy of the image by placing a lens in front of the pinhole."[13]) Petrie was not afraid

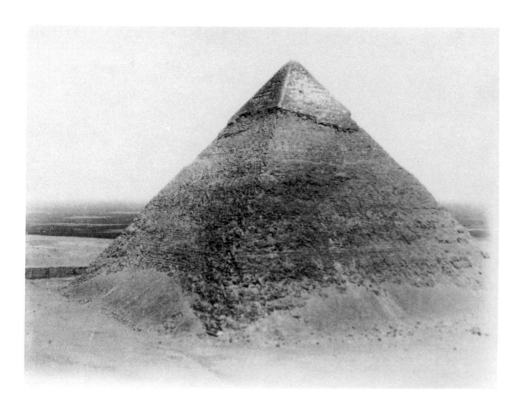

Figure 2.13a © *Flinders Petrie*, Khafre Pyramid, *pinhole photograph made from a 3" x 4" original glass negative, 1881. Courtesy of the Petrie Museum, University College, London.*

to take a nonconformist position in camera technology; he achieved exactly what he wanted in the most basic, direct way. Petrie wrote:

> Small stops can be made out of a strip of tin plate or blackened card; and the hand camera [placed on a tripod] can be stopped down with a pinhole stop stuck in front of the lens so as to work at almost any nearness and scale with exposures of $\frac{1}{2}$ or 1 minute in full sunshine.

> The instantaneous shutter is a useless article for all fixed objects. It is far better to work with a small stop which gives plenty of depth of focus, and exposed 2 to 20 seconds, which is long enough for f/100 on slow plates in Egypt. For direct enlargement of objects a stop of f/200 is excellent, and only needs 30 seconds exposure. If a shutter is wanted a simple drop can easily be extemporized.[14]

In his diary, dated 20 September 1881, Petrie wrote: "finished off camera and trying plates of newspapers as tests of definition. Got a line of $\frac{1}{1,600}$ inch wide on the plate."[15] Another pleasantly insightful observation on Petrie's camera and methods comes from M. V. Seton-Williams in *The Road to El-Aguezin*:

> He took all his photographs on the site. The objects and pottery were arranged on shelves draped with a black backcloth against the sides of the hut. Then the stand camera would be set up. . . . The exposures could take anything up to half an hour, but the

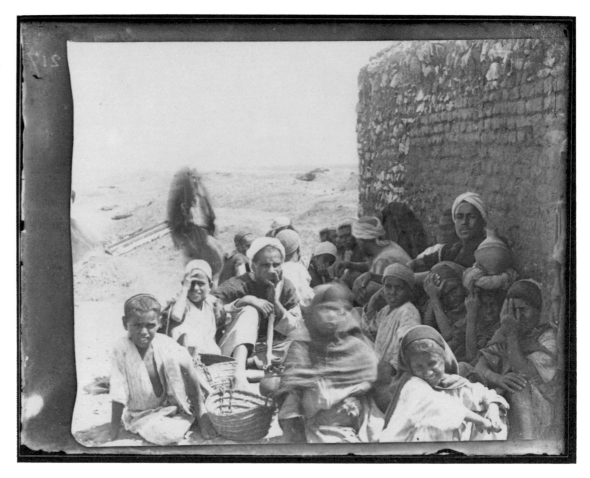

film was, speed 40 H & D, made specially for him by Kodak, that it did not matter if the whole expedition passed between the camera and the objects, as they sometimes did because the camera was set up in the only passageway into the mess room.[16]

PINHOLE'S POPULARITY IN EARLY "PICTORIALISM"

By the late 1880s, the impressionist movement in painting influenced a few of the more daring "art" photographers. For the first time, a sharply focused image was not deemed paramount by some; it was opportune to experiment with pinhole technique. This aroused intellectual antagonism. On one side were those from the old school, who believed in the sharpest focus and achieved it with highest-quality lenses. On the other side were those from the new school who admired atmospheric qualities, otherwise derided as fuzziness. Fuzziness later became known as *pictorialism*. There were factions within each group that reflected differences of opinion about the extent of sharpness or just how much fuzziness was desirable. In England, the most outspoken proponent of fuzziness was George Davison. At that time photography was not considered art. In 1889, in the new magazine *Photography*, Davison wrote:

> It need hardly be said that nearly all beginners and many old stagers simply go straight for the smallest stop they dare use in order to make sure of getting all sharp. If the object is what we may call scientific, well and good, but if there be anything worthy of artistic representation in the picture selected, such a procedure will certainly tend to lose, suppress, or distract attention from it. Some of those who are fond of chewing the word 'fuzziness' say that they quite see all this, and they express approval of many pictures shown them with soft out of focus backgrounds, and also of pinhole landscapes, but still they persist, apparently out of personal partisanship, in taking up a hostile position towards those who venture to call this artistic focus, and who point to the necessity for such treatment in every pictorial subject. Now, in regard to ninety-nine hundredths of the photographs turned out, it does not matter in the main how they are treated in this respect; they would be almost equally feeble however focused, but given a subject with really strong and poetic possibilities in it, sharpness and detail will go a long way to render it commonplace.[17]

A month earlier, Davison described his technique as follows:

> Our own apparatus is a thin flat piece of brass with a succession of holes of sizes $\frac{1}{20}$ in. to $\frac{1}{80}$ in., about $\frac{1}{2}$ in. apart, countersunk in it. This bar of brass slides across a hole in a special front to the camera, through slots made in a simple telescopic lens tube, which tube serves as a sky shade. . . . It will certainly do most photographers good to produce a few pinhole pictures. If they are not warped by prejudice, or blinded by ignorance, they cannot fail to feel the advantage that frequently is gained by such diffusion of focus.[18]

A year later Davison's pinhole photograph *An Old Farmstead* (Figure 2.14) won the highest award at the annual exhibition of the Photographic Society of London. (Davison later changed the title to *The Onion Field.*) Davison received praise; the pinhole received the following criticism:

> It is certainly a satire on the labours of the optician that after the resources of science have been exhausted to produce a perfect lens, the best work can be produced with no more elaborate optical instrument than a bit of sheet metal with a hole pierced in it.[19]

This award and criticism were the beginning of the schism in the Royal Photographic Society that resulted in formation of the Linked Ring—a group of art photographers dedicated to the ideal of pictorialism. George Davison was one of the original twelve founders. International exhibitions of art photography were presented by the group. Later the words *pictorial photography* were substituted for *art photography.*

By 1892, photographic enthusiasts in Europe, Japan, and the United States were purchasing varied types of commercial pinhole equipment. In London that year, four thousand pinhole cameras, known as Photomnibuses, were sold. (Oddly enough, not one of these cameras can be found in any historical collection.) Several years earlier, an American company invented the Ready Fotographer (Figure 2.15)—a camera a century ahead of its time, for it was the first disposable camera, and it was a pinhole camera. It contained one dry, glass plate, a pinhole in tinfoil, and a folding bellows (the entire camera folded flat). The first commercial pinhole camera came from France, designed by Dehors and Deslandres in 1887 (Figure 2.16). It, too, was unusual; it had a rotat-

Figure 2.14 © *George Davison,* The Onion Field, *1890. Courtesy of John and Elizabeth Fergus-Jean.*

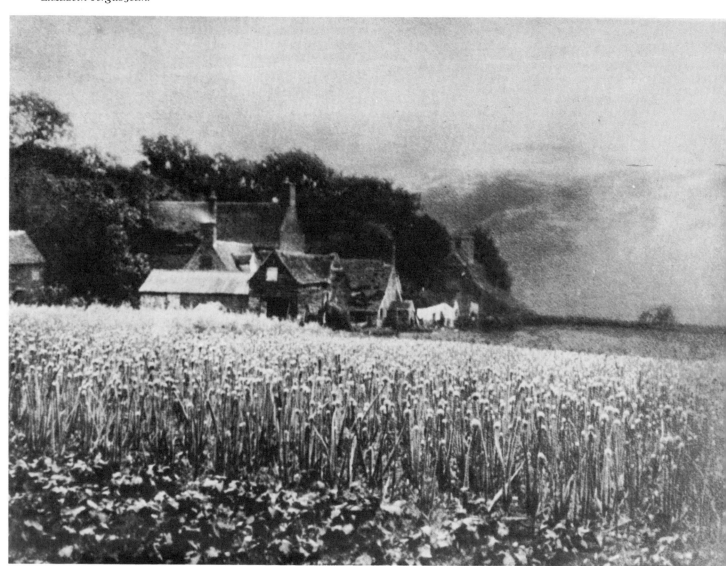

ing pinhole disc with six pinholes (three pairs of similar sizes) used singly or in stereoscopic pairs. Another American company sold the Glen Pinhole Camera, which included six dry plates (each $2\frac{1}{2}$ inches square), chemicals, trays, print frame, and ruby paper for a safe light (Figure 2.17). As if this were not enough, several companies sold rotating pinhole discs (Figure 2.18), which could be placed directly into a lens board (after the lens had been removed). All of these pinhole cameras and attachments are extremely rare today.[20] These cameras are remarkably inventive, and it is unfortunate they are no longer available.

AUGUST STRINDBERG

In 1892, the renowned Swedish dramatist August Strindberg (1849–1912) began experimenting with pinhole cameras. In his study of science and art, Strindberg became the creator of his own exotic branch of metaphysics. He distrusted lenses. Unfortunately, his pinhole psychological portraits from this period are lost. Strindberg's search within the photographic form had many unconventional approaches, one of which was to create images without a camera. For instance, Strindberg made Celestiographs by holding photographic paper in his hand and pointing it toward the galaxy or planet he was photographing. His manuscripts at the Royal Library in Stockholm give evidence that he often completed fifteen pages of mathematical calculations to arrive at how and when to aim the photographic paper.

Photo historians are still at a loss about how to place Strindberg in the history of photography. Although his work spanned forty years, only around 100 images exist today. Of these images, only three might be pinhole; two are in Strindberg's *Occult Diary.* The other is his photographic verification of Fraunhoefer diffraction. An additional two images were published in Frieda Uhl's book on Strindberg and are listed as being

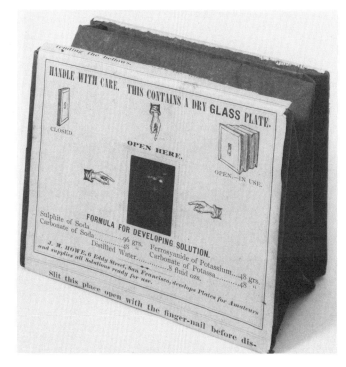

Figure 2.15 Ready Fotografer Pinhole Camera, *circa 1890. Courtesy of the Division of Photographic History, Smithsonian Institution, Washington, D.C.*

Figure 2.16 Messrs. Dehors and Deslandres' Pinhole Camera and Pinhole Disc *from "Photography without a Lens,"* Anthony's Photographic Bulletin *18(8 October 1887):599–601.*

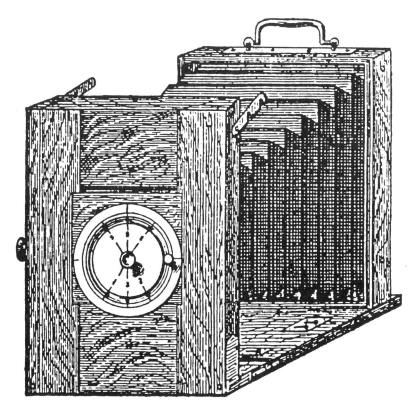

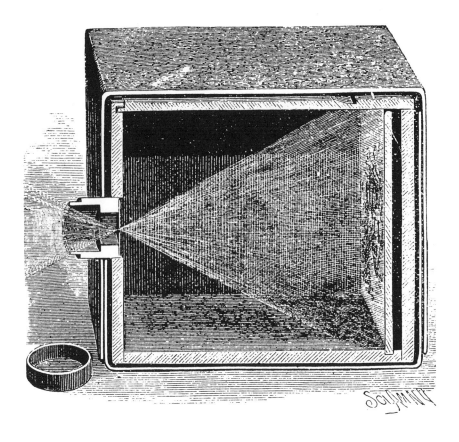

Figure 2.17 Glen Pinhole Camera *from "One Dollar Photographic Outfit,"* Scientific American 65(4 July 1891):5.

Figure 2.18 Watkins Universal Pinhole Lens, *circa 1905. Courtesy of Allen Sipprell.*

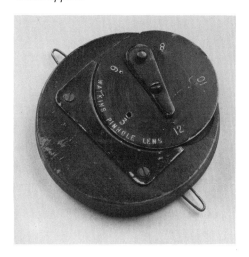

"made with a camera without a lens." In spite of the dearth of surviving images, we are fortunate indeed, for preserved in some of Strindberg's writings are explanations and investigations, although they are written with his cryptic, searching humor. Translated by Jan-Erik Lundström, a contemporary European photo critic, is the following excerpt from Strindberg's "On the Action of Light in Photography—Reflection on the Occasion of the X-Rays":

But: First speculate, then experiment! And I speculated as follows: Coming from the next room, the sound from an instrument touches my ear more forcefully if the door is open, than if it is closed. Analogy: The light ought to work more directly in the camera, if it doesn't have to pass through a solid medium, such as glass.

This was true and false at the same time; because sound is more easily transmitted in solid bodies than in the air. And yet, when I open the door, I can hear better!

And I do see clearer through glass lenses than through air! Here I stopped, amazed at the changeability of the unchangeable laws of nature, their capriciousness, their self-contradictions, and their looseness. But I then continued. Took away the lens from the camera, and inserted a diaphragm, drilled through with a sewing needle. I photographed a person, and received a result which in all aspects was more successful than in photographing with a good lens.

Against all rules, I had placed the man against a window—behind which was a landscape with fir trees in the foreground, and lakes and forests in the background.

The man appeared in clear detail; and so did the trees, in perspective all the way out to the distance.

Test with a lens and the same pose. The man now appeared flat, no detail, and of the trees not a trace—the whole landscape only a bright white background.

But my diaphragm gave me yet another advantage. The man's coat was white with blue stripes. These blue stripes should normally turn out white, but here they remained grayish, outlining themselves against the white coat. And this fact, that blue retained its value, became for me the starting point for further experiments with colour photography.

My speculation was correct when I took away the glass-lens, and allowed the light to work directly without passing through a medium.[21]

Elaborating on Strindberg's ideas about pinhole photography, Jan-Erik Lundström wrote:

Human vision is an artifact. Just like our understanding of nature is nothing but models that we construct, which are more or less feasible in our dealings with the world. And as a consequence the realism of the camera or photography cannot be easily trusted.

These are of course ideas that have many reverberations in contemporary cultural discourse—that realism is relative, that language constructs a world rather than reflecting one—in the heydays of deconstructivism, and a post-modernism that has given up the possibility of a sensory world, a world of direct physical experience. Strindberg's turn to pinhole photography might then be viewed as a counterpoint—a search for an unmediated world, an absolute realism.

Such was also his mode of photography—seldom expressionist or window-on-the-world realism, but rather conceptual, analytical, symbolic, metaphysical. The camera was an instrument with many ends. Photography a medium with endless applications.[22]

PINHOLE'S DEMISE IN THE EARLY TWENTIETH CENTURY

By the twentieth century, pinhole technique was pigeonholed and labeled impressionistic. The technique could find only limited use by pictorialists (Figure 2.19). New realism, mass-produced photographic equipment, and the cataclysmic need for speed left pinhole technique far, far behind. By the 1930s, the technique was

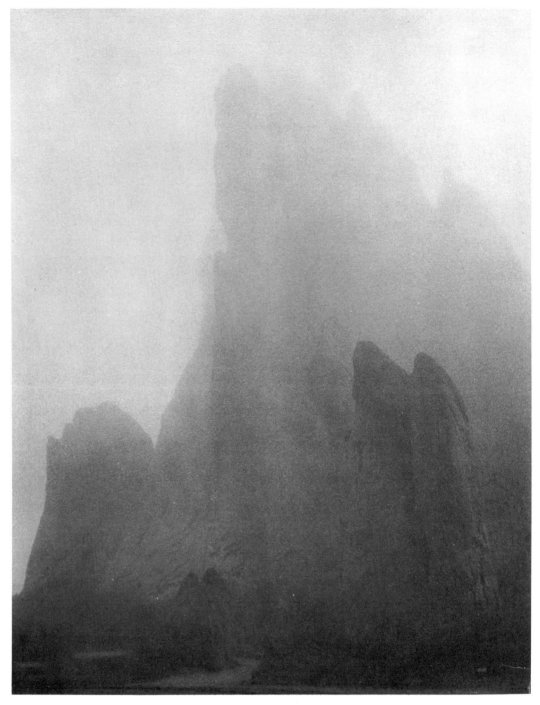

Figure 2.19 *Laura Gilpin,* Ghost Rock, Garden of the Gods, *1919, 8" x 10" platinum print, P1979.95.66. © Amon Carter Museum, Laura Gilpin Collection, Fort Worth, Texas. Used by permission.*

barely remembered. At best, in the photographic art world, it became merely a teaching tool. Frederick Brehm in the late 1930s at the college that would later become Rochester Institute of Technology was possibly the first college professor to emphasize the educational side of pinhole technique. Brehm also designed Kodak's only commercial pinhole camera—the Kodak Pinhole Camera (circa 1940s). This kit offered the first build-it-yourself commercial pinhole camera (Figure 2.20). Brehm unknowingly may have damaged pinhole's reputation; by the 1950s many people thought of pinhole as only the simplest of cameras, mostly useful because it could be made from a kit.

Between 1940 and 1960, pinhole was rarely used. Pinhole technique was practically forgotten in art. It has been written that the well-known British art photographer Bill Brandt (1904–1983) used a pinhole for his 1950s wide-angle nude studies.[23] However, Jim Barrow, who later owned the camera Brandt used for this series, stated that the camera definitely was not pinhole. I hope Barrow's letter, included here, will correct photographic history. Barrow wrote:

Here is the "story." Bill Brandt had two whole plate ($6\frac{1}{2}$" x $8\frac{1}{2}$") cameras made by Kodak in England (or made for them). The design would have made them useful to general purpose commercial photographers doing day, architectural or industrial work; it has been said that it was a popular camera with the police force, maybe so, but it has been described as a police camera and this is nonsense. It was nonfocusing, rigid construction, but a focusing bellows attachment was available as an extra. Basically it was designed around the Zeiss W. A. Protar series maximum aperture f 18 stopping down to f 45—the focal length of mine was 8.5cm—but he had others. The provenance of my camera, which I recently sold, was Brandt's widow. I am enclosing a picture of the camera identical to the one he used [Figure 2.21].[24]

By the end of the 1950s, the few articles published about pinhole trivialized the medium. A new awareness was needed.

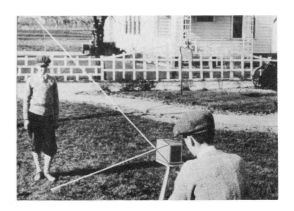

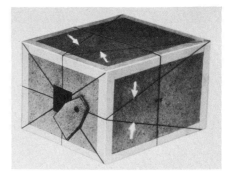

Figure 2.20 *Two details from Frederick Brehm's* Instructions for Building Kodak's Pinhole Camera *circa 1940. Gift of Richard Zakia, from the collection at Pinhole Resource.*

Figure 2.21 © *Jim Barrow,* Whole Plate Camera Similar to Bill Brandt's, *lens photo. From the collection at Pinhole Resource.*

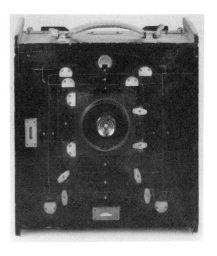

NOTES

1. Filarete (1400–1469), in Eugenio Battista, *Brunelleschi* (New York: Rizzoli International, 1981), 110.
2. Ibid., 102–13.
3. Fred Leeman, *Hidden Images* (New York: Harry N. Abrams, 1976), 21–22.
4. James Waterhouse, *"Camera Obscura,"* in Encyclopaedia Brittanica (1910), 102.
5. Leon Battista Alberti, *On Painting and on Sculpture* (1435; reprint, edited by Cecil Grayson, London: Phaidon Press, 1972), 69.

6. Battista, *Brunelleschi*, 110.

7. Leonardo da Vinci, *The Notebooks of Leonardo da Vinci,* ed. Jean Paul Richter (New York: Dover Publications, 1970). Leonardo's contributions to pinhole optics are in the following: D. 8a; A. 64b; Br. M. 174b; W. 19152a and b; D. 5r; A. 9b; C. A. 190a; A. 9b; W. 19150b; A. 42b; C. A. 135b; W. 19149a; B. N. 2038. 20b; Triv. 6b; F 5a; C. 6a; Leic. 1a; C. 7a (9b); W. 19148b; C. A.204b.

8. William Martin Conway, *The Writings of Albrecht Dürer* (New York: Philosophical Library, 1958), 208.

9. Ibid.

10. Stanley R. Page, "The Golden Age of Pinhole Photography 1885–1919," *Pinhole Journal* 2(1986):29. A complete description of pinhole photography in the 1890s.

11. Sir David Brewster, *The Stereoscope: Its History, Theory, and Construction* (London: J. Murray, 1856), 136–37.

12. Margaret Drower, *Flinders Petrie* (London: Victor Gollanca Ltd., 1985), 48.

13. M. H. Pirenne, *Optics, Painting and Photography* (New York: Cambridge University Press, 1970), 23.

14. Flinders Petrie, *Methods and Aims in Archeology* (New York: Macmillan, 1904), 74–75.

15. Flinders Petrie, diary, dated 20 September 1881, 1882, Petrie Museum, London, unpublished.

16. M. V. Seton-Williams, *The Road to El-Aguezin* (London: Kegan Paul Int., 1988), 3.

17. George Davison, "Softness in Photographs and Means of Obtaining It," *Photography* 1 (12 December 1889):684–86.

18. George Davison, "Softness in Photographs," *Photography* 1 (14 November 1889):634–35.

19. "Exhibition of the Photographic Society," *Times* (London), 29 September 1890, 4.

20. Stanley R. Page, "The Golden Age of Pinhole Photography 1885–1919," *Pinhole Journal* 2(1986):21–25.

21. August Strindberg, "On the Action of Light in Photography: Reflection on the Occasion of the X-rays," trans. Jan-Erik Lundström, *Pinhole Journal* 4(1988):19. The entire article was written circa 1894 and appeared in Strindberg's *Collected Works,* Vol. 26, ed. John Landquist (Stockholm: Bonniers, 1912–1920).

22. Jan-Erik Lundström, "Notes on 'On the Action of Light in Photography'…," *Pinhole Journal* 4(1988):21.

23. Weston Naef, *Handbook of Photographs Collection* (Malibu: The J. Paul Getty Museum, 1995), 208.

24. Jim Barrow, personal letter to the author, September 6, 1998.

The pinhole camera is basically a room or space with a window. Actually the first historical cameras that we know of were real rooms that one could walk around in. Their purpose was to observe the sun. The inside space of a pinhole camera is of course much smaller in relationship. Nevertheless, their simpleness and flawlessness offers a perfect photo apparatus that is free from unnecessary fittings and attachments. They are pure in their functional clarity.

PETER OLPE

We shape the clay into a pot, but it is the emptiness inside that holds whatever we want.

LAO-TZU

Pinhole's Revival in Art: The 1960s and 1970s

REBIRTH—THE LATE 1960s

In the late 1960s, a number of artists whose training was not necessarily photographic chose to explore pinhole photography. None of them was aware of the others' work. Who was first does not seem important. What sets all these people apart is that they chose to experiment in pinhole photography without instruction from others: Paolo Gioli in Italy; Gottfried Jäger in West Germany; and David Lebe, Franco Salmoiraghi, Wiley Sanderson, and I in the United States.

Why were these artists working in pinhole if pinhole photography had practically died at least two decades before? Because a changing reality in the air in the late 1960s prompted investigation of alternatives. Something as universally accepted as the sharpness produced by a lens camera producing a singular image needed to be reexamined. For most of the aforementioned photographers, the only alternative was multiple imagery using a pinhole camera. Some of the concerns, fascinations, and needs of these artists are clarified in the following statements, both personal and theoretical. Paolo Gioli wrote:

> There is in the history of writing, of graphics, a mark that continues to fascinate me: the dot. It's always amazing to see a dot made by a pencil and then the dot immediately become a pinhole. The eye of a needle is probably the most provocative design in the history of art. Most of my work goes through the eye of a needle, basically with a great variety of *camera obscuras,* not a 35mm camera. I have taken the *stenopeic* slit as an ideological as well as a plastic "point of view." The *photostenopeic* image came to me because I didn't have a camera. I am fascinated by the purity of the action of shooting "poor" and the equally pure

image that one gets back [Figure 3.1]. Mine is not a brief scholastic experiment, but a definite way of understanding space specifically through a point in space which, as we know, penetrated into caves with alarming rays, or, reflected on the walls perturbing the first Arab thinkers . . . and my sensitized papers.[1]

Gottfried Jäger, in his article "Pinhole Structures" (1988), proclaimed his pinhole photography from the late 1960s was simply democratic, not enigmatic or magical. He wrote:

> Toward the end of the 60s there was a pervading sense of change in the Federal Republic of Germany. . . . In 1968 I organized the exhibition "Generative Photography" in Bielefeld. It was a direct response to the prevalent trends in West German photography at that time. On the one hand it was a reaction to "Subjective Photography," dating back to the 50s and 60s and now on its last legs. The latter had been increasingly reduced to a formal level and had shown lack of innovation. . . . In contrast, generative photography [Figures 3.2a, 3.2b] aimed at clarity and transparence. It did not want to convey anything magical or mysterious in its pictures. On the contrary, it aimed at enlightenment and rationality. Using a methodical, step-by-step procedure and being completely open about its method, it endeavored to avoid the enigmatic in art; instead, it attempted to make inherent ideas and forms understandable to everybody at all times. The sequenced composition, based on a programme previously defined, was here one of its essential means. . . . Nothing was to remain obscure. An elementary abstract, systematic, constructive, indeed "democratic" picture language was the result. Form had no "top" or "bottom"; there was no hierarchy amongst the pic-

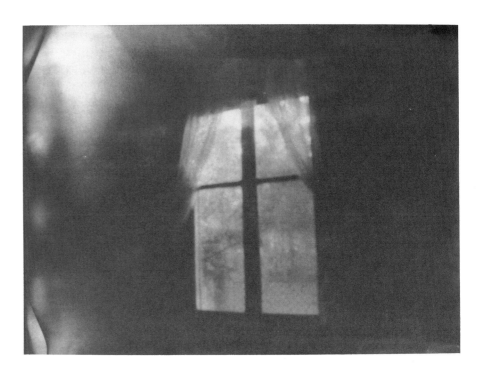

Figure 3.1 © *Paolo Gioli,* La Mia Finestra, *$3\frac{1}{2}$" x 5" pinhole photograph, 1969. From the collection of the photographer.*

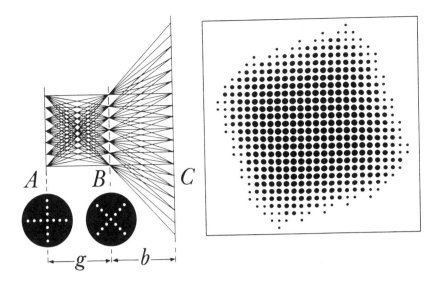

Figure 3.2a © *Gottfried Jäger*, Apparatus System of Pinhole Structures. *Multiple pinhole camera combined with light pattern subject. A: Light pattern subject, variable. B: Multiple pinhole, variable. g: Distance A-B, variable. b: Distance B-C, variable. C: Pinhole structure, result. From the collection of the photographer.*

tures. . . . Generative photography" thus presented itself as the continuation of the trend begun in the 20s, i.e. Constructivism and Elementarism, as defined by Theo van Doesburg, Moholy-Nagy and others. "Elementarism is an intellectual rebel, a trouble-maker, deliberately disrupting the tranquility of bourgeois life with its regularity and repetition at the cost of its own peace and quiet."[2]

David Lebe, who was doing pinhole photography in 1969 as a senior at the Philadelphia College of Art, stated:

> Reality moves so fast that everything is either an expectation or a memory. . . . We experience many fragmented and concurrent images and perceptions which flow together instantly, creating a picture [Color Plate 3.3] and a feeling of a scene. It is this flow of images and this sense of time that I want in my work.[3]

Franco Salmoiraghi in 1968 received a Master of Fine Arts Degree at Ohio University. In his thesis on pinhole photography (extremely rare for that time that the faculty would allow it), Salmoiraghi wrote:

> Photography has long been associated with the recording of fact and the representation to the viewer of something which he feels is real. Many photographers today are making an attempt to break with this traditional concept.

> The pinhole camera techniques seem to function better when used to produce a type of image which is not concerned with common-place reality but instead focuses on the world of dreams and fantasy.[4]

While teaching at the University of Georgia in 1966, Wiley Sanderson began making a 4-inch by 5-inch trifocal pinhole camera for the Jolly Screen process and in 1966 constructed a Jolly

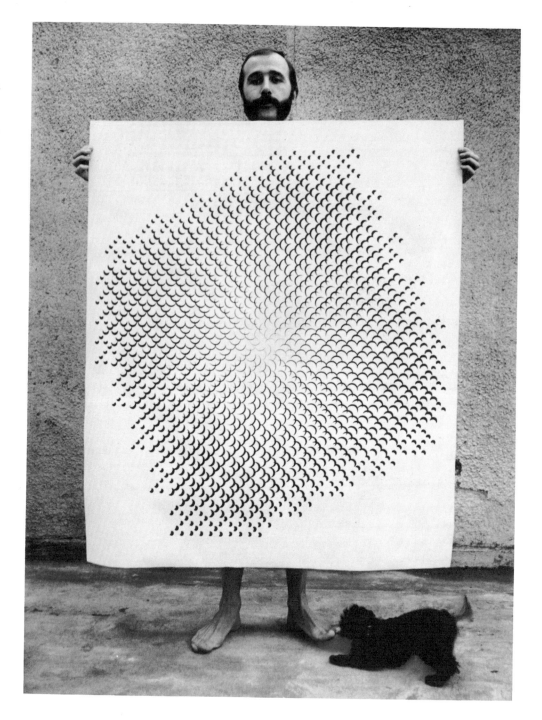

Figure 3.2b © *Gottfried Jäger with* Pinhole Structure. *Light graphic work, 3.8.14, modification F2.6, gelatin silver print on canvas, 118 cm x 110 cm, 1967. Photo: Ursel Jäger, circa 1968. From the collection of the photographer.*

Screen of 1,800 red, green, and blue diamonds. Sanderson taught photography from 1953 to 1988. During that time, his students built 4,356 pinhole cameras. Sanderson said:

> The incisive photograph [Figure 3.4] can assemble visual fragments of time, independent of the memory/sight combine. History can be now and the Universe can be here, photographically. By appreciating the limitations of visual logic and exploiting the camera to reveal facets of non-human vision, a multitude of recordable accuracies will be demonstrated. The egocentricity of constructing a camera to coincide with the limitations of human vision needs questioning. Moreover, the vast range of visual relationships between parts within a photograph far exceed man's notation by sight.[5]

For myself, much is a paradox and a puzzle. Just how did I end up with pinhole photography as my life's work? The following comes from an interview in 1987:

> In 1960, when I was in design school, I had to make a pinhole camera which was a standard kind of design school project. The professor didn't know anything about pinhole; he didn't know anything about photography—but he did have inspiring projects! We had to buy a piece of film from him for a quarter. We got only that one piece and he told everybody to load it in their cameras and to take them outside to expose for a designated length of time. I was the only person who didn't take my camera outside; I exposed through a window. Everybody else's was over-exposed and black—mine was the only one that worked! I didn't think anything more about pinhole photography for eight years. After graduate school, I realized I was no longer interested in design. Curiously enough, just before getting out of graduate school, I applied for a Fulbright to do camera design with Hasselblad in Sweden. Of course I didn't get it—it was kind of idiotic I applied for that kind of grant. Two days after graduating, I started to teach for the State University of New York. John Wood, who became a good friend of mine, was teaching photography there.

Figure 3.4 © *Wiley Sanderson,* Prow Menace in Venice. *A 3" x 9½" pinhole photograph, 1972. From the collection of the photographer.*

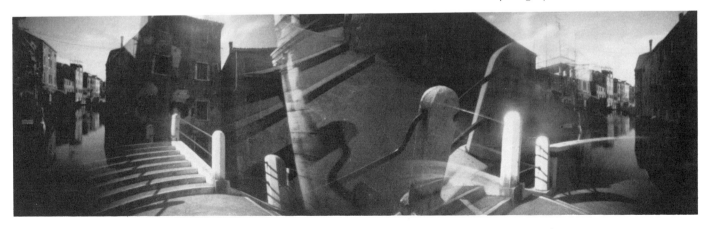

That may have had some influence on my beginning photography. One day in 1968, I was walking down the street, and I said to myself, or something said to me: "Why don't you make a camera that takes a whole environment into view?" I was sort of disgusted with what I had seen in photography—a single image that didn't say enough to me somehow. I remembered I knew something about pinhole photography. After about two months, I made a camera [Figure 3.5a] that used six pinholes to make a 360 degree image [Figures 3.5b, 3.5c]. . . . After about 6 years the people at *Afterimage* published an article about my work. After that, I didn't have to knock on doors. . . . I loved pinhole photography—it was like I had found a way to get inside myself—express what was inside of me. I've always depended upon artwork in lots of ways and had real feelings about people and this planet— the things that are on it—the sun, the moon, the clouds, the love. I've always wanted some way to sense these things; the way that seemed appropriate was pinhole photography.[6]

Two scientists were working with pinhole photography for the dual purpose of art and science: Kenneth A. Connors in the United States and Maurice Pirenne in England. Connors researched pinhole definition and resolution. His findings were printed in his self-published periodical *Interest* (1972–1980). Pirenne used pinhole optics to study perspective in his remarkable book *Optics, Painting, and Photography* (Cambridge University Press, 1970).

Pirenne was a physiologist and optical scientist who wrote widely. He had spent a lifetime studying the history of art, particularly the use of perspective. For decades he explored the complexities of viewing two-dimensional paintings using both eyes (as

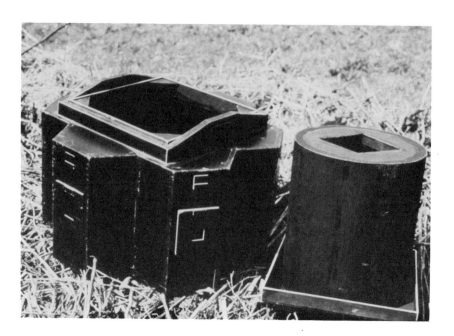

Figure 3.5a © *Eric Renner, Six-pinhole Camera, 1968. From the collection of the photographer.*

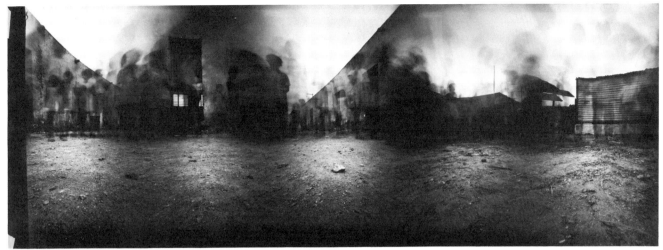

3.5b

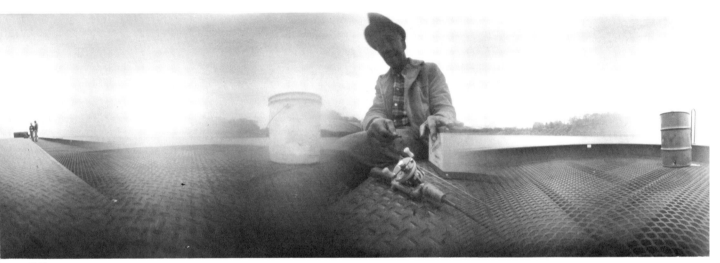

3.5c

in ordinary binocular vision) and with one eye (as in the fixed eye point required for Renaissance one-point perspective). He wanted an overview—one that explained how people have viewed two-dimensional paintings over past centuries. *Optics, Painting, and Photography* is Pirenne's synthesis. Within it are twenty-two pinhole photographs; most are couplets, each with a slightly shifted perspective. Pirenne prefaced his work by stating the following:

> In a sense, the present work constitutes a commentary on Leonardo. Instead of merely relying on texts, however, it deals on an experimental basis with problems which confronted Leonardo. Some of the experiments were specifically made for the present purpose. The book also deals with relevant aspects of the history of optics, from Euclid to Einstein.[7]

Pirenne also explained the pinhole camera:

Figure 3.5b *© Eric Renner,* Ticul Schoolyard, *9" x 25", a five-pinhole photograph, 1969. (This, my favorite pinhole photograph from the Ticul, Yucatan series, actually is only five overlapping pinhole images because the negative was accidentally chopped short in the darkroom before developing.) From the collection of the photographer.*

Figure 3.5c *© Eric Renner,* Fishing, Lake Erie *9" x 29", a six-pinhole photograph, 1974. From the collection of the photographer.*

Whereas each luminous point sends divergent rays into its surroundings [Figure 3.6a], the pinhole camera does select certain cones of rays [Figure 3.6b] from among all the rays which fill the whole of space, so that the main rays of these cones do now converge toward the centre of the pinhole. These main rays are shown in [Figure 3.6a] as the lines AH, BH and CH.

The fact that image-forming systems so select certain cones of rays in each of which the rays diverge from its object point, while the cones themselves all converge towards the image-forming system, is the crux of the matter with regard to the formation of "real" optical images.

The situation is essentially the same for the eye—except that inside the eye, as well as inside the lens camera, the rays of each cone are made to converge, whereas inside the pinhole camera they remain divergent. Outside the eye, the narrow divergent cones of rays coming from the different object points all converge towards the pupil. The main rays of all these individual cones thus form a visual pyramid or a pyramid of sight which geometrically diverges from the eye, even though physically the light goes toward the eye.[8]

Pirenne's "visual pyramid" refers to the pyramid of light, as seen directed toward the viewer's eye in Figure 2.6 and earlier pinhole perspective devices of Brunelleschi and Alberti, placed into a twentieth-century context. Pirenne's book, a must for anyone whose mind can intermingle perspective, optics, photography, and painting, covers an extremely complicated subject. In his own unpretentious way, Pirenne has resolved some of the intricate visual conceptualizations Leonardo questioned.

Like Pirenne, Kenneth A. Connors, professor of pharmacy at the University of Wisconsin, confronted the Brunelleschi-Alberti

Figure 3.6a *Maurice Pirenne,* Luminous Points of Light Sending Divergent Rays. *From* Optics, Painting, and Photography. *Courtesy of Cambridge University Press, London, 1970.*

Figure 3.6b *Maurice Pirenne,* Pinhole Camera Selecting Certain Cones of Rays. *From* Optics, Painting, and Photography. *Courtesy of Cambridge University Press, London, 1970.*

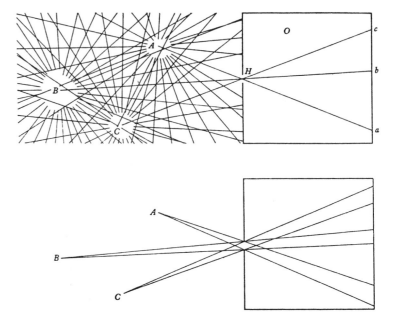

"visual pyramid" (a section of which is a photograph) and adjusted it for the context of twentieth-century optics. Connors stated:

> The pinhole is a "phase-selector," a recombination element that selects only waves that are (very nearly) in phase. In order to do so, of course, it must reject most of the light, so that image intensity is very low. The process of optimizing pinhole diameter for a given focal length consists of applying a criterion that specifies the range of phase differences that is acceptable in the admitted wave-front.[9]

THE 1970s

Toward the end of the 1960s, Nathan Lyons, curator of contemporary photography at the George Eastman House, confronted traditionalists in photography by espousing the idea that photography in a larger sense can encompass unconventional imagery and processes. He believed the entire field would gain a greater depth if the boundaries were broken. Lyons promoted his views internationally through publication of books that showed a wide variety of images and ideas, including pinhole photography. In 1971 Time-Life Books published *The Art of Photography* in its widely distributed Life Library of Photography series and included one of my panoramic six-pinhole images (Figure 3.5b), which was far from traditional. By 1972 the painter Willie Anne Wright (Figure 3.7) and others began to be intrigued by pinhole photography, although it was certainly not widely accepted until ten years later.

In 1973 Carlos Jurado, a painter from Mexico, began making pinhole cameras and images (Figure 3.8). A year later his book on pinhole and the history of the photographic process titled *The Art*

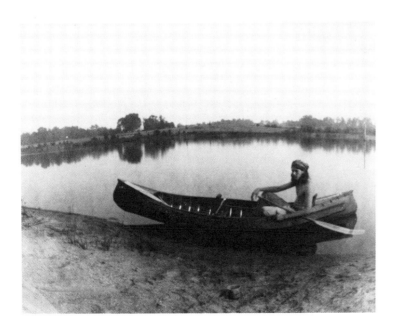

Figure 3.7 © *Willie Anne Wright, The Canoe, 8" x 10" sepia-toned pinhole photograph, contact printed from a paper negative, 1973. From the collection of the photographer.*

63

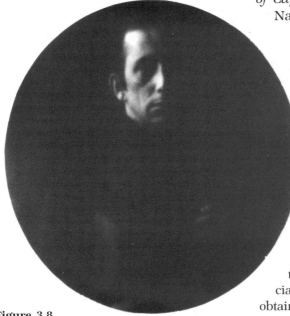

Figure 3.8
© *Carlos Jurado,*
Viejo Autorretrato, $4\frac{1}{2}$" *diameter*
pinhole photograph, 1973. From the
collection at Pinhole Resource.

of Capturing Images and the Unicorn was published by the National University of Mexico. Of his work, Jurado stated:

> I consider photography as a magical process in which alchemy is more important than technology. I don't particularly like mathematical systems or processes. That's why I make everything from scratch. To make pinhole cameras for example, I don't use pre-made materials like oat boxes or any other boxes. I build my own cameras according to my needs of expression. I don't rely on format or sizes that are already established. This allows me more versatility and creativity in my work. . . . It is like a way of "reinventing" photography. I feel the inventors of photography are true heroes of humanity. Today this process is basic to human life. Talbot, Niépce, and Daguerre made possible the path which today millions of people follow. To me these characters in addition to being heroes, were magicians. I imagine them in their laboratories experimenting to obtain marvelous results. In addition to this many of them were artists. Niépce was a lithographer. Daguerre was a painter. Ducos and Charles Cros, the inventors of the subtractive system of colour, were a pianist and a poet, respectively, but who knows it? I modestly try to follow their steps and I am sure that my images have some of their influence.[10]

In 1973, Phil Simkin, from Boston, created a conceptual humanistic "displacement project" with the Boston Institute of Contemporary Art in which twenty thousand hand-assembled preloaded pinhole cameras (Figure 3.9a) were stacked in tractor trailers and taken to drop-off points around the city where residents would pick-up (displace) a camera, then make a photograph with it. Prints from the camera were hung at the Institute. The project gained more exposure in 1975 when it was "redisplaced" at the Philadelphia Museum of Art. Fifteen thousand cameras were stacked in the foyer (Figure 3.9b) and an adjacent room in the art museum. Simkin organized this as another displacement project. People would come into the museum and take (displace) a camera out of the huge stack of cameras and make an exposure at home, preferably in their living space. A public darkroom was built in the museum, where with the help of museum assistants, each person could develop and print their image. During the month's duration of this project, images were continuously exhibited. The result offered a very human view of Philadelphia. Each camera was made from die-cut cardboard and had a taped-in brass shim with pinhole; 3-inch by 10-inch Ilford photo paper was used as

Figure 3.9a © *Phil Simkin,*
Displacement pinhole camera, *1973,*
lens photo by Phil Simkin. From the
collection at Pinhole Resource.

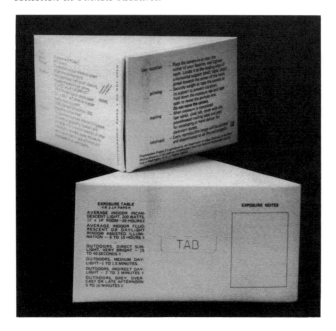

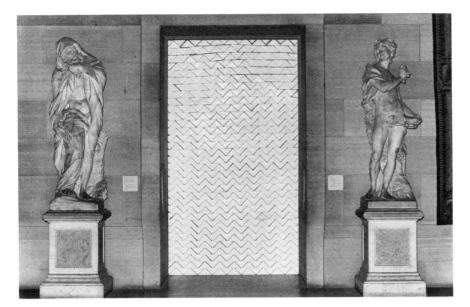

a negative. The entire project received much publicity when *Popular Photography* published the article, "Pinholes for the People" (June 1975). The triangular folded pinhole camera Simkin designed is probably the most unusual design of all the cardboard cameras from the latter part of the twentieth century. Never sold commercially, the design has not received the acclaim it deserves.

In the late 1970s, pinhole photography became increasingly popular, although multiple pinhole cameras, often designed by pinhole photographers in the late 1960s, were seldom explored. In the 1970s, most pinhole photographers chose to work with alternative printing processes, standard light-sensitive materials, and single-pinhole cameras. Their combined efforts produced pinhole imagery in almost every old or new process, such as cyanotype, gum bichromate, serigraph, platinum, dye transfer, Polaroid, Xerox, video, and 8mm film. Pinhole was an ideal starting point for any photographic printing process that required a large negative. A camera accommodating a large negative could be made from any type of box, can, or suitcase. Photographers needed only to coat their light-sensitive paper with platinum, gum, or cyanotype and contact-print the negative. Pinhole photography was gaining momentum, offering proof that this was the back-to-basics era.

By the mid 1970s, Jim Shull's cartooned introduction to pinhole titled *The Hole Thing: A Manual of Pinhole Photography* (Morgan and Morgan, 1975) was published, as were many widely read articles, such as "The Alternative Optic" by Wiley Sanderson in *Photographic Journal* (June 1975), wherein he proposed that the pinhole camera be the primary type of camera used in a college photography curriculum; "I Really Should Be Interviewing You" by Charles Hagen and Charles Kelly in *Afterimage* (December 1974), describing my pinhole photography; and "Are Pinholes a Threat to the Glass-Based Camera-Lens Industry?" by Bob Schwalberg, senior editor, in *Popular Photography* (October 1976). Stanley R. Page, from Utah, became pinhole's primary historian, collecting 450 articles on pinhole photography published after 1850, a monumental project that took more than five years to complete.

Even though a number of artists were seriously involved in making pinhole images, photography critics in the United States did not know of this contribution toward a broader photographic awareness, and at best pinhole photography was still trivialized as a primitive approach. In Europe, however, Paolo Gioli and Dominique Stroobant received much wider attention and consideration.

Dominique Stroobant, of Belgian descent and living in the marble-quarrying and sculpture-producing center of Miseglia de Carrara in Italy, spoke philosophically:

I got trapped by pinhole photography, once I discovered how obvious and pleasant it was to realize everything from the start.

Figure 3.10a © *Dominique Stroobant, January 8, 1978, one-day exposure, 7" x 9" pinhole photograph from camera H2-R. From the collection of the photographer.*

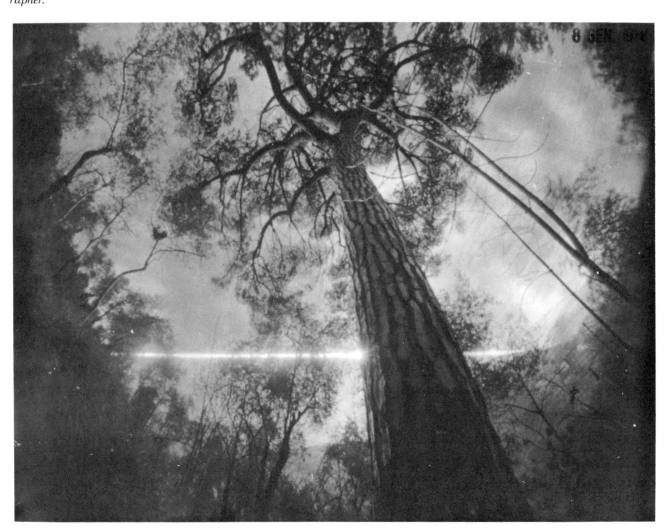

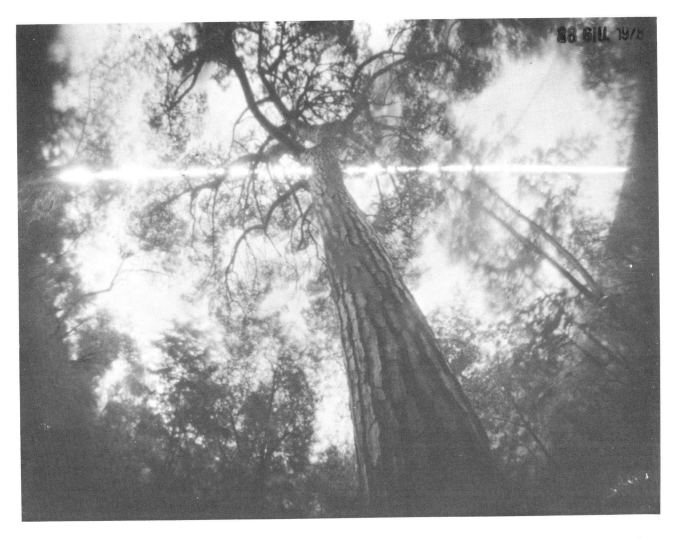

Figure 3.10b © *Dominique Stroobant,*
June 28, 1978, *one-day exposure, 7" x 9"*
pinhole photograph from camera H2-R.
From the collection of the photographer.

My tools could not be ready-made. Why try to conceive of anything more sophisticated than the cameras presently in use: there
is more enjoyment to go the other way. Since Niépce in photography nothing else has been done but reduce space and time to
smaller fragments at each step. . . . Once I showed people what I
could realize with these clumsy, heavy, but still handsome devices
of mine, they thought it was sorcery. However, I believe, all they
are accustomed to use is real sorcery! Just try to dismantle any
camera of today. We live in an age where many peasants do not
even know how to grow a salad, or anything else, without very
specific chemicals. There is no trick to what is shown here. I see
it as my duty, however, (or rather my pleasure) to dissolve the
boundaries of consciousness [Figures 3.10a, 3.10b], wherever people think they should be fixed. The first photographers did what
real painters did and are still doing: they tried to fix not just
what they saw, but in order that they could see it. Since one sees
only what one thinks one sees, there is no way of seeing things
the way they are. Not only do we see 99% with our memory but
even whatever we use to visualize what we see or feel, is almost
entirely programmed by some preconceived idea of what we

should see. One can also build devices to visualize things one cannot see, which one can only imagine in an indirect way. It took me time to see—not just understand as an abstraction—how the sun affects us. Most people understand things by rationalization, through spatial geometry for example, but they still do not "see.". . . Many things are not obvious. Most ready-made images give us a fragmented view of things. This fits easily into the field our eyes can embrace at once. Perhaps part of Alberti's perspective system, and many existing prejudices about what is a deformed or non-deformed image in photography, are due to accepting as a norm the limitations encountered in human optical perception.[11]

Peter Olpe, Professor at the Basel School of Design, Switzerland, began making pinhole cameras as part of his film technique course in the mid-1970s. Of his work (Figures 3.11a, 3.11b) Olpe stated:

Perhaps it is not a coincidence that in the 70s with the emergence of video that my passion for all kinds of mechanical-optical picture machines started. I have never developed any interest in electronic machines beyond their immediate practical necessity. It is by no means a way of protecting a traditional technique because of the arrival of a new one. I have felt that nowadays the old mechanical-optical methods are not evaluated for their practical value and their usefulness. They should be looked at again, taken apart and put together in a new way.

All of my pinhole cameras accept roll film. In this way they are independent from the darkroom. This is my only concession in respect to the modern camera. Because these pinhole cameras are set up for roll film, correspondingly there are three successive interior rooms or compartments. These spaces serve, in a logical

Figure 3.11a © *Peter Olpe,* Lago Maggiore, Italy, *1978, 5" x 8" pinhole photograph. From the collection of the photographer.*

order, the purpose of housing the light sensitive materials, to produce pictures and to also store the exposed materials before development. The largest and most central compartment is perhaps the most important. This is the *camera obscura*. It is here around this dark room with the small window where I build houses, fortresses, bunkers, temples of light and image picture factories.

With a series of self-built cameras I search through photography to show the close relationship between motion film and still film. The pinhole camera technique represents the common basis between the two types of cameras. Its concept is essential for both.[12]

Ruth Thorne-Thomsen, of Chicago, wrote:

The photographs in *Expeditions* are what I call "environmental collages," consisting of small props and photographic cut-outs . . . assembled in the environment, and photographed with a pinhole camera and paper negatives [Figure 3.12]. I attempt to create photographically convincing realms.[13]

Nobuo Yamanaka from Japan, who died in 1982 when he was 34, started making pinhole *camerae obscurae* in the early 1970s (Figure 3.13). His *camera obscura* work predates that of photographers in the 1990s who made *camera obscura* imagery so widespread. Of his work Janet Koplos, art critic for the *Asahi Evening News*, wrote:

His next "movie" *Pinhole Camera* (1972) was a decisive change that introduced the approach he pursued for the remainder of his life: Yamanaka made his first *camera obscura*. He is best known for using entire rooms as *camera obscuras*—photographing scenes outside his home and catching his presence inside the camera at the same time. He recorded the view from a ninth-floor apartment as the image fell on the back and side walls, and on the floor and ceiling. He held two-part exhibitions in which the exposure process went on for several days, and the results were shown precisely where they had been made. Not surprisingly, Yamanaka also worked with a pinhole camera (a 35mm camera with a copper plate over the lens opening), thus taking his *camera obscura* on the road. He made a series of color prints taking the sun as his theme—a new expression of his fascination with light.

His last several works made his photographs into objects: the image was fractured into fragmentary planes and wrapped around the interior of one or more black-painted wooden boxes. Though the box was supposedly just a more convenient way to send his work to the Paris Biennial, he was actually recapitulating both the camera-room and the camera-device in a literal and symbolic black box.[14]

Some pinhole photographers felt no need to explain their work. This was best stated by Clarissa Carnell of Pennsylvania in her cryptic, yet wonder-filled, statement:

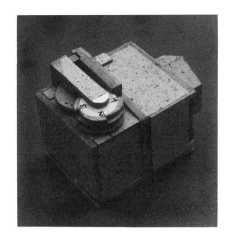

Figure 3.11b © *Peter Olpe*, 135mm Pinhole Camera, *used for the image in Figure 3.11a. Mechanism on top keeps film from going backward. Lens photograph. From the collection of the photographer.*

There is a song that gets stuck in my mind that goes, "You think we're diving for gold; we know we're diving for pearls.". . . No matter what you are up to, someone will always think you are up to something else. So, all I'll tell you is I'm having fun. What is the point of using a pinhole camera if it's not fun. Otherwise, it is too confusing.[15]

The following statement by Dale Quarterman of Virginia epitomizes the reason most people become involved in pinhole photography:

The pinhole camera is so simple and direct in its creation of a photograph that it allows the artist to shed the technical trappings of modern photographic equipment and concentrate on the development of very personal imagery. . . . Pinhole cameras are all about freedom. The freedom to create a unique vision of the world, by going back to the basics of photography in order to have the total control of this magical and enjoyable act of painting with light.[16]

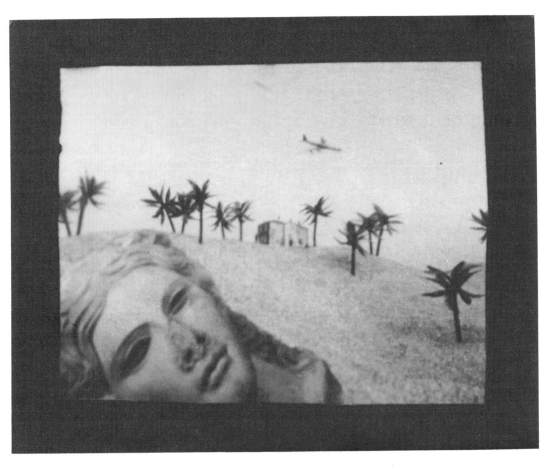

Figure 3.12 © *Ruth Thorne-Thomsen,* Head and Plane, Chicago, *$4\frac{1}{2}$" x $5\frac{3}{4}$" pinhole photograph from* Expeditions, *1979. From the collection at Pinhole Resource.*

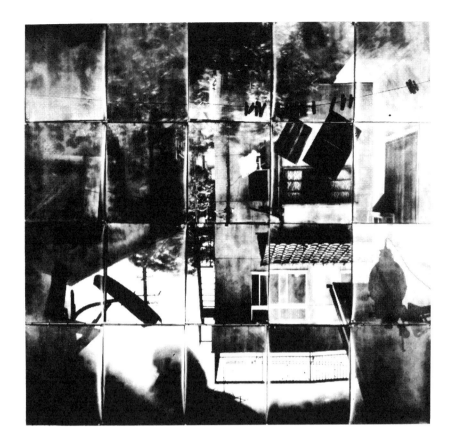

Figure 3.13 © *Nobuo Yamanaka,* Pinhole Room, *1973. From the collection of the estate of the photographer.*

Peggy Ann Jones of California may have been the first artist to make pinhole cameras as sculptural objects only—some were never meant to capture images. In 1977 she placed a group of seven of her cast-lead nonfunctioning cameras into a photographer's carrying case. The case weighed forty-four pounds and was titled *One Thing Lead to Another!* Jones was playing on the idea that most photographers think they need an overabundance of equipment. By the time their carrying case is full, it's too much.

Even though pinhole photography and the making of pinhole cameras as an art form gained popularity during the 1970s, very few pinhole photographers knew much of the others' photographs. This lack of communication resulting from geographic isolation provided a diversity of approaches to pinhole imagery and cameras.

NOTES

1. Paolo Gioli, "Photographs/Cameras," *Pinhole Journal* 2(1986):16–17. Two books are available on Paolo Gioli's pinhole photographs. They are *Paolo Gioli Obscura, la natura riflessa* (Milan: Electa, 1991) and *Paolo Gioli Gran Positivo nel crudele spazia stenopeico* (Florence: Alinari, 1991).
2. Gottfried Jäger, "Pinhole Structures," *Pinhole Journal* 5(1989):22–23.

3. David Lebe, "Artist's Statements," in *The Visionary Pinhole,* ed. Lauren Smith (Layton, Utah: Peregrine Smith Books, 1985), 76.

4. Franco Salmoiraghi, "An Exploration of the Inherent Qualities of the Pinhole Camera," (graduate M.F.A. thesis, Ohio University, 1968):26, 49.

5 Wiley Sanderson, "Artist's Statement," in *The Pinhole Image: Eleven Photographers* catalogue (Richmond, Va.: Institute of Contemporary Art of the Virginia Museum, 1982), 14. Organized by Willie Anne Wright, this was the first group exhibit of pinhole photographers working throughout the United States.

6. Eric Renner, "Interview," *Pinhole Journal* 3(1987):25–26.

7. Maurice Pirenne, *Optics, Painting, and Photography* (London: Cambridge University Press, 1970), xxi.

8. Ibid., 17.

9. Kenneth A. Connors, "Resolution and Definition in Pinhole Photography," *Pinhole Journal* 2(1986):10.

10. Carlos Jurado, Letter to the author from Zinzuni Jurado from an interview by Dr. Kathleen Kadon Desmond, 21 April 1998, part of "Artist's Statement" in the *International Pinhole Exhibition,* June, 1998, New Zealand Museum of Art.

11. Dominique Stroobant, "Solar Recorders," *Pinhole Journal* 4(1988):18–19.

12. Peter Olpe, letter to the author, June 29, 1998.

13. Ruth Thorne-Thomsen, "Artist's Statement," in *The Pinhole Image: Eleven Photographers,* 15. For a complete discussion of Ruth Thorne-Thomsen's pinhole photographs, see *Within This Garden* (New York: Aperture, 1993).

14. Janet Koplos, "Made in Japan," *Afterimage* 16(1989):20.

15. Clarissa Carnell, "Artists' Statements," in *The Visionary Pinhole,* 40.

16. Dale Quarterman, "Artist's Statement," in *The Pinhole Image: Eleven Photographers,* 12.

I have been photographing out here [the American West] for eleven years and I have found that I could go back to all the same places I had worked before with a pinhole. It was as if I was photographing in a completely different world. It seems almost as if the pinhole camera takes you beneath the surface of reality as we know it into another dimension, another place. . . . The whole convergence of light to the center was a fascinating concept to me and the whole idea of a passageway going to a different place, a different reality—it all seems to have mystical overtones for me. I'm not really sure where I'm going with it. It was really good for me to leave the whole idea of the control that I was exerting over my photography through the 8" x 10". I felt in some cases I got tired of that control, I wanted to let go of some of it. I found that pinhole photography has freed me to a great degree. Whether I stay with pinhole or go back to lenses some day, pinhole has forever altered the way I see the world.

DOUGLAS FRANK
Interview, *Pinhole Journal*, 1991

I wondered if I could do pinhole images, but I was always afraid of doing them because I was such a control oriented person. But then I did my first shot of my friend who was going through a very difficult divorce, who was trying to be more of a person than her husband. In my very first shot, I had her wrists tied. She came off looking like half man, half woman—I couldn't even read the negative. I thought I really couldn't understand this at all. And I made the print and I thought oh my God, pinhole photography captured so much more than I was able to see with my naked eye.

DAVID PLAKKE
Interview, *Pinhole Journal*, 1990

Pinhole's Revival in Art: The 1980s

THE PETER PAN PRINCIPLE, OR "I CAN FLY"

Pinhole photography can be the art of surprise, like looking at the world through a child's eyes. It is a continual wonder, and surely magical, that time after time pinhole cameras can make an intriguing image. This curious attribute is the pinhole camera's greatest gift to its user. I truly appreciate that something as easy to make as a pinhole camera performs such a seemingly complex task as producing an image. Here within mere minutes is a camera and in a few more minutes an image! Some people have tried to make pinhole photography complicated, but it is not, and it should not be. Knowing *f* stops and exact pinhole diameters, making viewfinders, and using light meters are not necessary considerations. The inherent simplicity of a pinhole camera is the basis of its character. The excitement of making and using something so simple appeals to a childlike innocence within all of us. Those who have retained this innocence are in accord with pinhole photography (Color Plate 4.1). It has taken me thirty years of thinking about what a pinhole camera really is to arrive at this explanation. This very "innocence" often has been overlooked by photo historians, photo critics, and other writers who have attempted to define the "why" of pinhole photography. Lauren Smith's *The Visionary Pinhole,* published in 1985 by Peregrine Smith Books, documented for the first time that many serious artists were making pinhole photographs.

THE BODY AS CAMERA

A pinhole camera consists of four parts (more or less): the aperture, the camera body, the light-sensitive material placed inside the camera, and the shutter. The artist can vary each part enormously according to artistic need. The completed pinhole camera and image undoubtedly reflect their maker's thought processes. For example, in a darkroom, Thomas Bachler, of West Germany, in 1986 placed short, cut pieces of 35mm film in his mouth. He left the darkroom and stood in the light in front of a mirror. Opening his lips to resemble a pinhole for an instant, he formed a self-image on the film. In this process, the lips acted as the aperture and as the shutter. Returning to the darkroom, Bachler took the film out of his mouth, which had been the camera body, and reloaded. The entire process was recreated at least sixty-three times and the images later contact-printed onto one sheet of black-and-white paper (Figure 4.2a). The completed piece was physiologically titled *The Third Eye, pinhole photographs made with the mouth, using lips as an aperture, film in mouth, standing in front of a mirror, all self portraits.*

In a shifted new reality, Bachler physically became the camera when he placed unexposed film inside himself. Exposing the film, he imaged his "camera-self" in the mirror, thus becoming the "photograph" too, in much the same manner of Narcissus, who saw his mirrored image reflected on the surface of the pool, as mentioned by Alberti in the quotation at the beginning of Chapter 2. Through this purposeful redefinition of photography, Bachler makes the camera, image, and himself one. The "third eye" in his title makes reference to this oneness. The unconventionality of this type of artistic endeavor can be typical of pinhole photography. In 1992, Jeff Guess, an American living in Paris who did not know Bachler's work, made a series titled "From Hand to Mouth" (Figure 4.2b) using his mouth as a camera body and lips as a pinhole.

In a similar conceptual manner, Paolo Gioli in 1989 used his fist as a camera, pinhole, and shutter (Figures 4.3a and 4.3b) to produce images appropriately titled *Window in my Fist* and *Fist Against Myself.*

A tangential idea of "oneness" exists in my plaster face cameras. I made my first plaster face camera in 1985 by the usual process of having someone pour plaster over my face, which had been covered with petroleum jelly. After removal of the dried

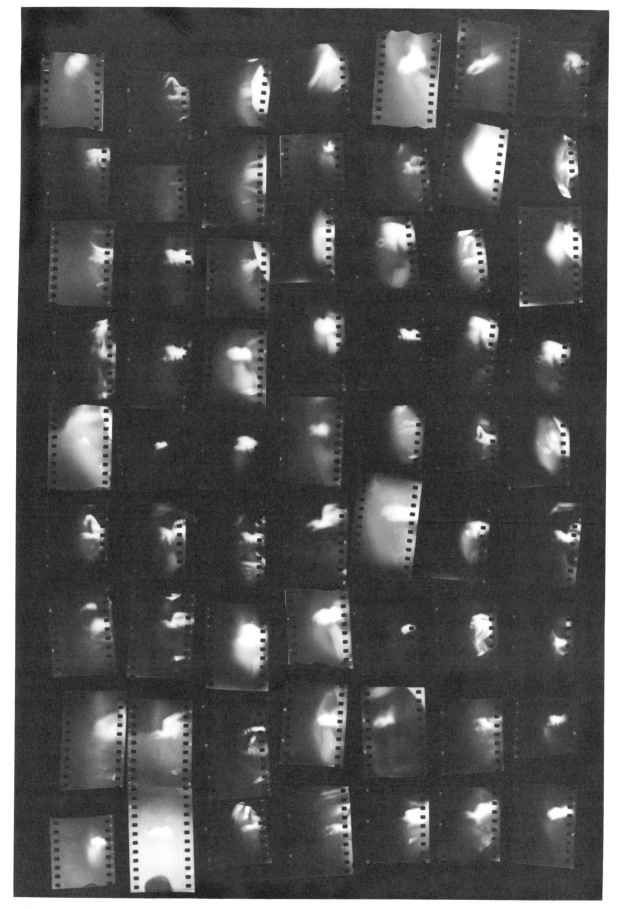

Figure 4.2a © *Thomas Bachler,* The Third Eye, *pinhole photographs made with the mouth, using lips as an aperture, film in mouth, standing in front of a mirror, all self-portraits, 15" x 20" contact print of 63 mouth photographs, 1986. From the collection at Pinhole Resource.*

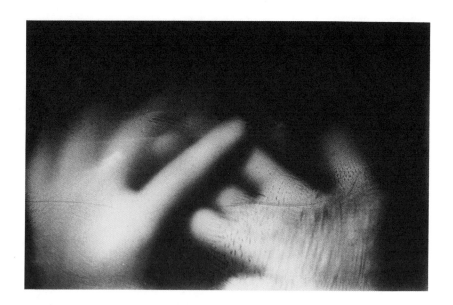

Figure 4.2b © *Jeff Guess,* From Hand to Mouth, *7" x 11" pinhole photograph, 1992. From the collection at Pinhole Resource.*

Figure 4.3a © *Paolo Gioli,* Window in my Fist, *fist used as a pinhole camera, 4" x 7" lens photograph, 1989. From the collection of the photographer.*

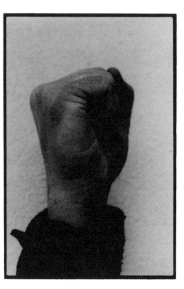

plaster, this casting became a mold for the face camera. In this first plaster face camera, the pinhole was in my right eye only, making reference to things I had seen from within. For many years, I have seen what I refer to as "little movies" in my right eye when the lid is closed. An example of these "little movies," which Jung probably would have called "lucid dreams," happened late one night in 1983 after I put my two-year-old son Zephy back to bed for the eighth time (no exaggeration, I counted). When I got back in bed, in my right eye I saw a pyramid with a door in it, which opened. Out of the door came a small figure (Zephy?) who walked along a long, low wall extending from the pyramid. At the end of the wall, the figure stopped and turned, looked around, and said to me, "Everything is going to be alright." The figure then retraced its steps back into the pyramid.

The first plaster face camera was an attempt to make tangible the "little movie" experience. This pinhole camera was used for self-portraits—the camera was "I." In later versions of the plaster face cameras, there were pinholes in both eyes and photographs were not always "self" oriented. It took me almost twenty years of working in pinhole photography to come to the realization that I should make my face and mind into a camera—for that is what I really am! I did not want the camera to have a back, as if, metaphorically, my mind were free. When making a photograph, I held the camera upside down (Figure 4.4a), so that the image would be right side up on the Ilfochrome Classic color paper held against the flattened back. The pinhole image area was quite sharp and clear (Color Plate 4.4b), even though I held the camera in my hand for five- to seven-second exposures. Sunlight always worked its way under the edges of the plaster face, in photogram fashion, making a variety of planned accidents. When the camera was used in low sunlight, the inner dark area remained black and unexposed; when it was used in bright sunlight, the exposure was

76

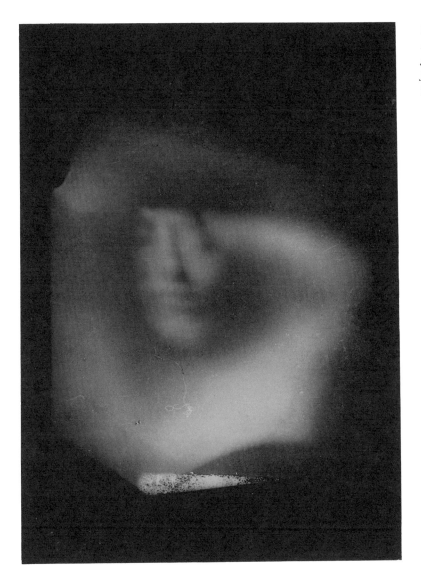

Figure 4.3b © *Paolo Gioli*, Fist Against Myself, 4" x 5" *pinhole photograph, negative made inside the artist's fist, 1989. From the collection of the photographer.*

purple-blue. In 1989, after Nancy and I were married, I made plaster face cameras of both of us (Figure 4.5a) and used these for double self-portraits (Color Plate 4.5b) with the idea that we were one and were looking at each other through each other's eyes.

A primal and uniquely symbolic manner of portraying self was invented by Jeff Fletcher of Austin, Texas. In his photographic series *Bromide Eggs* (Figures 4.6a and 4.6b), we are invited to enter a dozen aspects of his private world, which have been imaged onto the anamorphic cave-like inner surfaces of opened egg shells. Of this wonderful idea Fletcher wrote:

> The whole idea of eggs—a symbol of new life, the human figure, life/death cycles, regeneration, etc., just seemed to me the perfect conceptual match. With a little thought the emulsion of choice became Liquid Light which comes in a bottle and can be applied to almost any surface. The camera was easy. Built out of an aluminum pepper shaker, it has a pinhole in what was the bottom and the holes that made the "P" on the lid have been blocked.

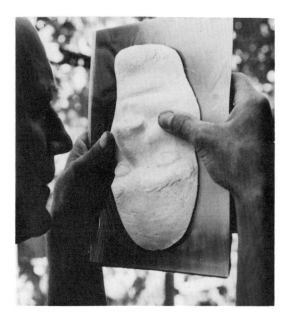

Figure 4.4 © *Eric Renner*, Plaster Face Camera, Pinhole in One Eye, *1985, lens photograph. From the collection of the photographer.*

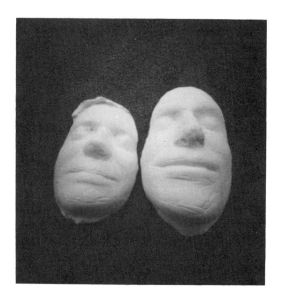

Figure 4.5a © *Nancy Spencer and Eric Renner*, Plaster Face Cameras, *1988, pinhole photograph. From the collection of the photographers.*

Because each shell has a different size and/or shape, there is a piece of felt used to hold the shell firmly in place. It seemed I was all but done. All that remained was to start eating a lot of eggs.

Unlike the gelatin on normal film and papers, Liquid Light is a soft gelatin. To use it, one heats the bottle until the emulsion melts, applies it to the desired surface, allows it to cool and set, makes an exposure, then develops the image in the same manner as conventional photographic papers. This technique may work well in most cases but proved to be a disaster when used the way I had in mind. The temperature inside a camera, in direct sunlight, gets quite high. The first image or two I tried just oozed out of the shell into the developer. A treatment in a weak formaldehyde solution solved that problem and eliminated a rather disgusting sight.

So that's it, or almost it. Somewhere along the line a problem with chemical fogging developed. After more than a year of tinkering with the variables—chemistry, egg sources, etc., I came to the conclusion that the egg shells themselves vary—not from shell to shell, but from season to season. It seems that only late spring, early summer eggs will work well. I have no idea as to why. Kodak has been in the poultry business for over a hundred years. Perhaps it's true, "You are what you eat."[1]

CAMERA AND PHOTOGRAPH AS ONE

One of the first photographers to intertwine camera and photograph into a singular art object is Julie Schachter, of Washington State. She placed a Boraxo camera (Figure 4.7a) in the sands of Death Valley (harking back to the old television commercial for Borax soap, which featured a twenty-mule team that trudged across the desert) to portray biographically the violent mentality of "Death Valley Days" television actor and "Star Wars" U.S. President Ronald Reagan (Figure 4.7b). It was vital that Schachter's pinhole camera be constructed out of the soap can made by the company that sponsored Reagan's television program and be placed in an appropriate landscape for a revealing portrait of the man and his gun.

Other Schachter cameras sculpturally combined tripod, pinhole camera, and photograph into one: Tinkertoy pieces supported a Tinkertoy box (Figure 4.7c) to photograph her son Marlon (Figure 4.7d), pink newspaper television sections covered a pod supporting a television

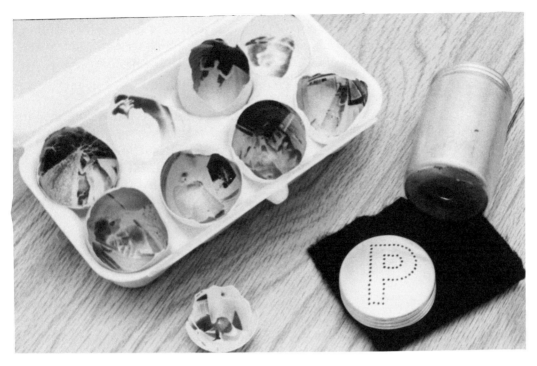

Figure 4.6a © *Jeff Fletcher*, Pepper Shaker Pinhole Camera with Eggs, *1989, lens photo. From the collection of the photographer.*

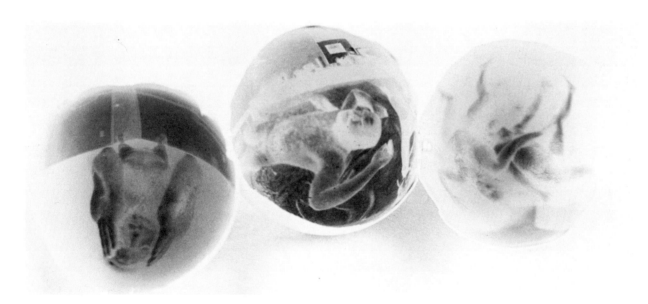

Figure 4.6b © *Jeff Fletcher*, Bromide Eggs, Self Portraits, *1989, pinhole photographs in eggs. From the collection of the photographer.*

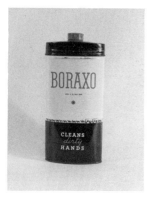

4.7a

(Figure 4.7e) to photograph someone watching soaps while ironing, and a solid, carved-oak pod supported a hollowed-out 1939 *Who's Who* (Figure 4.6f with detail) to photograph one hundred of her friends. Below the surface of humor and whimsy lie Schachter's serious attempts to broaden the photographic art form.

Delving into tongue-in-cheek humor, Larry Bullis, of Washington State, took the biblical statement "It is easier for a camel to go through the eye of a needle, than for a rich man to enter into the kingdom of God" (Matthew 19:24) and deliberately transformed his conventional Polaroid camera into a soul-saving Polaroid needle-hole camera to instantly redeem those who eternally suffer from monetary greed. How? Bullis explained:

> Thinking about the nature of life and the need for magic, it occurred to me I could for once and for all answer an age old

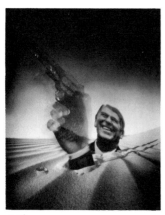

4.7b

Figure 4.7a © *Julie Schachter,* Boraxo Pinhole Camera, *1980s, lens photo. From the collection of the photographer.*

Figure 4.7b © *Julie Schachter,* Ronald Reagan, $3\frac{1}{4}$" x $4\frac{1}{4}$" *pinhole photograph from Boraxo pinhole camera, 1980s. From the collection of the photographer.*

Figure 4.7c © *Julie Schachter,* Tinkertoy camera with wood, cardboard, and string pad, *1980s, lens photo. From the collection of the photographer.*

Figure 4.7d © *Julie Schachter,* Self-Portrait with Marlon, $5\frac{1}{2}$" x 7" *pinhole photograph made with a Tinkertoy camera, 1986. From the collection of the photographer.*

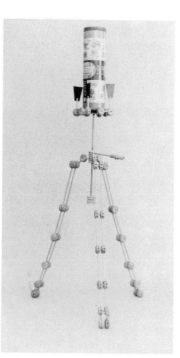

4.7c

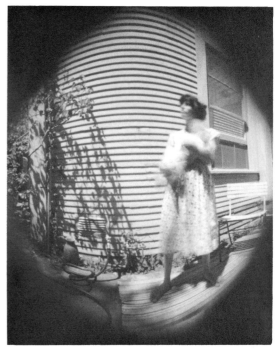

4.7d

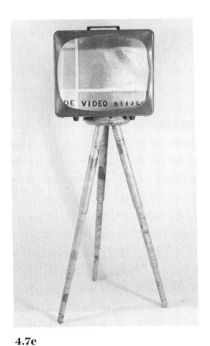

4.7e

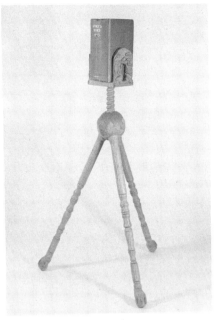

4.7f

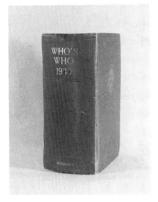

4.7f

Figure 4.7e *© Julie Schachter,* TV pinhole camera with wood covered with pink newspaper TV sections, 4 pods, *1980s, lens photo. From the collection of the photographer.*

Figure 4.7f *© Julie Schachter,* Who's Who Pinhole Camera with solid carved-oak pod, *1980s, lens photo. From the collection of the photographer.*

question and revive hope for countless otherwise helpless individuals, who, because of their unfortunate wealth had resigned themselves to eternal suffering. I know that I will be able to photograph using the eye of a needle [Figures 4.8a, 4.8b] as imaging device. The only proper subject for this device would be a camel.

There were some difficulties here, which were not expected. When you need a camel you go to the zoo, right? Wrong. Neither Woodland Park, nor the Portland Zoos have camels anymore. Too boring. Fortunately, there is a camel ride concession at the dunes in Florence [Oregon] (Lawrence of Florence?). Originally, I greeted this with some measure of despair, because Florence is such a long way for such a dumb idea. But the more I thought about it, the better it got. Think of it. This guy rents out his camels for folks to climb atop to have their pictures taken, so I can get on top of the camel, thus getting a free trip through the eye of the needle myself.

I'm working on the camel project. It is more difficult than one might expect. The first subject photographed with the needle eye camera was the Trojan Nuclear Power Plant. Perhaps this is our contemporary equivalent of a camel; another kind, another quality of transformation.[2]

After making the images, Bullis continued:

A quick note to let you know history has been made. I drove 850 miles with my younger daughter for that image last weekend. Of

Figure 4.8a *Larry Bullis,* Camel Photographed with Needle Eye Camera, $2\frac{3}{4}$" x $3\frac{3}{4}$" *pinhole photograph, 1987. From the collection of the photographer.*

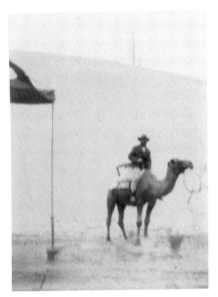

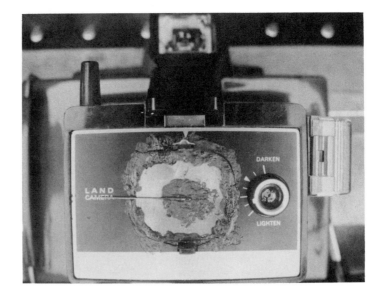

Figure 4.8b © *Larry Bullis,* Needle Eye Camera, *1987, lens photo. From the collection of the photographer.*

course, the camel had decided to take that day off—the first in three summers. So we drove to Coos Bay and sat on the rocks at Cape Arago. Came back for the camel on Tuesday.

I had built a needle eye camera out of a Polaroid Color Pack II; just pulled the lens off and replaced it with a piece of brass shim stock with a needle glued into a gash in it with black Duro rubber. So I had an automatic exposure, too. It was great! 3000 speed Polaroid is wonderful material for pinhole work.[3]

As with all superb ideas, someone was working on the same concept somewhat simultaneously. In 1990 we received photographs from Paolo Gioli, of Italy. In 1986, he had made a needle-hole camera (Figures 4.9a, 4.9b) to photograph camels with the same biblical statement in mind! Soul saving is worldwide.

During the 1980s, Paolo Gioli created other unique pinhole cameras. Many were Duchampian "ready-mades," for which Gioli used objects such as crackers, shells, buttons, with holes in them that would act as pinholes (Figures 4.10a, 4.10b).

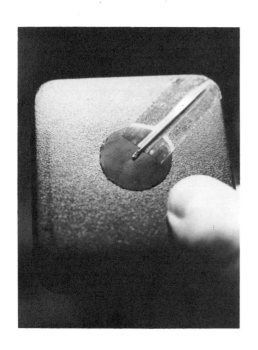

Figure 4.9a © *Paolo Gioli,* Camera Agostenopeica, *1986, lens photo. From the collection of the photographer.*

CAMERAS AND IMAGES IN THE 1980s

Much in art is intuitive. Without viewfinders, light meters, and other technical tools, we can arrive at the barest essentials necessary for a pinhole camera. Inherent in this simplicity is the photographer's sense of intuition. Some pinhole photographers have gone so far as to let their pinhole cameras operate as basic light receptors. These photographers gain insights from each the specific light-gathering

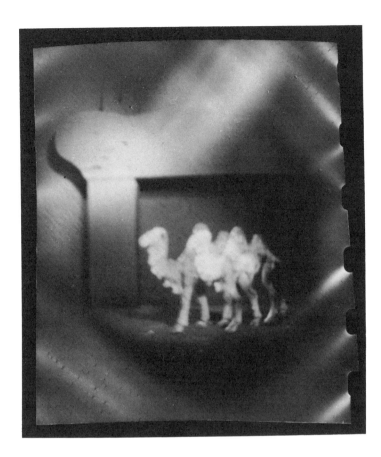

Figure 4.9b © *Paolo Gioli*, Il Cammello della Cruna Stenopeica, *1986, $3\frac{1}{2}$" x 2" needle-hole photograph. From the collection of the photographer.*

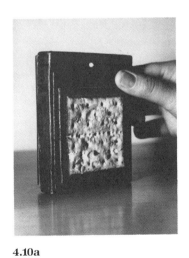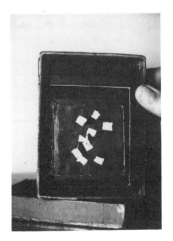

4.10a   4.10b

Figure 4.10a © *Paolo Gioli*, Camera Crackerstenopeica, *1981, lens photo. From the collection of the photographer.*

Figure 4.10b © *Paolo Gioli*, Interno di Camera Crackerstenopeica, con filtri colore di carta trasparente, *1984. Filters are placed over some of the holes. Lens photo. From the collection of the photographer.*

Figure 4.11a © *Terrence Dinnan and Dominique Stroobant*, Pinhole Earth Camera while Digging, *May 1980, Miseglia de Carrara, Italy, lens photo. Terrence Dinnan in front. From the collection of the photographers.*

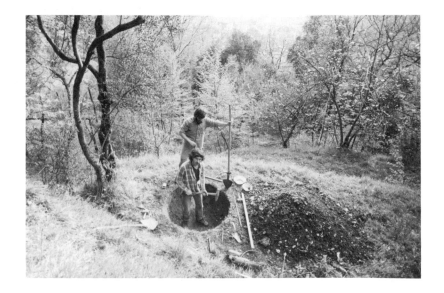

Figure 4.11b © *Terrence Dinnan and Dominique Stroobant*, Setting of Black Plastic on Pinhole Earth Camera, *1980, lens photo. From the collection of the photographers.*

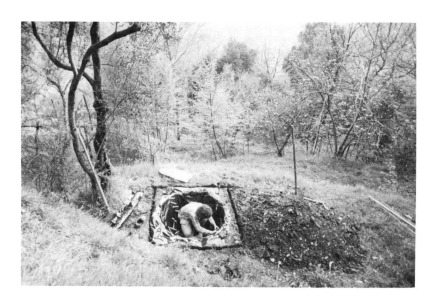

Figure 4.11c © *Terrence Dinnan and Dominique Stroobant*, Pinhole Earth Camera on Exposure, *1980, lens photo. From the collection of the photographers.*

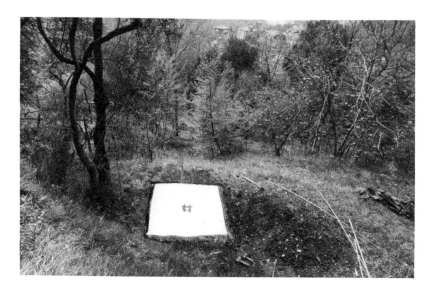

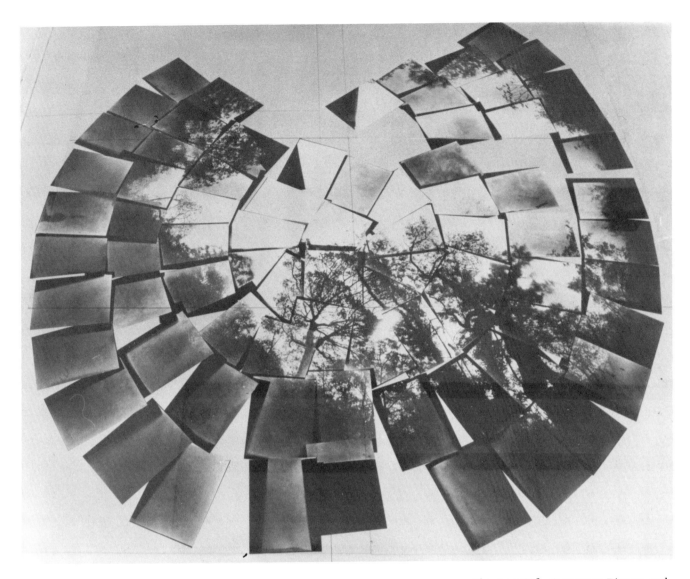

Figure 4.11d © *Terrence Dinnan and Dominique Stroobant,* Earth Camera Photographs, *ICC, Antwerp, June 1980. From the collection of the photographers.*

qualities of each camera and the specific latent-imaging sensitivities of each film. A pinhole camera produces an image of what is projected through the opened aperture onto light-sensitive material inside rather than an image of what the photographer sees and expects to be recorded. An example is the pinhole suitcases Thomas Bachler shipped from cities in Germany to his home city of Kassel, Germany. The pinhole was open during the entire shipping process. Whatever amount of light projected onto the photographic paper inside became Bachler's final image.

In Miseglia de Carrara, Italy, in the clearing of a hillside wood, Terrence Dinnan, of Vermont, and Dominique Stroobant, of Belgium, dug a four-foot-diameter hole shaped like a globe (Figure 4.11a) and covered it with black plastic and an entry bag (Figure 4.11b) for loading and unloading photographic paper. In the middle of the cover was a pinhole (Figure 4.11c). Dinnan crawled into the hole to line the interior with eighty sheets of unexposed

85

photographic paper. After Dinnan crawled out, an exposure was made (Figure 4.11d). The process was suggestive of the astronauts' leaving their space capsule to make a photograph; however, the entire had been inverted to take place on Mother Earth—yet the final image has the look of a stellar composite.

During the 1980s, Dominique Stroobant continued his work photographing the sun. He made many cameras that could remain outside for extended periods of time, even as long as six months. For many of his projects he used multiple cameras, each of which was aimed at different angles from the horizon to a zenith in the sky. One such set is shown in Figure 4.12; the camera was left to photograph for six months. What is amazing is that Stroobant can still achieve a correctly exposed view of the landscape while photographing the sun for as long as six months. Stroobant used very slow litho film to make these images.

Capturing the sun's path across the sky with a pinhole image has a beautiful precedent in the Kogi, a native tribe from the lower Colombian Andes. Their concept of the cosmos is demonstrated in their conical temples. According to ancient Kogi beliefs, the earth is an immense, four-cornered loom on which the sun weaves two pieces of cloth each year.[4] The temple floor models this loom in miniature; the four corners of the earth are fireplace designations. This is further explained by the archaeoastronomer Gary Urton as follows:

> This temple loom is operated by the sun. At the apex of the conical temple is a small hole which is usually covered by a pot-sherd. On certain occasions, the shaman of the temple removes the pot-sherd and allows the sunlight to enter the temple. At the beginning of the Kogi year, on the morning of the June solstice, the pot-sherd is removed at 9:00 A.M. and sunlight strikes the fireplace in the southwest; during the day, the shaft of light [the pinhole solar image] moves along the temple floor from west to the east until, at 3:00 P.M. it rests in the southeastern fireplace. On the morning of the December solstice, the shaft of sunlight makes a line on the ground from the fireplace in the northwest to the fireplace in the northeast. The Kogi say that in this way the sun is weaving a fabric on the loom of the temple. The warp threads of the fabric, running north-south, are laid down by the Earth Mother, and the sun completes the textile by weaving in the east-west threads of the weft. Thus, during the daytime throughout the year, the sun weaves a white fabric. During the night however, the sun weaves another fabric, but this fabric is black.

> The weft of the black fabric is woven during the night when the light of the night sun (what the Kogi refer to as the "black sun") passes through the apex of the inverted subterranean temple. The night sun, however, lays down the black weft of the temple fabric in lines moving from right to left, as opposed to the left-to-right pattern of the white weft of the daytime fabric. Throughout the year, then, the sun weaves one black and one white fabric by the alternation, or opposition, of the left-to-right moving rays of the

daytime sun and the right-to-left moving rays of the nighttime sun.

This theme of resolution of oppositions is reflected in virtually every aspect of Kogi life and thought.[5]

In 1987 Catherine Rogers, of Australia, built a portable darkroom (Figure 4.13a) to be used in the field with a group of friends and students who were hiking in the outback. Because they were hiking about sixty miles, their heavier supplies were hauled by car and dropped at certain points along the route. The group made pinhole cameras out of existing materials. For example, one camera was made of bark, mud, straw, and glue. Negatives were loaded and processed in the portable darkroom, which was set on the ground in the shade. The negatives were then hung to air dry (Figure 4.13b). Alternative process emulsions, such as Van Dyke, were painted on watercolor papers by starlight. The print was contact-printed the next day by sunlight and washed in the river upside down in the maker's shadow (Figure 4.13c) so that the least amount of light would fog the image during processing.

In the early 1980s, Willie Anne Wright, of Virginia, and Lauren Smith, of Ohio, began using large sheets of Ilfochrome Classic paper in their cameras. Ilfochrome Classic is a direct positive color paper (used without a negative) and is intended to be used with tungsten light under an enlarger for printing color slides. Wright filtered her Ilfochrome Classic to balance it to daylight color (Color Plate 4.14), whereas Smith used the paper unfiltered (Color Plate 4.15).

Wright in 1982 organized the first national pinhole exhibition, *The Pinhole Image: Eleven Photographers,* at The Institute of Contemporary Art of the Virginia Museum. Of her imagery, Wright said:

> Plato's image of a world of shadows inhabited by prisoners has, for me, layers of meaning concerning the nature of reality and has a direct relation to the concept of the *camera obscura*. Plato says:
>
>> And now, I said let me show in a figure how far our nature is enlightened or unenlightened: Behold! Human beings living in an underground den, which has a mouth open toward the light and reaching all along the den; here they have been from their childhood, and have their legs and necks chained so that they cannot move, and can only see before them, being prevented by the chains from turning round their heads. Above and behind them a fire is blazing at a distance, and between the fire and the prisoners there is a raised way; and you will see, if you look, a low wall built along the way, like the screen which marionette players have in front of them, over which they show the puppets.
>>
>> I see.

Figure 4.12 © *Dominique Stroobant, 6 Months Photographs, December 22, 1981, to June 22, 1982. Four 7" x 9½" pinhole cameras were set at different angles. Pinhole photograph made with litho film. From the collection of the photographer.*

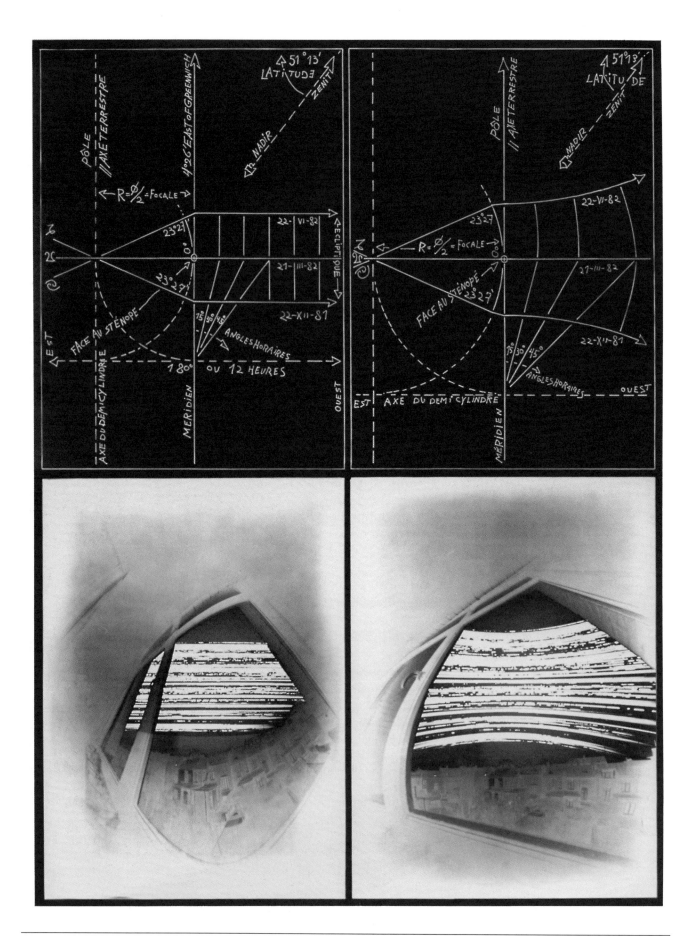

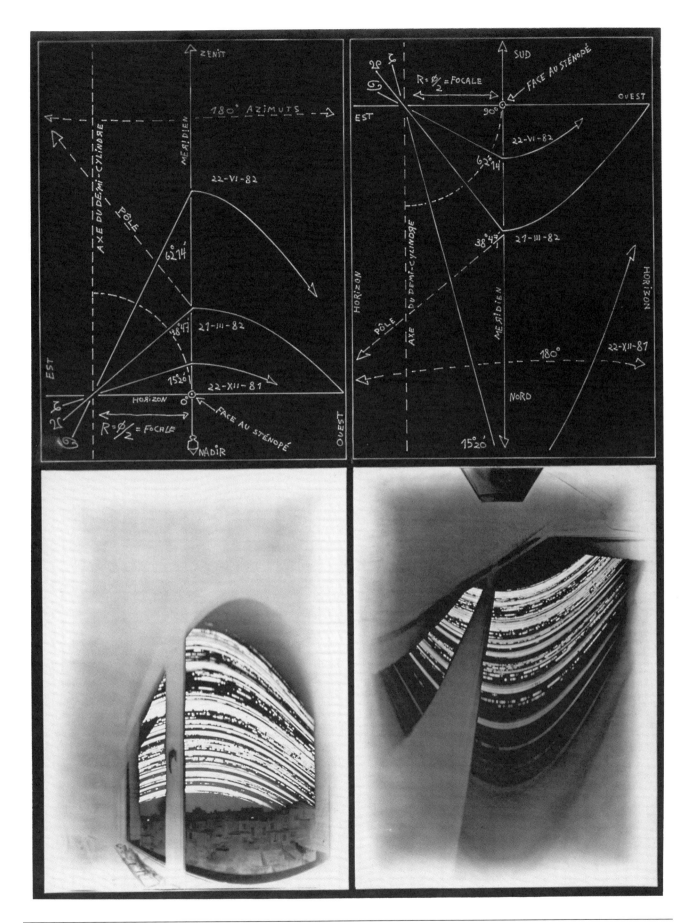

And do you see, I said, men passing along the wall carrying all sorts of vessels, and statues and figures of animals made of wood and stone and various materials, which appear over the wall? Some of them are talking, others silent.

You have shown me a strange image, and they are strange prisoners.

Like ourselves, I replied; and they see only their shadows, or the shadows of one another, which the fire throws on the opposite side of the cave.

Wright completes her explanation:

To me if you vaguely compared the den to a *camera obscura*—the sun would be the fire and the people would sit (inside) facing the back of the camera (making room for the pinhole, of course) and would watch the figures thrown on the back (inside) of the camera. Now going a step further this could be considered a metaphor for life in this world—where appearances are not always true and we see as through "a mirror darkly" truth to be revealed in its entirety perhaps in another world. It's probably better not to try literally to interpret the simile, but to grasp it intuitively. [6]

Figure 4.13a © *Catherine Rogers,* Portable Darkroom, *lens photo, 1986. From the collection at Pinhole Resource.*

Figure 4.13b © *Catherine Rogers,* Negatives Drying in the Wind, *lens photo, 1986. From the collection at Pinhole Resource.*

4.13a

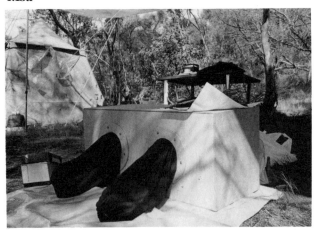

4.13b

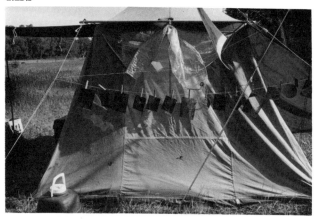

Clarissa Carnell, of Philadelphia, used gold-toned printing-out paper to express subtle or mysterious qualities that often appear as part of the image when lengthy time exposures are deliberately used in pinhole photography. Carnell's photograph at Jim Morrison's Paris grave intentionally made use of the blurred unknown sitter who awaits the moment of resurrection (Figure 4.16).

Barbra Esher has chosen to show layers of color to speak for the layers of intrigue she found while living in Japan. Of her *Kimono Heart/Mind* series (Color Plate 4.17) she stated:

The Japanese word *kokoro* means both heart and mind, not separated but seen together as a whole. This series, in which I've chosen the kimono to explore the Japanese *kokoro*, was conceived and begun during a year's stay in Japan and nine months in America. When I first arrived in the countryside near Mt. Fuji, ideas of what I thought Japan would be like jumbled with my surroundings. I was staying with Japanese people who didn't speak English and everything I did seemed to be wrong. As I frantically searched my dictionary for explanations, they patiently corrected me. Their kindness and consideration was amazing, embarrassing and confusing. Learning Japanese was a step toward understanding what was going on but only because it changed the way I thought and felt.

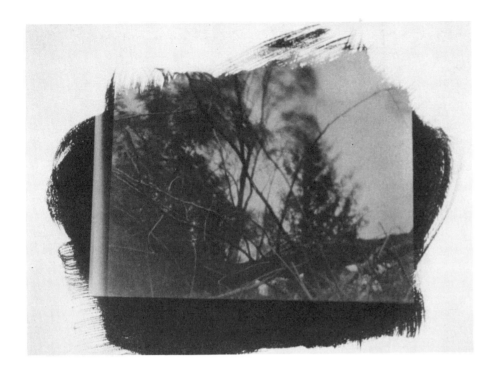

Figure 4.13c © *Catherine Rogers, Untitled, 5" diameter Van Dyke pinhole photograph, 1966. From the collection at Pinhole Resource.*

Permeating the language is an unselfish sensitivity to the "other," whether another person or nature. Deference is expressed through a complicated system of honorific speech, which means you could address a person when you first meet them on a choice of about 13 different levels. These forms of speech have to gradually be changed according to age, social position and the amount of familiarity developed.

As a buffer to this "other," directness is considered rude. Japan's is a culture of wrappers, postcards and books or concealed jealousies and desires. Layers upon layers to peel through only to get to more wrappers. As well as privacy this creates a curious mystery. Nothing is spelled out; it must be discovered. There's an unseen drama in the shadows which hides as well as describes. It's important in Japanese to talk around the subject; something is lost in being direct. If the area around the subject is described and defined, then what you have left is the thing intact; not broken down but as it actually exists—as a beautiful perfect whole.[7]

One cold morning in December of 1982, I made a glass pickle jar into a pinhole camera by painting the inside black, wrapping the jar with three layers of duct tape, and making the pinhole in the glass. I placed the camera under the icy water in a pool near my house in New Mexico. Naively, I was trying to photograph the landscape above the water. The camera was sitting upright, the pinhole about one-half inch under the water. To my complete surprise, the camera photographed underwater what is known in physical optics as "total internal reflection." Reflections underwater!

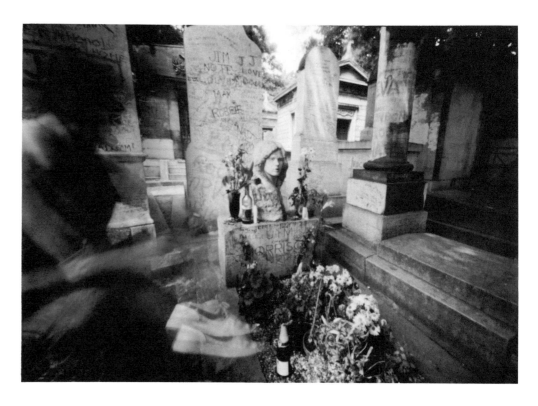

Figure 4.16 © *Clarissa Carnell,* Waiting for Jim, *5" x 7" gold-toned printing-out paper pinhole photograph, 1984. From the collection at Pinhole Resource.*

For the next two years, I worked on a series of images obtained by placing the camera underwater with a heavy rock on top to counteract its buoyancy. The camera simply photographed what was in front of it—the image was a combination of the pool bottom to the edge and a reflection of the pool bottom on the underside of the surface (Figures 4.18a, 4.18b, 4.18c). The exposures were twenty minutes long. I used photographic paper as a negative. The pool had to remain still for the reflection to be clearly mirrored; otherwise it blurred. I became so intrigued with the blended bilateral symmetry in the images that I began to look in old optics books hoping to find information on "underwater reflection," as I called it. I found that early optical scientists, from Alhazen onward, had used pinholes in their window shutters for intimate studies of isolated light rays. This knowledge was my first introduction to the idea that pinholes are a primary tool. I never did find anyone credited with the discovery of underwater reflection, but I did trace the discovery of "total internal reflection" (in glass) back to Theodoric of Freiberg (1290) and the discovery of "the critical angle of total internal reflection" to Johannes Kepler (1600).

It was profound for me to realize a reflection existed underwater that was similar to the reflection on the surface above the water. It was even more profound for me to consider how these

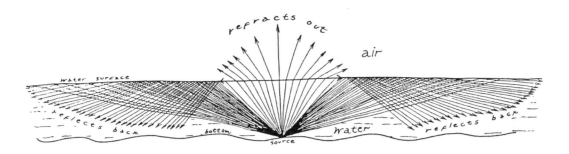

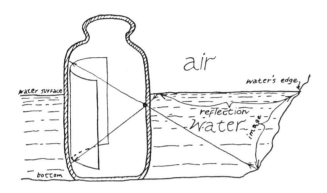

Figure 4.18a © *Eric Renner,* Drawing Illustrating Underwater Reflection, *1984. From the collection at Pinhole Resource.*

Figure 4.18b © *Eric Renner,* Drawing Illustrating Underwater Reflection, *1984. From the collection at Pinhole Resource.*

two reflections are physically placed against one another and that their interface must be of infinitesimal thickness!

Pierre Charrier, of Montreal, uses layers of cameras stacked one on top of another to the height of the person he photographs (Figure 4.19a). Each of the cameras uses an entire roll of color film stretched horizontally with seven pinholes in the front. All together, the entire camera has approximately ninety pinholes. The model poses about a foot from the camera. Charrier opens one pinhole at a time over a period of six to twelve hours (each exposure is about twelve seconds). Each strip of film is processed, and all of the strips are contact-printed together as they were in the original layer of cameras (Color Plate 4.19b).

Charrier said of his work:

> The way I work is to pile them [the cameras] up one over the other. They go to about 6 foot 4 inches. Sometimes I use 12, sometimes 13—all depending upon the height of the person I'm photographing because I'm interested in head to toe recording. If you add all these pinholes, it's 84 or 91 pinholes. In my first photographs I exposed all the pinholes. The type of image I was obtaining was very dense. I call them, I don't know if the English term is very good—very charged. I was looking for an image I could look at for a very long time and not just glance at the image and turn away from it. I could find detailed parts that I could look at longer to find out more about what was happening.

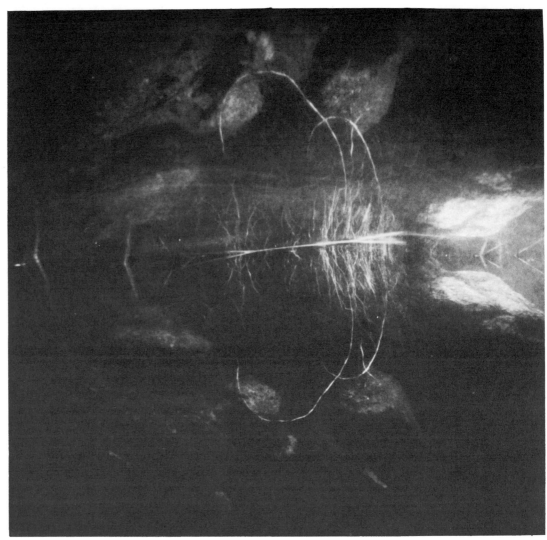

Figure 4.18c © *Eric Renner,* Under the Sod Bank, *underwater reflection, 8" x 8" pinhole photograph, 1984. From the collection at Pinhole Resource.*

It was sort of a vision I would use when looking at a painting. But I would never look at a photograph as long. So I wanted to solve this problem—to look at my photos longer. In my photographs now, I don't expose all the pinholes, I may expose 50 or 30 or 70 depending on how I compose the picture.[8]

Also from Canada, Paul Cimon uses single-frame pieces of cut 35mm film placed in thirty-six match boxes (Figures 4.20a, 4.20b). After processing, each black-and-white image is enlarged and hand-colored, then placed panoramically in three dimensions (Figure 4.20c).

During solar eclipses Jim Jones, of Missouri, uses a ten-foot-long plastic plumbing pipe to photograph the sun (Figures 4.21a, 4.21.b). Jones explained:

> The solar eclipse camera was made of a 3" plastic pipe with pinhole and shutter at one end and an improvised springback for a 4" x 5" film holder at the other. In use, the camera is pointed at the sun so that the shadow of the front is centered on the back. A string attached to the shutter runs the length of the camera for convenient operation. A self-cocking shutter from old folding cameras usually has adequate speeds. 1/100 of a second with a .070" pinhole worked on outdated Kodalith film developed in Dektol.[9]

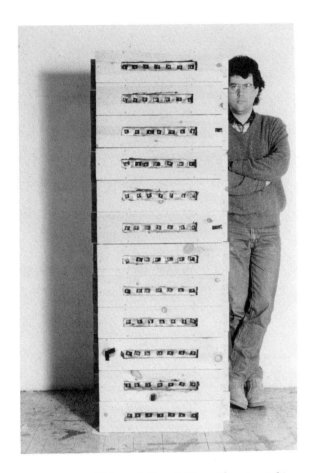

Figure 4.19a © *Pierre Charrier,* Self-portrait with Pinhole Camera, *lens photo, 1986. From the collection at Pinhole Resource.*

This camera would not work for landscape images, because there would be too much reflection along the pipe. For photographing a bright spot such as a solar eclipse, however, it is perfect.

Some of the most interesting cameras made from unusual objects come from Professor Sanchez Gaetan's class at the University of the Sacred Heart in San Juan, Puerto Rico. The land crab camera (Figure 4.22) is by Guillermo Gonzalez. All of the cameras made by Gaetan's students must produce an image.

Sarah Van Keuren, of Pennsylvania, uses 8-inch by 10-inch film holders that attach to the end of a wooden box. Of her introduction to pinhole photography and her evolving philosophy (Color Plates 4.23a and 4.23b), Van Keuren observed:

> I got more and more involved with it partly because I needed a large format negative for my non-silver processes. I had been enlarging 35mm negatives on copy film, commercial film, or duplicating film. That seemed kind of phony to me. Pinhole was so beautifully simple and so inexpensive. I've had kind of a reaction against the high-priced equipment; I'm not an equipment jock. I liked the fact I could make a pinhole camera for almost no money at all and get a large negative. It was only after I'd

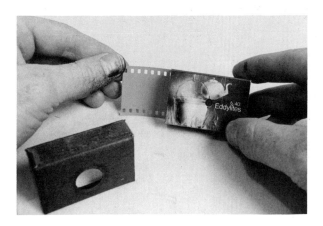

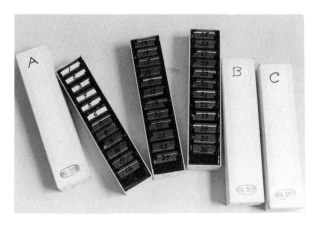

Figure 4.20a © *Paul Cimon, New Generation Matchbox Pinhole Camera, lens photo, 1986. From the collection of the photographer.*

Figure 4.20b © *Paul Cimon, New Generation Matchbox Pinhole Camera, 12 to a box, 36 in all, lens photo, 1986. Each box contains a viewfinder. From the collection of the photographer.*

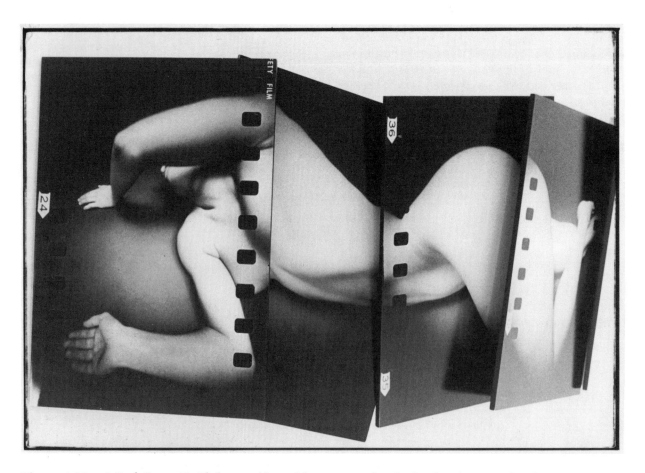

Figure 4.20c © *Paul Cimon, Untitled, assemblage of four 11" x 14" hand-colored and sequenced pinhole images from 35mm film placed in a new-generation matchbox pinhole camera, 1989. From the collection of the photographer.*

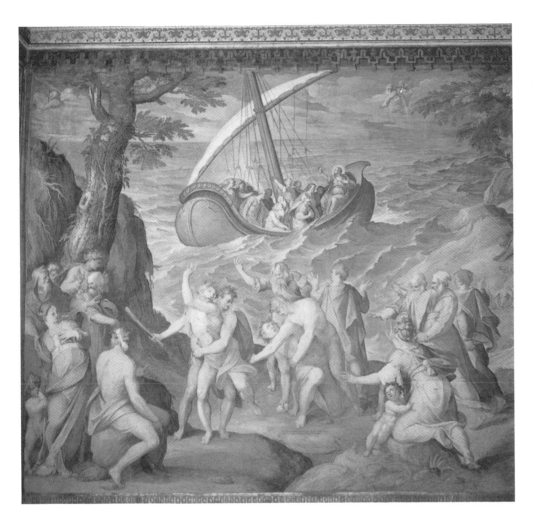

Color Plate 1.13 La Tempesta Sedata, *Pinhole in the mouth of the God of the South Wind. Courtesy of Secret Archives, the Vatican.*

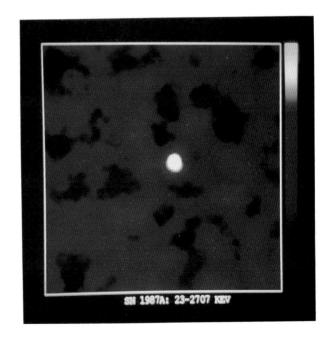

SN 1987A: 23-2707 KEV

Color Plate 1.27b *Thomas A. Prince*, First Gamma-ray Image of Supernova 1987A. *Coded-aperture pinhole image, November 18, 1987. Courtesy of the California Institute of Technology, George W. Downs Laboratory of Physics, Pasadena.*

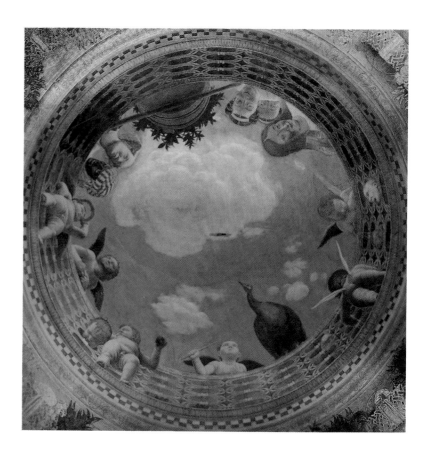

Color Plate 2.5 *Andrea Mantegna,* Oculus in the Ceiling, *circa 1470, in Camera degli Sposi, Palazzo Ducale, Mantua.*

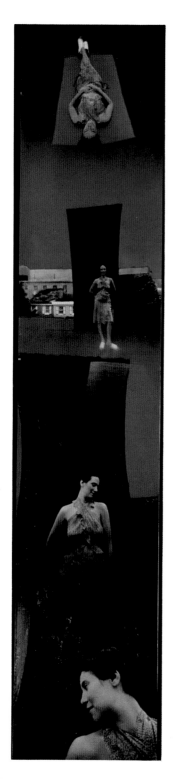

Color Plate 3.3 *© David Lebe, Susan, $2\frac{1}{2}$" x 12" hand-colored pinhole photograph, 1973. From the collection of the photographer.*

Color Plate 4.1 © *Margaret L. Harrigan,* The Marble Picture, *12" x 18" type C print pinhole photograph, 1988. From the collection at Pinhole Resource.*

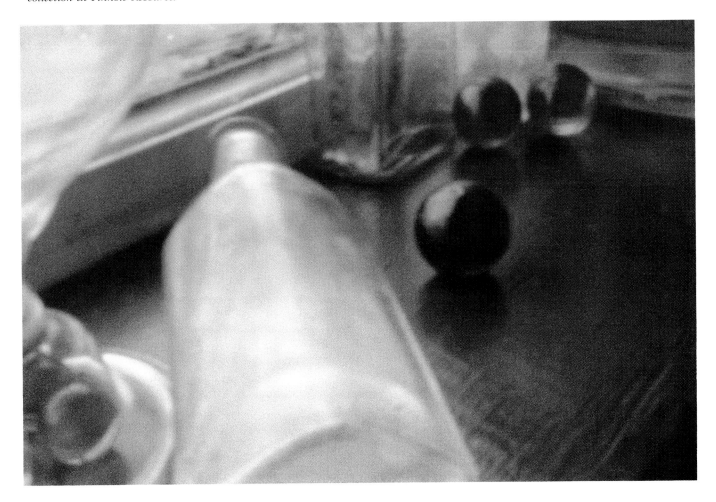

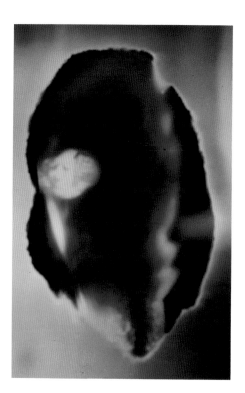

Color Plate 4.4b © *Eric Renner,* Self, *8" x 10" unfiltered Ilfochrome Classic pinhole photograph, 1985. From the collection of the photographer.*

Color Plate 4.5b © *Eric Renner and Nancy Spencer,* Self-Portraits, *8" x 10" unfiltered Ilfochrome Classic pinhole photograph made from a seven-second exposure, 1989. From the collection of the photographers.*

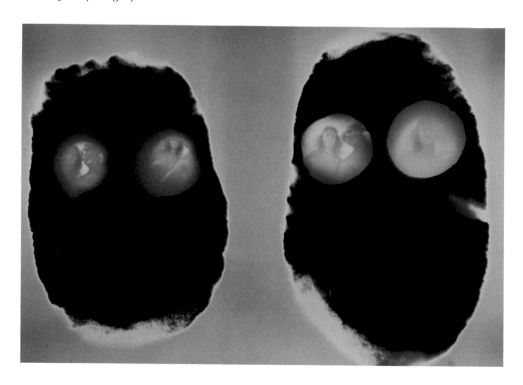

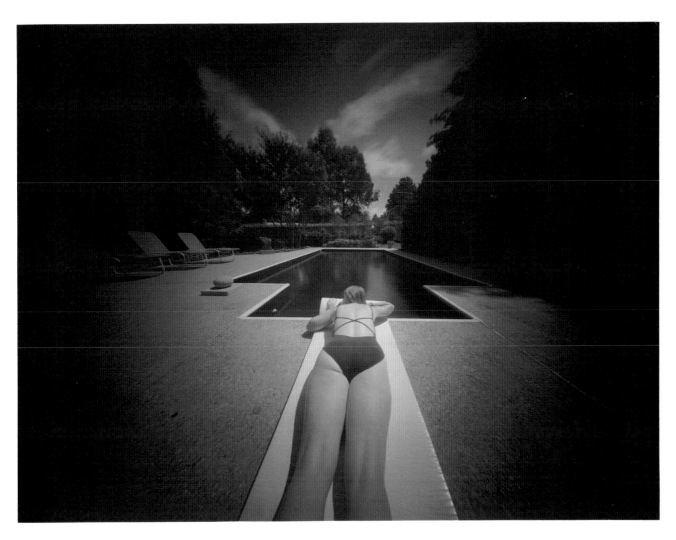

Color Plate 4.14 © *Willie Anne Wright*, Anne S. in Front of Jack B.'s Pool, *9" x 13" Ilfochrome Classic pinhole photograph, 1984. From the* Pools *series. From the collection at Pinhole Resource.*

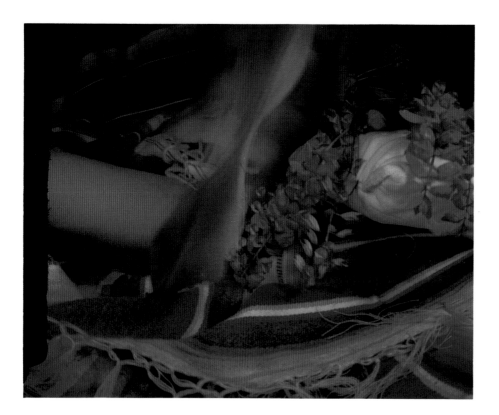

Color Plate 4.15 © *Lauren Smith,*
Untitled, *8" x 10" unfiltered Ilfochrome*
Classic pinhole photograph made from
a Charlie Chip Potato Chips can pinhole
camera, 1982. From the Spring Passion
series. From the collection of the photog-
rapher.

Color Plate 4.17 © *Barbra Esher,*
Kimono Heart/Mind *series, 30" x 40"*
type C pinhole photograph, 1980s. From
the collection of the photographer.

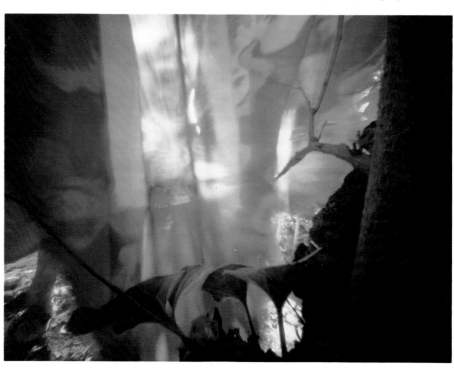

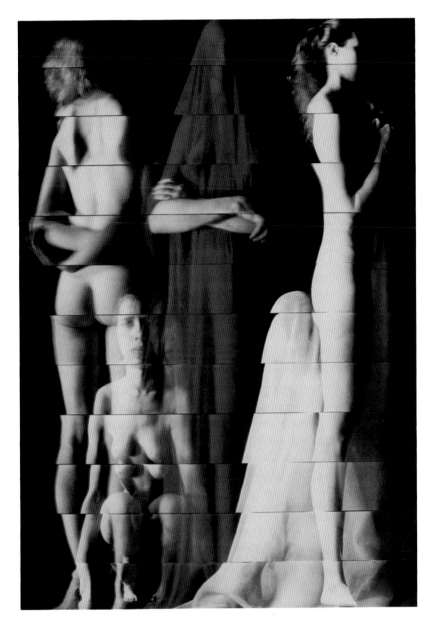

Color Plate 4.19b © *Pierre Charrier,* Untitled, *20" x 30" type C pinhole photograph, 1986. From the collection at Pinhole Resource.*

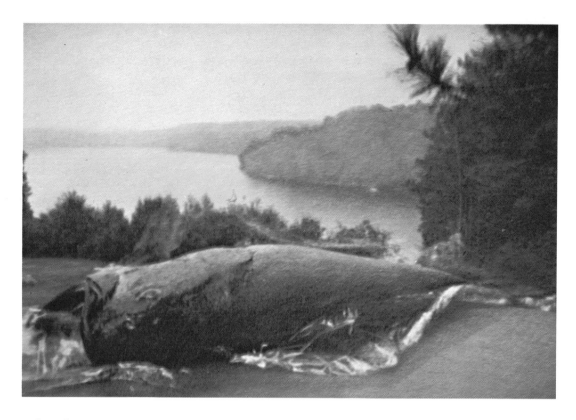

Color Plate 4.23a © *Sarah Van Keuren,* Fish by Lake, *8" x 10" cyanotype and gum pinhole photograph, 1986. From the collection of the photographer.*

Color Plate 4.23b © *Sarah Van Keuren,* Figure by Pool, *8" x 10" cyanotype and gum pinhole photograph, 1986. From the collection of the photographer.*

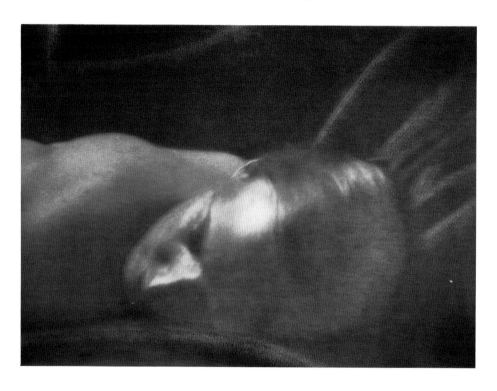

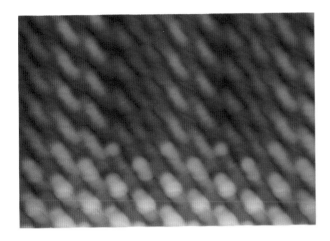

Color Plate 4.27 © *Sandy Moss, TV,
14" x 17" unfiltered Ilfochrome Classic
pinhole photograph, ten-minute exposure, 1987. From the collection of the
photographer.*

Color Plate 4.28 © *Jo Babcock,
Alcatraz, 40" x 54" type C pinhole photograph, 1988. From the collection of the
photographer.*

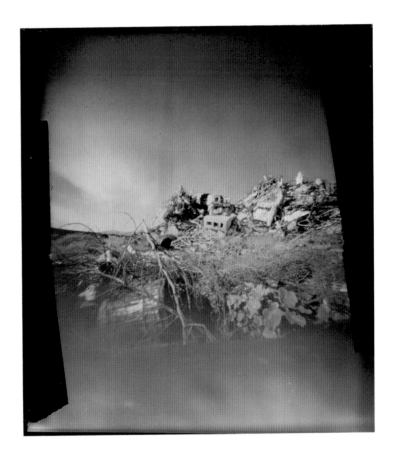

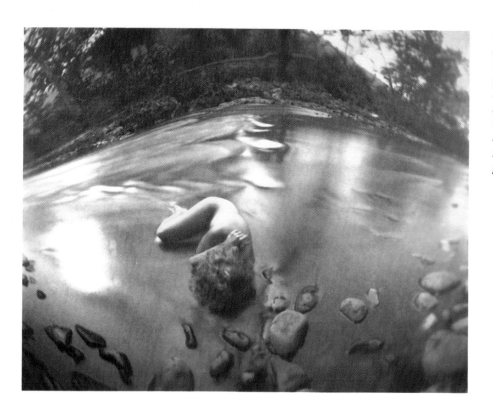

Color Plate 5.12 © *Nancy Spencer and Rebecca Wackler, Flight Series, 8" x 10" hand-colored pinhole photograph, 1986. The cylindrical camera has been angled slightly downward (not perpendicular to the ground), which creates an exaggerated curved-earth effect. From the collection of the photographers.*

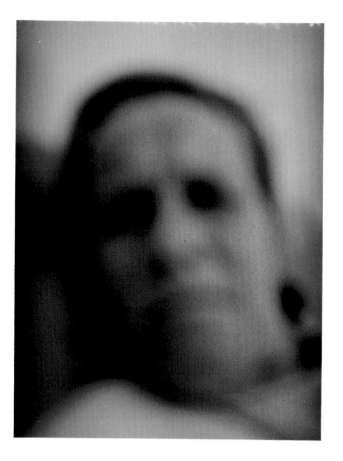

Color Plate 5.19 © *Thomas Kellner, Untitled, $3\frac{1}{2}$" x $4\frac{1}{2}$" type C pinhole photograph, 1992, made with a Kodak Quick-Snap Camera with pinhole added. The pinhole is ten times the size it should be for optimal sharpness. From the collection of the photographer.*

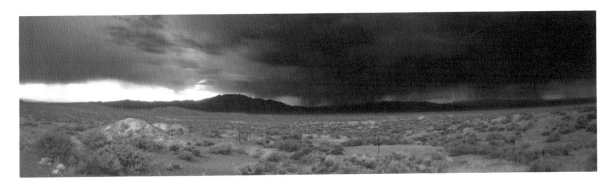

Color Plate 5.27 © *Denis Farley*, Tonopah, Nevada, *2" x 7" type C pinhole photograph, 1990. From the collection* *at Pinhole Resource.*

Color Plate 5.30a © *Paolo Gioli*, Tondo di pupilla riaperta, *3" x 4" stereo Polaroid Polachrome,* *microstenopeica stampota su Ilfochrome Classic, 1986. From the collection at Pinhole Resource.*

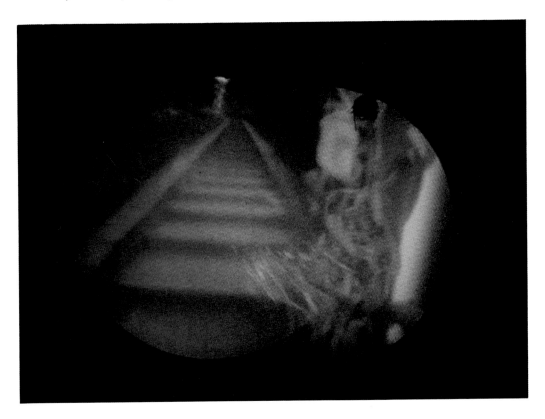

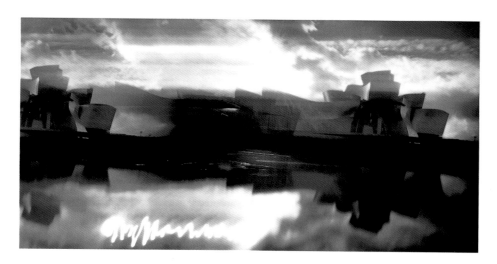

Color Plate 5.31 © Herbert Bötcher,
Guggenheim Museum, Bilbao, Spain,
*three pinhole color photograph from the
Architecture + Energy series, film
Ektachrome 100 developed in C41, 1997.
From the collection of the photographer.*

Color Plate 5.33 © Rita DeWitt, Elvis Visits Lake Michigan, 20" x 30" type C pinhole
*photograph from a plastic camera with a pinhole, 1989. From the collection of the pho-
tographer.*

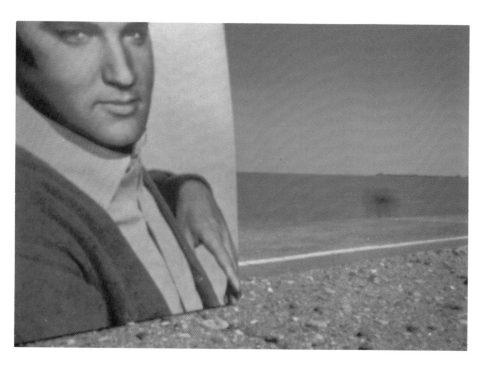

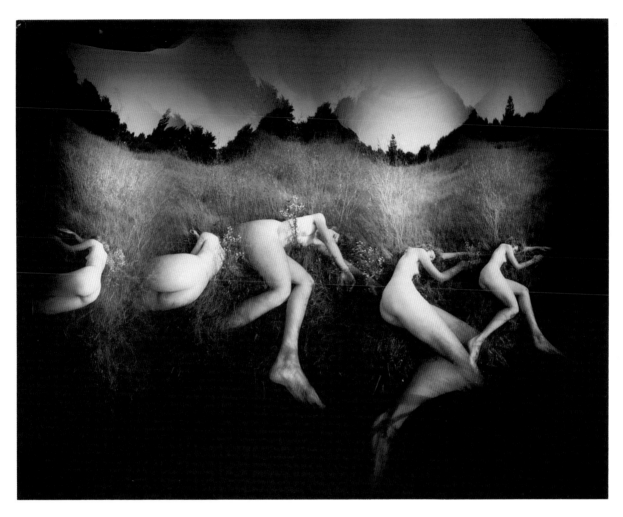

Color Plate 5.40   © *Jim Cherry,* Katie, *8" x 10" Ilfochrome Classic pinhole photograph, five-pinhole panorama, 1987. From the collection at Pinhole Resource.*

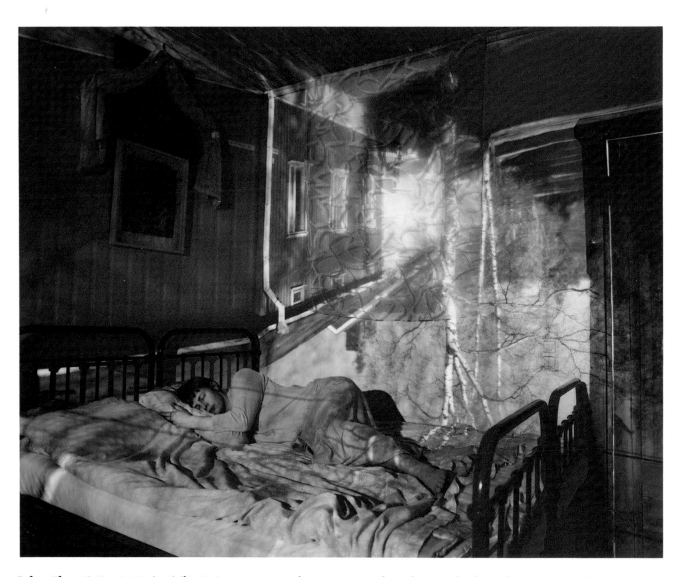

Color Plate 5.43 © *Marja Pirilä*, Sarianna, *camera obscura portrait, lens photograph of a pinhole image inside the room, 1996. From the collection of the photographer.*

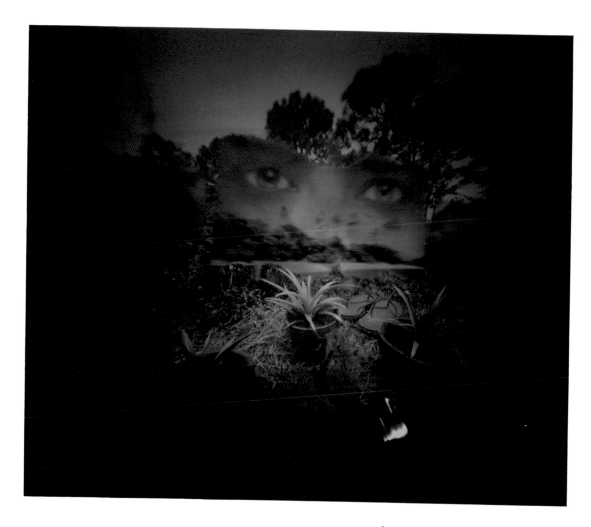

Color Plate 5.47 © *Howard E. Williams*, Untitled, *20" x 24" Ilfochrome Classic pinhole photograph filtered with Lee filter #102 light amber, 1987. Two-hour exposure on a cloudy day from a* $6\frac{1}{2}$" *focal-length camera. From the collection of the photographer.*

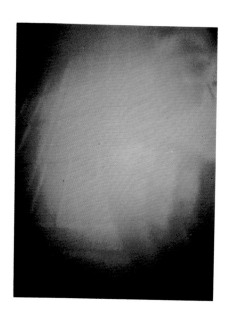

Color Plate 6.8 © *Eric Renner*, John Wood, *11" x 14" unfiltered Ilfochrome Classic slit photograph, 20-second exposure, 1985. If you view it long enough, you can see a face in the upper right-hand corner and an enlarged hand below. From the collection of the photographer.*

Color Plate 6.9 © *Harry Littell*, Slit camera obscura images, *12' x 100', 1989, Omaha, Nebraska, lens photo. These images are being viewed from front of rear-projecting screen. From the collection of the photographer.*

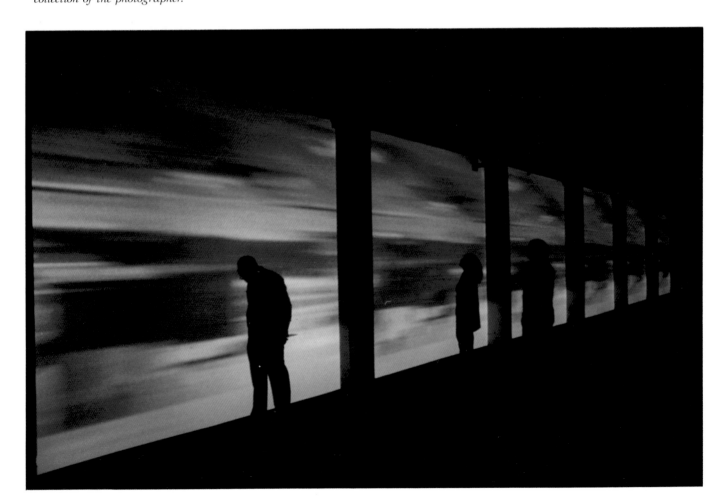

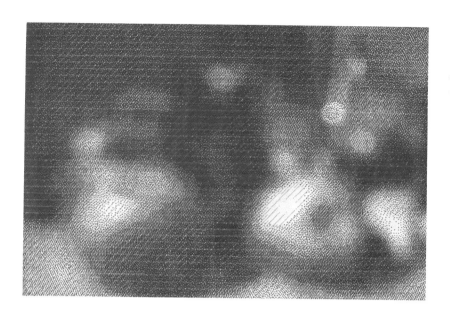

Color Plate 6.12 © *Sam Wang*, Untitled Still Life, $4\frac{3}{4}$" x 7" *nail-hole color-separated computer print, Macintosh ported to Atari ST, printed on Star, 1989. From the collection at Pinhole Resource.*

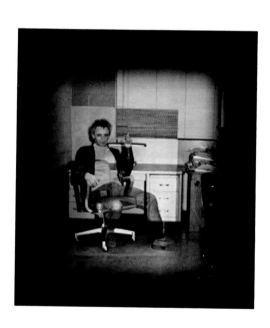

Color Plate 6.13a © *Gillian Brown*, Painted Image Seen through Hole, *lens photo, 1989. From the collection of the photographer.*

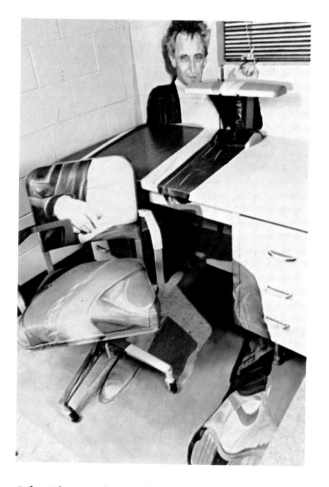

Color Plate 6.13b © *Gillian Brown*, Painted Image Seen from Angled View, *lens photo, 1989. From the collection of the photographer.*

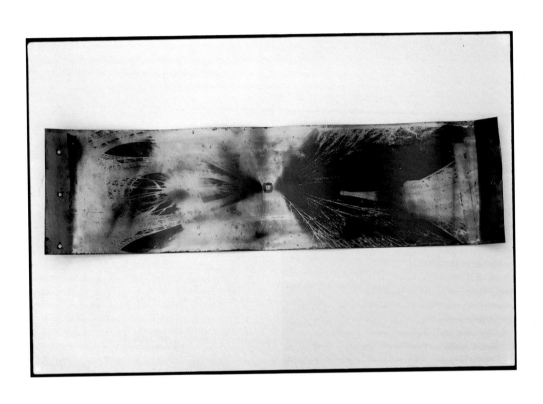

Color Plate 7.1 © *Ilan Wolff*, Architecture in Paris *(work in progress), pinhole photograph using Liquid Light inside a metal container with pinhole, pinhole camera taken apart and exhibited flat, 1994–1995. From the collection of the photographer.*

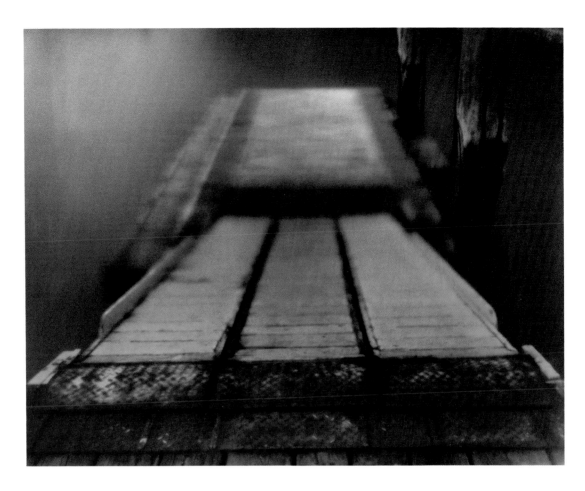

Color Plate 7.9 © *David Gepp*, Fondamenta Zattere, 7-*minute exposure from a 4" x 5" color negative, 1995. From the collection of the photographer.*

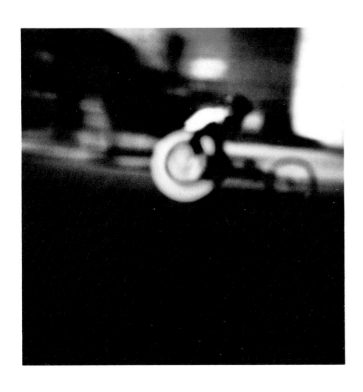

Color Plate 7.11 © *Robert Oehl*, Wheelchair Marathoner, NYC Marathon, $3\frac{1}{2}$" *square Polaroid SX-70 pinhole photograph, 1996. From the collection at Pinhole Resource.*

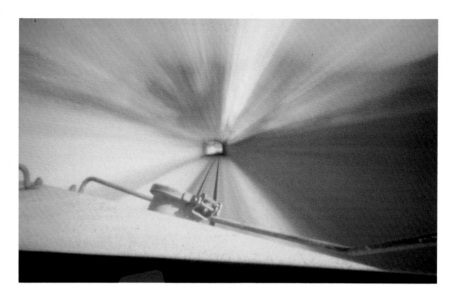

Color Plate 7.13a © *Joseph Jakusz,* Motion Blur . . . Tunnel 10 (West of Caliente, NV), *pinhole photograph made with Fujichrome 50 film, 1991. The pinhole was mounted in a C3 Argus camera and shot from a Union Pacific cab. From the collection of the photographer.*

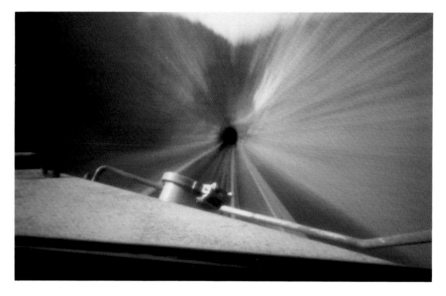

Color Plate 7.13b © *Joseph Jakusz,* Motion Blur . . . Tunnel 7 (Approach to Stine, NV), *pinhole photograph made with Fujichrome 50 film, 1991. The pinhole was mounted in a C3 Argus camera and shot from a Union Pacific cab. From the collection of the photographer.*

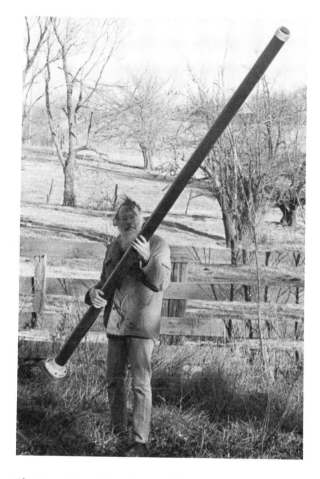

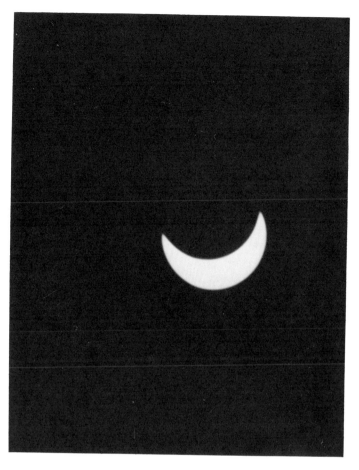

Figure 4.21a © *Jim Jones,* Self-Portrait with Solar Eclipse Camera, *lens photo, 1984. From the collection at Pinhole Resource.*

Figure 4.21b © *Jim Jones,* Solar Eclipse, 30 May 1984, $3\frac{3}{4}$" x $4\frac{1}{4}$" *pinhole photograph. From the collection at Pinhole Resource.*

been doing it for awhile that I began doing portraits. I had always done portraits as a lithographer—for years and years. I began to realize that a pinhole photograph provided a composite image of a person—like what you get when you're drawing a model over a period of time. It's a collection of expressions. The body of the model slumps into a characteristic pose, if I'm doing a full figure during the 6 or 7 minute duration of my indoor exposures. You don't get a fleeting expression of someone's face; it's very different in feeling, kind of like the early photos where the people had to pose for a long time. To me it seems to get at a certain inner truth—like a psychological x-ray.[10]

Ian Paterson, a Canadian living in Paris, also uses a simple box to make pinhole landscapes. Paterson's photographs (Figure 4.24) from Luxembourg Gardens received wide attention in his Paris exhibition at Musee Carnavalet in 1989.

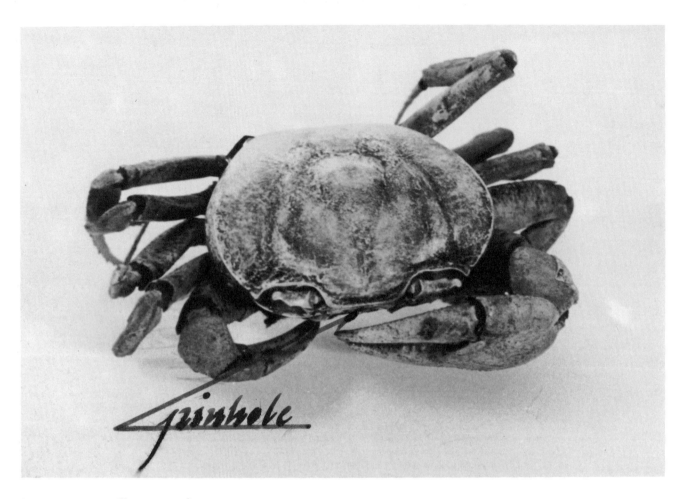

Figure 4.22 © *Guillermo Gonzalez, Land Crab Pinhole Camera, lens photo, 1980s. From the class of Professor Sanchez Gaetan, Universidad del Sagrado Corazon, San Juan, Puerto Rico. The pinhole is at the crab's mouth. From the collection of Osvaldo Garcia.*

In the late 1980s, photographer Nancy Spencer worked in collaboration with playwright and actress Rebecca Wackler. One of their series, *Gospel of Mary*, concerns the disrespect and lack of appreciation that Christ's disciple Mary Magdalene receives in the Bible compared with her honored place in the Gnostic Gospels—a set of thirteen books written nearly two thousand years ago, but only discovered in 1945, unearthed from inside a buried vase in Egypt.

One of their pinhole photographs, made to accompany a stage production, shows a woman crucified (Figure 4.25), symbolizing Mary Magdalene on the cross. Spencer explained the controversial image:

> It possibly may be offensive to many people, but what we were trying to say in *Gospel of Mary* was that Christianity crucified women, but the Gnostic Gospels don't.[11]

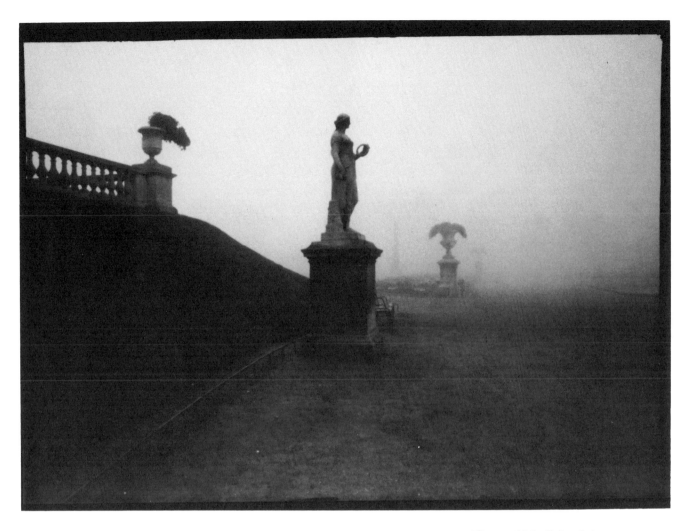

Figure 4.24 © *Ian Paterson, Luxembourg Gardens, $5\frac{1}{4}$" x $7\frac{1}{4}$" pinhole photograph, 1989. From the collection of the photographer.*

1980s Commercial Pinhole Cameras

Not everyone who does pinhole photography makes a specialized type of pinhole camera. Many people use a very simple, reliable camera such as an old oatmeal box, a large-format camera with lens removed and pinhole attached, or one of the readily available commercial pinhole cameras. At least six different commercially produced pinhole cameras were manufactured during the 1980s. The first to appear was the four-inch by five-inch Pinhole Camera Kit designed collaboratively by Jerry Stratton and Bob Witanowski, of Ohio. Containing an acid-etched pinhole, the camera can be assembled in about two minutes; five thousand have been sold. Next was the PinZip, designed by David Pugh, of Delaware, with 126 Instamatic cartridges. Pugh's use of the PinZip is shown in Figure 4.26. Almost ten thousand were sold through an outdoor catalogue. By 1986, the World Famous Lenseless

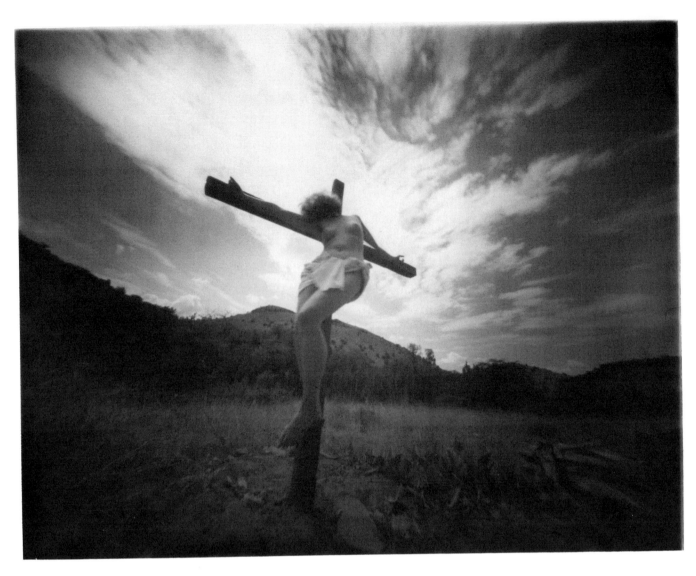

Figure 4.25 © *Nancy Spencer and Rebecca Wackler,* Untitled, Gospel of Mary *series, 11" x 14" pinhole photograph, 1989. From the collection of the photographers.*

Camera of Santa Barbara, handcrafted by Walter Boye using four-inch by five-inch film holders and refined plywood, was available. In 1988, the Make Your Own Working Camera kit manufactured in book form arrived on the market. A pinhole stereo camera shaped to resemble a block of Swiss cheese apparently was available from Switzerland, although I have never seen one. In England, John Adams Toys produced a three-inch by three-inch kit called Pinhole Camera that included photo paper and chemicals.

International Pinhole Shows

In 1988, the first international exhibition of pinhole photography, *Through a Pinhole Darkly,* was organized by the Fine Arts Museum of Long Island. The idea was suggested to the museum by the pinhole photographer Bernice Halpern Cutler. Cameras and photographs from forty-five artists were shown.

A second international exhibition soon followed. In Spain in May 1988, the Museum of Contemporary Art of Seville showed the work of nine pinhole photographers. Four months later, a third exhibition, the *International Pinhole Exhibition,* was organized by the Center for Contemporary Arts of Santa Fe, New Mexico, and showed the work of twenty pinhole photographers. The most thorough analysis of 1980's pinhole photography from the standpoint of photo criticism came from James Hugunin's essay "Notes toward a Stenopaesthetic," in the catalogue of this show. Many of Hugunin's insights are of great value in understanding specific artists' sensibilities, thoughts, and directions. Excerpts from Hugunin's essay follow (reproduced by permission of James Hugunin).

On Sandra Moss:

Sandra Moss, who lives in Sweden, has been exploring the four elements—earth, air, fire and water—in order to "de-construct them and to observe how they contrast with each other."[12] Due to the all pervasiveness of electronic media, she decided to add a "fifth element"—television [Color Plate 4.27], an element of the "bad life"—which she sees as inexorably diminishing our relationship to the original four. As Guy Debord put it in *Society of the Spectacle,* the media promoted "a counterfeit life requir[ing] pseudo-justification."[13] Moss explains her modus operandi "I don't want to photograph at earth, or at TV . . . I want to photograph through it."[14] For her study of water, a container of it was put right up against the pinhole of a home-made camera for twenty minutes, an hour exposure through dirt placed over the pinhole and Moss had obtained *Earth* (1987).

In this show, Moss only displays work exploring that "fifth element," television. TV Landscape, #1–6 (1987) is part of a larger

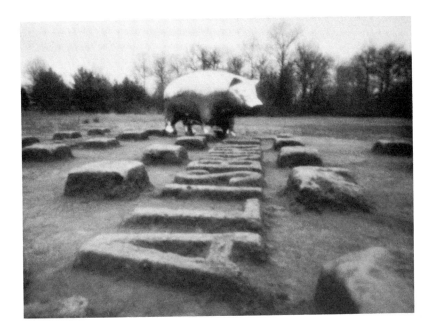

Figure 4.26 © *David Pugh,* Pig on a Manhole Cover, $6\frac{1}{4}$" x $8\frac{1}{2}$" *pinhole photograph, 1982. This image was made from a PinZip camera f/110, 4-second exposure of a 3" high brass piggy bank standing on a utility hole cover. The raised letters (part of the word "Salisbury") are about $\frac{1}{8}$" high, and the square bumps are about $\frac{1}{4}$" high. From the collection at Pinhole Resource.*

series she calls *Vanishing Senses* and was photographed at various distances from the color TV screen. When the pinhole was right against the screen, as in *TV Landscape #5*, the stenope worked as a magnifying lens enlarging a minuscule area, resolving only the raster's "phonemes": the red, blue and green constituents of the full color image.

. . . By this juxtaposition, Moss contrasts the traditional window-onto-nature scene with television's "obscenity," where (as Jean Baudrillard reminds us): "the body, landscape, time all progressively disappear as scenes."[15] If the window-onto-nature is our Western model for representation, then the obscenity of the visible that television participates in puts an end to such representation. It is this Baudrillardian dystopia Moss symbolically attacks.[16]

On Jo Babcock:

In a large 30 x 40 inch type C color print titled *Alcatraz* [Color Plate 4.28], Babcock aims his pinhole at the remains of the once infamous, impregnable penitentiary where "The Birdman" perched for many years. The middle third of the image depicts chunks of crumbling white concrete whose twisted, tortured rebars suggest the agonies of the many inmates who suffered behind those walls. The disorder Babcock sees in this subject—a "clash of uncoordinated orders," as Rudolph Arnheim reminds us, and "not the absence of all order"—is echoed in the composition.[17] Unified pictorial space is cut into three quasi-autonomous zones— the blue sky in the top third of the print, the concrete remnants, an area of magenta colored fogging at the bottom. This, and the irregularly shaped edges of the image, suggest yet a deeper reading of this image. May not Babcock be pointing to the inexorable entropic "running down" of all matter, even that of such formidable institutions as Alcatraz and, by implication, the decline of authority and power garnered by these institutions? Herein lies the essence of Babcock's political commentary.[18]

On Martha Casanave:

Martha Casanave did her first pinhole photographs in 1984, affixing a pinhole on the front standard of her 4 x 5 inch camera. Her reason for using the device? "I've often heard myself say that if I could made a photograph with just my eyes and brain," she has commented, "and not this clumsy and noisy mechanical device, I would be very happy. Using a pinhole camera comes closer to this ideal [Figures 4.29a, 4.29b]."[19]

Casanave's portrait-narratives deal with what the photographer confesses are "uncomfortable and ever traumatic memories."[20] Yet, as Casanave found upon exhibiting this work and getting responses to it, her imagery also "spoke" of similar memories by women other than herself. Not merely interested in form, Casanave tries to implicate her personal expression with a universal feminism.[21]

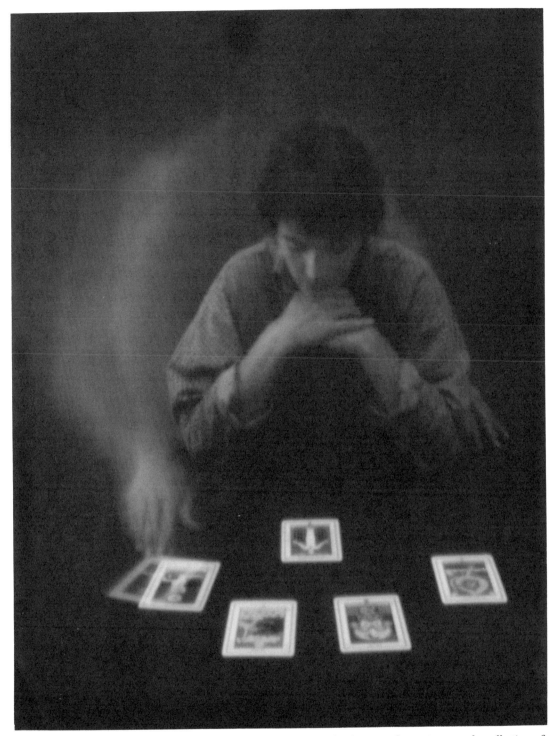

Figure 4.29a © *Martha Casanave, Untitled, 16" x 20" pinhole photograph, 1986. From the collection of the photographer.*

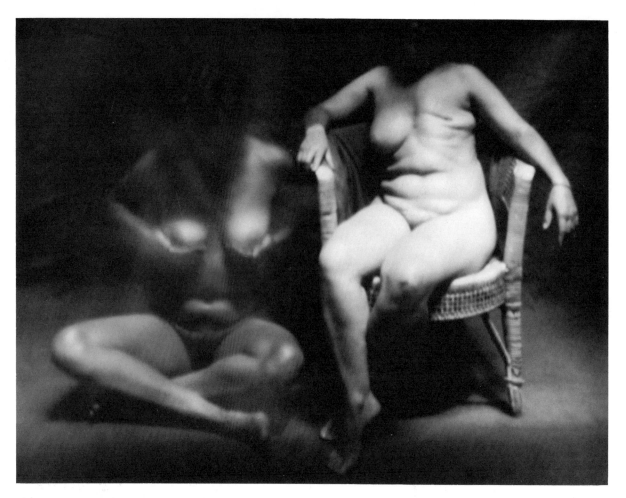

Figure 4.29b © *Martha Casanave*, Untitled, *16" x 20" pinhole photograph, 1986. From the collection of the photographer.*

On Peggy Ann Jones:

In her *Kakemono* series, Southern California artist Peggy Ann Jones combines her interests in printmaking, fiber arts, sculpture, and pinhole photography with her delight in Japanese artifacts.... What Jones wanted to build was a device capable of holding a piece of light-sensitive paper folded out like a Japanese fan, so that marked distortions would occur during image projection. At first, in her series *Preconceptions of Japan* [Figure 4.30], Jones did not attach the fan-photo to a scroll. Soon, however, the flattened out fan-image was to become the starting point for the construction of the long vertical *kakemono* scrolls. . . . The composition of the print itself blends so well with the fan-fold shape that the subject photographed and the object upon which it is rendered fuse into a

Figure 4.30 © *Peggy Ann Jones*, Taos Pueblo Church, *from* Preconceptions of Japan #1, *8" x 16" pinhole photograph, 1988. From the collection at Pinhole Resource.*

Figure 4.31 © *Douglas Frank*, Untitled, *11" x 14" platinum pinhole photograph, 1990. From the collection of the photographer.*

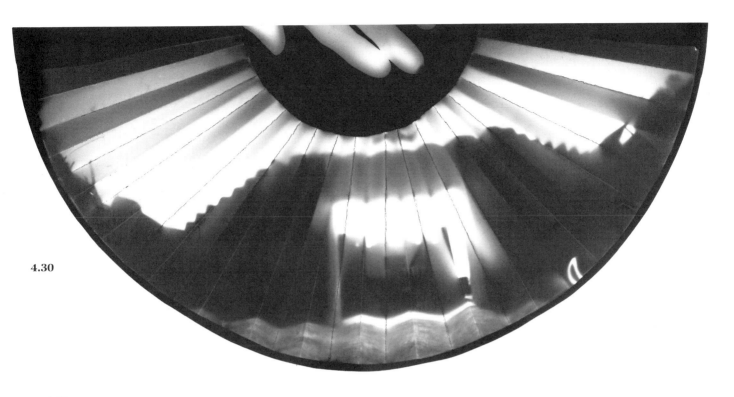

4.30

4.31

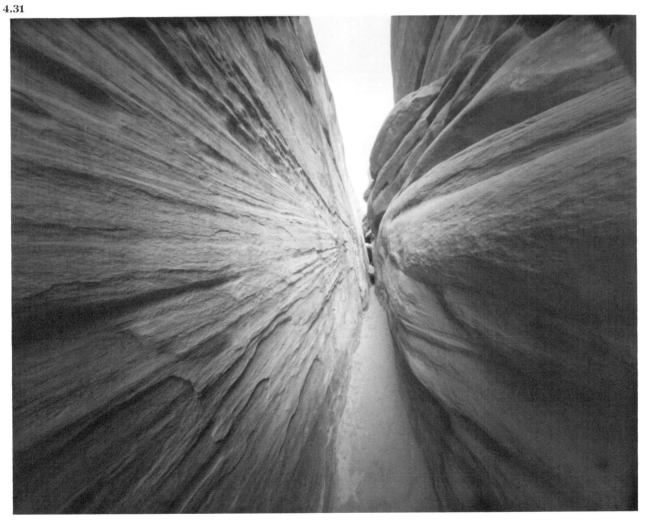

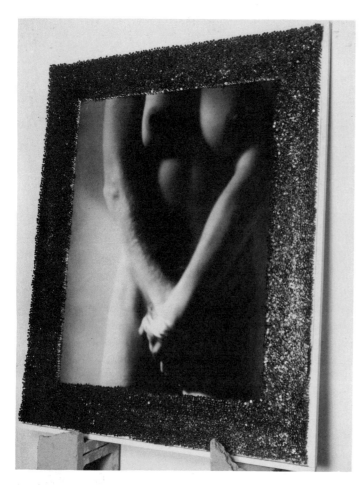

Figure 4.32 © *David Plakke,*
Untitled, 40" x 50" pinhole photograph
and nails, 1988. Courtesy of the Witkin
Gallery, New York City.

single visual entity. Pictorial space becomes ambiguous: at times it advances to the picture plane, then it recedes back into the illusory third dimension. Empty space is permitted to have great impact, conforming to the Japanese conception of *mu* (which anticipated Gestalt psychology), the intuition that negative space is not merely empty, but active, as worthy of esthetic attention as the figure. This *kakemono* invites the kind of quiet contemplation urged upon us by Zen brush paintings and rock gardens.[22]

By the end of the 1980s, many photographers who might have otherwise known only lens photography chose to try pinhole. Many were accomplished photographers and brought with them a strong sense and knowledge of the medium. Douglas Frank, of Oregon, had used lens cameras to make large-format platinum prints for years. In the late 1980s, he turned to pinhole; his sophisticated wide-angle pinhole landscapes employ a series of masks to either accentuate or deaccentuate the edges of the image (Figure 4.31). Similarly, David Plakke, of New Jersey, brought a prior sense of the medium to pinhole photography. His emotionally intense pinhole images (Figure 4.32) deal with AIDS and contemporary issues of sexuality.

Politically, the 1980s ended abruptly—communism leapt toward democracy. In one brilliant statement West German Marcus Kaiser used holes that had been torn through the Berlin Wall as pinhole cameras (Figure 4.33a). On one side of the hole in the wall, he taped a pinhole; on the other side he taped a film holder (Figure 4.33b). For the first time in decades, a person could photograph through this cherished light toward the East (Figure 4.33c)—or move his pinhole and film holder around and photograph toward the West (Figure 4.33d). Long-dreamt-of freedom had arrived. So had the pinhole arrived.

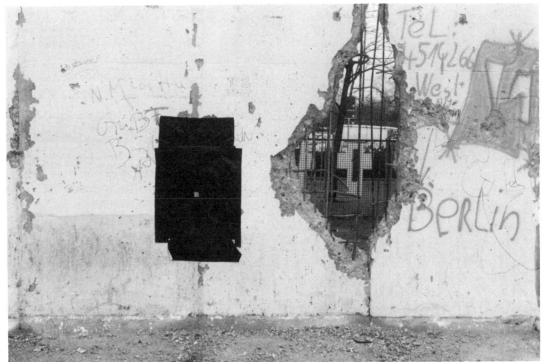

4.33a

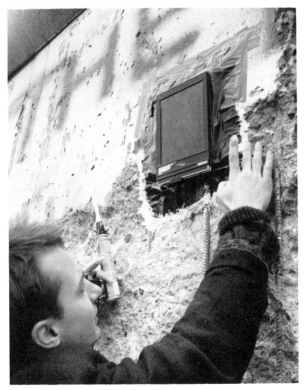

4.33b

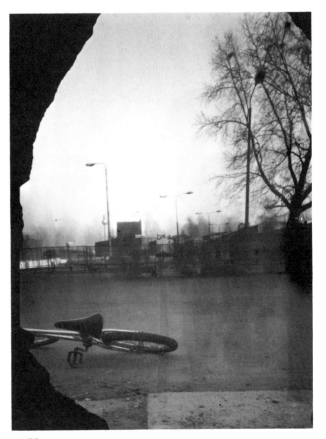

4.33c

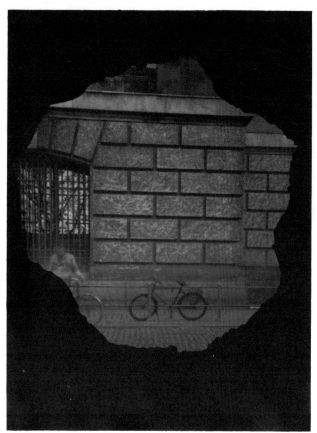

4.33d

Figure 4.33a © *Marcus Kaiser,* Pinhole Camera Made in a Hole in the Berlin Wall, Mauerblicke *series, lens photo, 1990. From the collection at Pinhole Resource.*

Figure 4.33b © *Marcus Kaiser,* Placing film holder (back of pinhole camera) over a hole in the Berlin wall, *lens photo, 1990. From the collection at Pinhole Resource.*

Figure 4.33c © *Marcus Kaiser,* Mauerblicke Looking East, 5" x 7" *pinhole photograph, 1990. From the collection at Pinhole Resource.*

Figure 4.33d © *Marcus Kaiser,* Mauerblicke Looking West, 5" x 7" *pinhole photograph, 1990. From the collection at Pinhole Resource.*

NOTES

1. Jeff Fletcher, "Bromide Eggs," *Pinhole Journal* 7(1991):17.
2. Larry Bullis, "Letters to the Editor," *Pinhole Journal* 3(1987): inside front cover.
3. Ibid.
4. Gary Urton, "The Use of Native Cosmologies in Archaeoastronomical Studies: The View from South America," in *Archaeoastronomy in the Americas,* ed. Ray A. Williamson (Los Altos, CA, and College Park, MD: Ballena Press Anthropological Papers and The Center for Archaeoastronomy, 1981), 296.
5. Ibid., 297.
6. Willie Anne Wright, "Photographs: Pools," *Pinhole Journal* 2(1986):25.
7. Barbra Esher, "Artist's Statement," *Pinhole Journal* 5(1989):20.
8. Pierre Charrier, "Interview," *Pinhole Journal* 3(1987):10–11.
9. Jim Jones, "Artist's Statement," *Pinhole Journal* 2(1986):2
10. Sarah Van Keuren, "Interview," *Pinhole Journal* 3(1987):18.
11. Nancy Spencer, "Interview," *Pinhole Journal* 6(1990):9.
12. James Hugunin, "Notes Toward a Stenopaesthetic," *The International Pinhole Photography Exhibition Catalogue* (Santa Fe. NM: Center for Contemporary Arts of Santa Fe, 1989), 16.
13. Guy Debord, *Society of the Spectacle* (Detroit: Black and Red, 1983), section 48.
14. Sandra Moss, "Light paths/Planetary Elements: Sandra Moss Interview," *Pinhole Journal* 4(1988):30.
15. Jean Baudrillard, "The Ecstasy of Communication," in *The Anti-Aesthetic: Essays on Postmodern Culture* (Port Townsend, WA: Bay Press, 1983), 129.
16. Hugunin, 16.
17. Rudolph Arnheim, "Order and Complexity in Landscape Design," in *Toward a Psychology of Art* (Berkeley: University of California Press, 1966), 125.
18. Hugunin, 13.
19. Martha Casanave, "Interview," *Pinhole Journal* 3(1987):2.
20. Casanave, Artist's statement in communication to James Hugunin, unpaginated, 1988.
21. Hugunin, 12.
22. Ibid., 19–20.

5

*One of my teachers recalled a memory of a discarded refrigerator box.
Climbing inside the box and closing up the flaps, he and his brother found
images of an upside-down world. Soon they had all the kids on the block
assembled to view the spectacle for a penny and then jump up and down outside for the benefit of the other viewers.*

HARRY LITTELL
personal letter to the author, 1990

The How-to of
Pinhole Photography

MAKING A SIMPLE PINHOLE CAMERA

A pinhole is basically a very sophisticated light leak. An image is produced because the hole is small (Figure 5.1) and many light rays pass through it. The pinhole is one of two "natural" systems that form an image—the other system is a lens, as in our eyes. One animal uses pinhole eyes for sight, the mollusk *Nautilus* (Figures 5.2a, 5.2b), which has been a species on this planet since the dinosaurs. The open aperture in each eye can accommodate (enlarge or shrink) and sea water goes directly through its opened pinhole eyes.

A simple pinhole camera can be made in about ten minutes. The simplicity of pinhole cameras was demonstrated by John Wood, of New York, who painted the inside of a paper grocery bag black, placed photographic paper inside, and poked a hole in the bag with a pin (Figure 5.3).

For many years the classic box to make into a pinhole camera was an oatmeal box with a heavy paper lid. But that changed; the cereal companies replaced paper lids with plastic, which is very difficult to make light tight. As of this writing the best box to transform into a pinhole camera is a small cylindrical or rectangular tin, the kind that candies or cookies come in that has a tight-fitting tin lid. This kind of container works well in a classroom situation. Choices for decorative tins are almost endless in the candy departments of discount stores. Another useful container is a box that holds one hundred sheets of four-inch by five-inch film. These boxes are perfect for pinhole cameras because they have three parts, making them light tight.

A cookie box or film box is a good starting point because it is easy to transform into a pinhole camera. After you have learned the

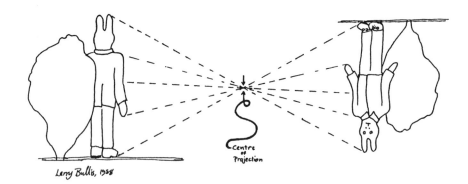

Figure 5.1 © *Larry Bullis*, Drawing of image entering a pinhole and being projected onto the film plane, *1988. From the collection at Pinhole Resource.*

Figure 5.2a Nautilus *(eye is oval in upper right). From Arthur Willey,* Zoological results based on material from New Britain, New Guinea, Loyalty Islands and elsewhere collected during the years 1895, 1896, and 1897. *London: Cambridge University Press, 1900).*

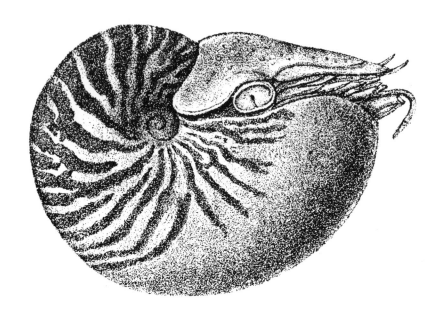

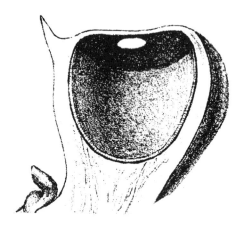

Figure 5.2b Enlarged view of the eye in vertical section. *From Arthur Willey,* Zoological results based on material from New Britain, New Guinea, Loyalty Islands, and elsewhere collected during the years 1895, 1896, and 1897. *London: Cambridge University Press, 1900).*

principles, you can adapt other containers. What you don't want to use is a box with a loose-fitting lid, such as a shoebox, because it is difficult to make light tight. If you can find a cylindrical grits or cornmeal container with a cardboard lid, use it. Unfortunately, they are becoming very difficult to find.

Materials Needed

- A cylindrical or rectangular tin box about three inches wide or a one-hundred-sheet four-inch by five-inch cardboard three-part film box two inches deep
- An electric drill with a one-half-inch drill bit, if you use a tin box
- 0.002-gauge metal
- A small sewing needle
- A sheet of no. 600 emery sanding paper
- One roll of black vinyl electrical tape or black photographic tape (preferably Scotch no. 235 available at large photo stores)
- A pair of scissors

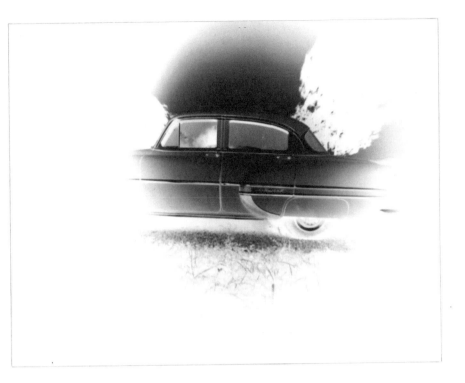

Figure 5.3 © *John Wood*, Paper Bag Pinhole Photograph of the Chevy, *6" x 7½" pinhole photograph, 1975. From the collection at Pinhole Resource.*

- A single-edged razor or mat knife
- A ten-sheet package of RC multigrade mat-surfaced photographic paper
- *Flat* black spray paint
- A conventional darkroom with chemicals for black-and-white photography

Adding the Pinhole

The most readily available materials for pinholes are semidisposable baking sheets or pie pans, which come in a variety of sizes and shapes in most food markets. The aluminum is approximately 0.002 gauge, and one pan will supply many pinholes. Those who want "higher class" pinholes can buy 0.002-gauge brass shim stock at an automotive or bearing store, but this is more expensive and not always readily available. Inexpensive pie-pan aluminum is very similar to the expensive brass in both workability and gauge. (Aluminum from a soft drink can also is approximately 0.002 gauge, but it is hard metal and more difficult to use.)

After getting the metal you want for pinholes, cut out a one-inch square. Under this square place a sheet of cardboard like the kind that comes on the back of a writing pad; this makes the best working surface for drilling the pinhole. Get a small sewing needle—I'm not suggesting a certain numbered needle size, because they are difficult to find. (Numbered needle-shaft diameters are shown in Figure 5.18a.) Tape a piece of masking tape across the eyed end of the needle to prevent it from pressing into your finger.

Hold the needle in the center of the piece of one-inch square metal and spin the metal, while you hold the point of the needle against it. The metal should be on top of the cardboard. With some amount of pressure and spinning, you will see the needle begin to drill a hole into the metal. Spinning the metal keeps the hole round. Continue spinning until the needle point sticks through the metal almost one-eighth inch. The hole will be less than 0.5mm. The optimal-size pinhole for a three-inch focal length box is 0.3150mm, or 0.0125 inch. The optimal-size pinhole for a two-inch focal length box is 0.2625mm, or 0.0115 inch. When you drill the pinhole, it is better to make it slightly too small than too large. *Don't worry about making a perfectly sized hole—a less than optimal pinhole will make an image.*

With a piece of no. 600 grit emery paper, sand off the burr that remains on the back side of the pinhole. Then sand the front side of the metal, which helps to thin the metal and make the hole cleaner. The thinner the metal, the less diffraction bounces off the edge of the metal—what you don't want is a pinhole that is like a tunnel. Clean out the sanded metal that has been trapped in the pinhole by placing the needle in the pinhole and spinning it gently.

If you have access to a small hand comparator, use it to measure the pinhole or try using Tom Fuller's homemade comparator (Figures 5.4a, 5.4b). Fuller explained:

> The pinhole plate to be measured is placed on a light box, a thin steel rule is laid over it, and an 8x loupe is set on top. Pieces of thin cardboard are used to shim the stack so that the transparent base of the magnifier rests evenly. I move the pinhole so that it can be seen through the exact center of the lens, then jog the rule slightly so that one of its graduation marks meets the left edge of the hole. I then read the diameter by merely counting the number of rule marks. Hardly a patentable idea, but it works. The drawback is that the thickness of the rule introduces some error, making the hole appear smaller than it really is, but you can learn to estimate this difference. Examine a hole of known size to see what it measures on your rule.[1]

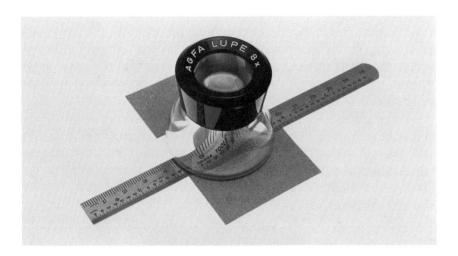

Figure 5.4a © *Tom Fuller,* Homemade Comparator, *lens photo, 1991. From the collection of the photographer.*

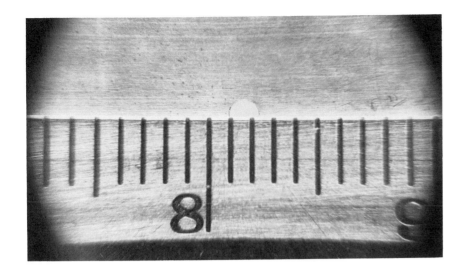

Figure 5.4b © *Tom Fuller*, View of Pinhole through Comparator, *lens photo, 1991. From the collection of the photographer.*

The photograph [Figure 5.4b] shows a hole that is about 1.5mm in diameter. If you use this technique, buy a rule with the finest possible graduations for best accuracy. This utility rule is graduated in full millimeters along one edge, with $\frac{1}{64}$" markings along the other. Edmund Scientific #C35,321 Optician's Rule has a metric scale graduated in $\frac{1}{2}$ mm increments, and an English scale marked to $\frac{1}{100}$".[2]

A second method for measuring the diameter of a pinhole was devised by Jay Bender, of Washington State, using an enlarger. Bender wrote:

> Since most of us do not have access to 100x microscopes, and since many of us do have enlargers, a method has been devised to use the enlarger to measure pinholes. At the side of this page are two scales and calibration lines [Figures 5.5a, 5.5b]. Make a [photocopy] and place Scale #1's calibration line in a negative carrier in your enlarger as you would a negative. Place Scale #1 on the baseboard and project the image of the calibration line down onto the scale. By moving the enlarger head up, or down, and refocusing, make the line 5.0mm long according to the scale. Once the calibration line is 5.0mm long, when sharply focused, your enlarger is calibrated and the scale is accurate. If you find that you cannot get the line to 5.0mm long, even with your enlarger all the way up, switch to a shorter focal length enlarging lens or use Scale #2 and calibration line.
>
> Now place your pinhole in the negative carrier (tape or some support may be needed to suspend it there) and project the tiny round spot onto the scale. Focus it carefully and measure it on the scale. Simple! Obviously, the smaller the pinhole, the less accurate your measurement will be.
>
> Put a grain focuser at the baseboard and line up the image of the pinhole in it. *Voila!* You have a 100x (or thereabouts) microscope! You can see if your pinhole is clean, round, and free from burrs.[3]

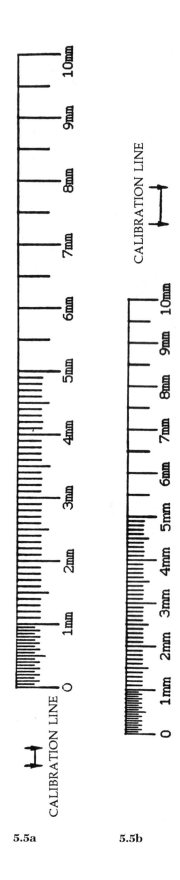

Mounting the Pinhole

If you are using a cookie tin:

Drill a big hole half way up the front of the tin container using a one-half-inch drill bit in an electric drill. To do this place a foot-long block of wood such as a two-by-four horizontally in a vise. Put the inside of the tin over the wood and drill the hole against the wood. Make sure the metal on the back side of the hole is cut cleanly.

If you are using a cardboard four-inch by five-inch 100 sheet film box or a grits box:

With a sharp single-edged razor blade or a mat knife, cut a one-half-inch or larger square hole in the center of the front of the box. That is, the largest of the three compartments of the film box. Make sure the cardboard and paper are cut cleanly; otherwise left-over material will block part of the image entering the box. Cut a one-inch square hole in the smallest of the three compartments; this hole will end up right behind the pinhole. Don't cut the middle-sized box; this becomes the back of the camera.

Using black vinyl electrical tape, tape the pinhole onto the outside of the box. (Black vinyl electrical tape is light proof). As you are doing this, look inside of the box to make sure that the pinhole is placed in the center of the cut opening. The back of the pinhole should face inward. Cut an extra piece of tape to act as a shutter over the pinhole.

If you are using a grits box, before loading the camera, take a strip of masking tape and encircle the container just below the edge on the lid. Also encircle the edge of the lid with masking tape. These two surfaces will then give you an area around which to run black electrical tape to stop any light leaks that may occur with a loose top. (If you don't tape this area with masking tape, the electrical tape will tear into the paper on the box each time it is removed.)

Painting the Inside of the Camera Black

Paint the interior with *flat* black spray paint. If you want to be assured of nonreflectivity, particularly useful if you are using film, use *ultraflat* black, although it is not as easy to find as flat black. Any object or box that is being transformed into a pinhole camera should be painted black if the interior is white or reflective. When in doubt, paint it. The inside of a one-hundred-sheet film box is black already. The back of the pinhole metal (facing inside the camera) does not have to be painted black, but if you

Figure 5.5a © *Jay Bender,* Scale #1 for measuring pinholes, *1990. From the collection of the photographer.*

Figure 5.5b © *Jay Bender,* Scale #2 for measuring pinholes, *1990. From the collection of the photographer.*

do want darken it, use black photographic tape or a black felt-tip marker to cover most of the area. Do not allow paint in the pinhole or tape too close to it.

LOADING THE PINHOLE CAMERA

In a darkroom under a red or yellow safe light, load the camera with a piece of photographic paper. Why photographic paper? Because you can see the image develop in the tray, and it's a lot more fun than film and a lot easier at first. Film requires total darkness. Use a paper cutter to cut small sheets from the eight-by-tens. The best type of paper to use for negatives is an RC multigrade mat-surfaced paper. Why RC? Because it dries perfectly flat for making positive contact prints from your negative. Why multigrade? Because it works best both on gray days and in sunshine. Why mat surfaced? Because it doesn't produce a reflected fogged strip the way shiny-surfaced papers do (Figures 5.6a, 5.6b) when curved inside a cylindrical pinhole camera.

When loading, curve the photographic paper around the inside of the cylindrical box opposite the pinhole. If you are using a three-part film box, the midsized box holds the paper or film in place. If you have a different kind of flat-backed box roll small pieces of tape into circles and apply these to each corner of the nonemulsion side of the paper.

The emulsion side of the photographic paper should face the pinhole. It is difficult to distinguish the emulsion side of RC multigrade mat-surfaced paper from the nonemulsion side, although the emulsion side has a slightly shinier surface. Kodak packs its black and white paper emulsion side up in the box. So does Ilford; however, Ilford flips the top sheet so the nonemulsion side is up. Figure 5.7a shows what happens when photographic paper is put in correctly; Figure 5.7b shows what happens when it is inserted backward.

Make sure the black electrical tape is over the pinhole to act as a shutter. After the camera is loaded, seal around the top with black electrical or photo tape (not necessary if you are using a three-part box). You are now ready to make a photograph.

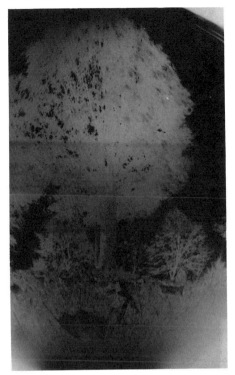
5.6a

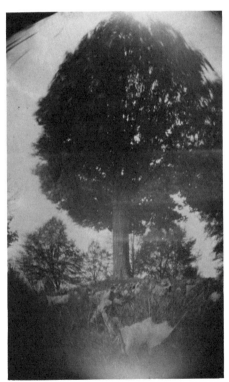
5.6b

Figures 5.6a, b *Pinhole photographs (paper negative and positive print) illustrating reflective fogged strip across center of glossy RC paper. Note: This will usually happen when using glossy-surfaced paper as a negative. This reflective area is one of the most common mistakes with first pinhole images. With a one-minute exposure in the sun, the camera was placed on its side approximately ten feet from the tree. Photographs by author.*

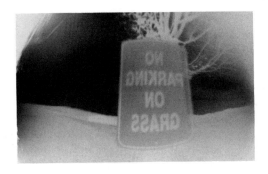

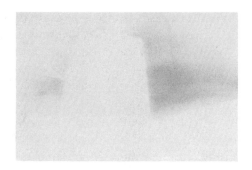

Figure 5.7a *Pinhole photograph (paper negative) illustrating photographic paper loaded correctly with emulsion side toward the pinhole. A one-minute exposure with a hazy, bright sky. Photograph by author.*

Figure 5.7b *Pinhole photograph (paper negative) illustrating photographic paper loaded incorrectly. Paper was put in backward, that is, emulsion side away from pinhole. One-minute exposure with hazy, bright sky. Photograph by author.*

MAKING A PHOTOGRAPH

There are certain "don'ts" to making a pinhole photograph for the first time. These don'ts can be experimented with later, for many unusual results come from breaking rules. For now, it is important to see whether the camera is working and to get an idea of exposure times. The don'ts are as follows:

1. Don't have the sun directly on the pinhole when exposing (Figure 5.8).
2. Don't hold the camera in your hand; exposure time and sharpness should be considered first. Set the camera on a wall, the ground, or another solid base. If it's windy, place a weight on the camera to hold it steady (Figures 5.9a, 5.9b).
3. Don't photograph into total shade, for example, near a tree that is completely in the shade. It's best to try to photograph with brightness, partial shade, and shadow in the same image.
4. Don't try to photograph indoors while making your first images; inside exposures can be very long and difficult to estimate.
5. Don't place the camera too far from the subject you are photographing. You should be much closer than you would be with a lens camera (Figures 5.10a, 5.10b, 5.10c).

To expose, simply remove the shutter tape. The image will be a very wide angle. Use a watch or count seconds so that you can repeat, lengthen, or shorten the time on your next exposures. With the size pinhole described earlier, your grits- or cornmeal-box camera should make an image outside in full sun in about thirty to forty-five seconds; if it's cloudy or overcast, exposure should be one to three minutes, depending on just how dark it is. As the sun goes

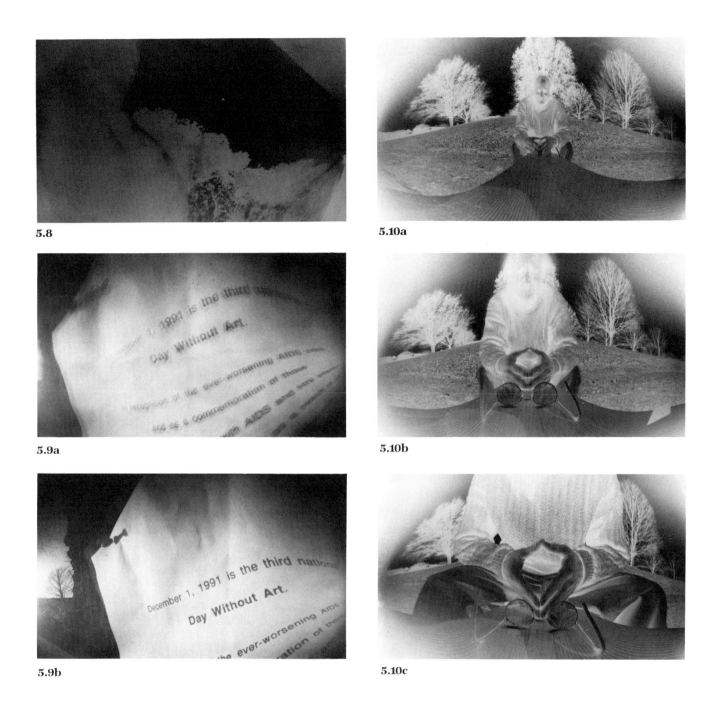

5.8

5.10a

5.9a

5.10b

5.9b

5.10c

Figure 5.8 *Pinhole photograph (paper negative) illustrating the sun on a pinhole. The camera was placed on the ground with the sun shining directly onto the front of the camera. Even with this short exposure of 25 seconds, the image is overexposed. Because of its brightness, the sun becomes the solarized dot in the center. Feathery streaks on left and right sides of image are places where the sun has diffracted light off the edge of the pinhole. Photograph by author.*

Figure 5.9a *Pinhole photograph (paper negative) illustrating results of photograph with camera in hand, 25-second exposure in sun. Photograph by author.*

Figure 5.9b *Pinhole photograph (paper negative) illustrating results with camera on firm surface, 25-second exposure in sun. Photograph by author.*

Figures 5.10a, b, c *Pinhole photographs (paper negatives) illustrating distances between camera and subject: (a) six feet from subject; (b) four feet from subject; (c) two feet from subject. All exposures are 30 seconds in full sun. Bench looks curved because photographic paper is wrapped around inside of camera. Photographs by author.*

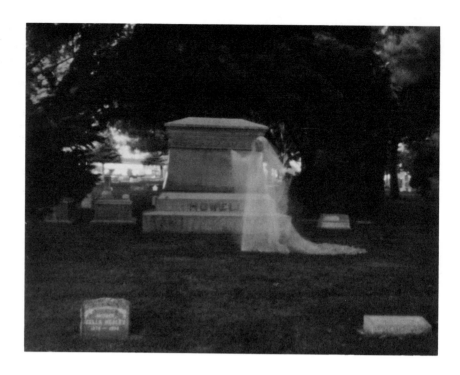

Figure 5.11 © *Stanley R. Page,* The Ghost, *8" x 10" pinhole photograph, 1978. From the collection at Pinhole Resource.*

down in the afternoon, exposure times lengthen. A little bit of rain won't hurt this camera, so don't be afraid to try it for a two- to three-minute exposure in the rain. Moving objects will not image unless they are moving very, very, slowly—if you walk in front of a thirty-second exposure, you won't appear in the image. If you want to make an image with a "ghost" (Figure 5.11), you have to remain motionless in the image for at least half of the exposure time, depending on the background.

Back in the darkroom, develop your paper as you would any black-and-white RC paper (probably two minutes in the developer, thirty seconds in a stop bath, and three minutes in the fixer). The resulting image is a paper negative that you can see develop in the tray. Usually the darkest area to show up first will be the sky; areas that remain light are the deep shadows.

It is easy to make contact-print positives from your negative because RC paper dries flat. Simply place your negative with the image side down on top of an unexposed piece of photographic paper with its emulsion side up. Both should be pressed together under a piece of glass or in a contact-print frame. If they are not pressed tightly, the image will be blurred where the sheets don't fully touch. Expose for about five seconds under an enlarger with its lens wide open, making sure the circle of light covers the paper area. Different photographic papers can be used for positive prints, because RC mat paper is certainly not the best for tonal values in positives.

Because this camera makes only one image at a time, you might consider carrying more than one box. I've seen someone carry as many as ten boxes at a time, all in a basket and each marked as it was exposed!

If a cylindrical camera is angled slightly toward the ground, the horizon line becomes more distorted. In Color Plate 5.12 the water appears silky because the exposure time is long.

5.13a

ADDITIONAL MISTAKES

If there is a light leak in your pinhole camera, the paper negative will overexpose and be black when developed (Figure 5.13a). One way to check whether your camera leaks light is to load it with photographic paper, place the black tape shutter over the pinhole, and place the camera in the sun for five minutes. Develop the paper; if it turns gray or black, the camera leaks light.

If the cardboard or tin in the area where the pinhole is mounted is not cut cleanly, a flap of cardboard or an edge of tin may block some of the image (Figure 5.13b). The cardboard should be cut clean at least one-fourth inch away from the pinhole. Sometimes when drilling a pinhole, you may accidentally drill two pinholes very close to one another, resulting in an image that looks blurred (Figure 5.13c). You can check this by looking at your pinhole through a magnifying glass.

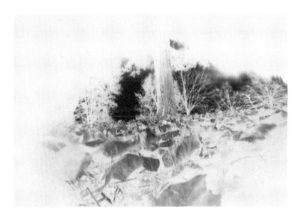

5.13b

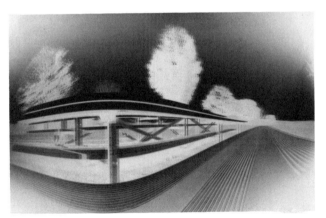

5.13c

Figure 5.13a *Pinhole photograph (paper negative) illustrating light leak. The photographic paper solarizes near the light leak. Photograph by author.*

Figure 5.13b *Pinhole photograph (paper negative) illustrating result when cardboard flap partially blocks a pinhole, forty-five-second exposure in full sun. This occurs when cardboard behind the pinhole is not cut clean or totally removed; cardboard should be cut clean at least one-fourth inch away from the pinhole. See Figure 5.35 for an unblocked version of this image. Photograph by author.*

Figure 5.13c *Pinhole photograph (paper negative) illustrating two pinholes accidentally drilled close to one another. Each pinhole is one-half millimeter in diameter and placed 1mm apart. Fifteen-second exposure in full sun. Photograph by author.*

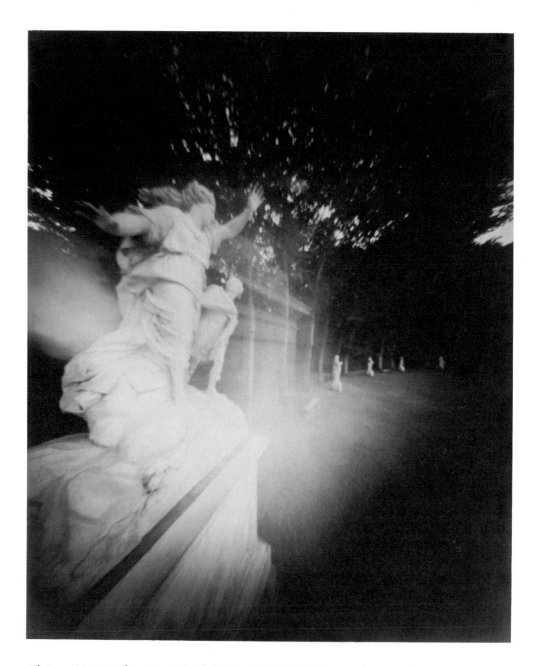

Figure 5.14 © *Adam Füss, Untitled, 20" x 24" pinhole photograph, 1986. The camera was placed on a high light stand, which moved in the wind causing some blurring of the image. Collection of the photographer.*

ADDITIONAL POSSIBILITIES

You might want to make use of blur caused by the wind's slightly shaking your camera. For Figure 5.14, Adam Füss placed his camera high on a light stand. While the paper was being exposed, the wind caused enough camera movement to add an interesting motion blur to the image.

If you use a short exposure time, the sun can be photographed. In a black-and-white image, feathery streaks appear; in a color image, spectral rainbows appear. In *Self-Portrait* (Figure 5.15), I set the pinhole camera face-up on the ground. I knelt over it with the sun directed in a line toward my slightly opened fingers and the pinhole. Exposing onto photographic paper, I let the direct sun hit the pinhole for about fifteen seconds, then I closed my fingers for the entire four-minute exposure. Because long exposure times usually are an integral part of pinhole photography, many possibilities are open to the photographer.

In the close up photograph *George Washington on a One Dollar Bill* (Figure 5.16), the bill was taped one-fourth inch in front of the pinhole. The camera was set on the ground with the sun on the

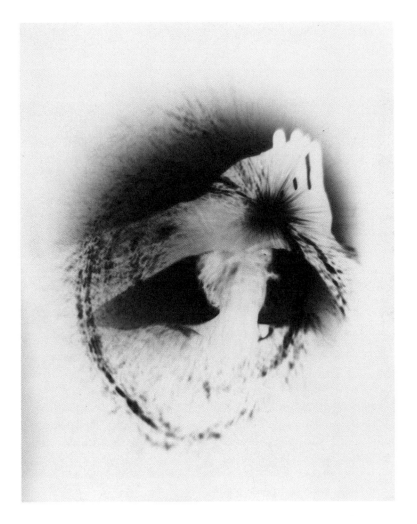

Figure 5.15 © *Eric Renner*, Self-Portrait, *16" x 20" pinhole photograph (direct negative on paper). Courtesy National Gallery of Canada, 1977.*

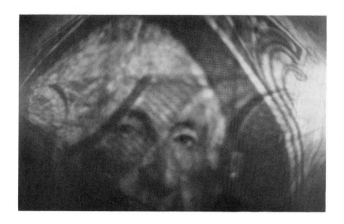

Figure 5.16 © *Eric Renner*, George Washington on a One Dollar Bill. *Pinhole photograph (positive print) illustrating ability of the pinhole camera to photograph very close to the object. Four-minute exposure in full sun.*

dollar bill. The printing on both the front and back of the bill show up in the image because the sun makes it translucent. The lines across Washington's face are actually from the back of the bill. The image *Grandma Becomes the Moon* on the dedication page at the beginning of this book was made from a 1919 photograph taped over a pinhole as with the Washington dollar bill photograph. In the old photograph of my grandmother, her face was approximately one-fourth inch wide. The pinhole camera was able to enlarge it to ten inches across—a 40x magnification!

Unpredictable solarization can result with the use of outdated Polaroid materials (Figure 5.17).

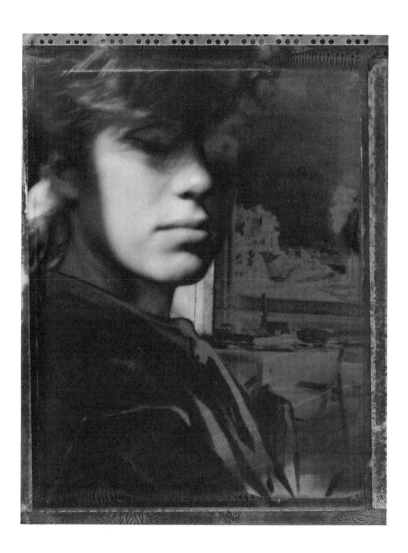

Figure 5.17 © *Pinky Bass*, Untitled Portrait, 4" x 5" Polaroid pinhole photograph, type 55, 1986. *Unpredictable solarization (see the subject's eye) can occur with the use of outdated Polaroid materials subjected to long exposure times. From the collection at Pinhole Resource.*

Popular Misconceptions

There are several popular misconceptions, held even by some who have done pinhole for many years. These are as follows:

Misconception 1. *The smaller the pinhole the sharper the image.* This seems to prevail among those who have used short focal length pinhole cameras, say none over 75mm, in which a small hole still makes a somewhat sharp image. Beyond 75mm it is readily apparent that the correctly sized hole should be slightly larger as focal length increases. An optimum chart is supplied later in this chapter.

Misconception 2. *A small pinhole will give a wide-angle image.* This seems to be a confusion held by those who have not experimented enough with different film sizes at the same focal length. Every pinhole does makes a very wide-angle image. It's a matter of how much of the image is captured on the size of film you are using. For example, a six-inch focal length four-inch by five-inch pinhole camera gives a normal image, but a sixteen-inch by twenty-inch piece of photographic paper in a six-inch deep suitcase (with pinhole on one side) gives a very wide-angle image.

Misconception 3. *Only black and white photo materials can be used with pinhole, not color.* Just about every light-sensitive material works in a pinhole camera. The only emulsions that are almost impossible to use directly inside a pinhole camera are papers coated with nonsilver processes, such as cyanotype, Van Dyke, or platinum.

Misconception 4. *The first photographers used pinhole cameras.* As far as I am aware, the first cameras had simple lenses; for instance, Talbot's "mousetraps" used a single lens over a large hole.

OPTIMAL PINHOLE FORMULAS

The larger the pinhole, the more light will enter.

Light intensity decreases the farther it travels from the pinhole. For instance, a four-inch focal distance takes more time to expose than a three-inch focal distance, and so on, given the same size pinhole.

For every focal length, there is an optimal pinhole diameter. Robert Mikrut and Kenneth A. Connors (Figure 5.18a) developed a chart of focal distances and corresponding optimal pinholes. Needle shaft diameters are shown in Figure 5.18b. The longer the focal length, the larger the pinhole should be. An example of an optimally sharp pinhole image is shown in Figure 1.22. If the pinhole

Pinholes   10 mm
Increment   10 mm

0.037 used in function

Focal Length(mm)	Pinhole Diam.(mm)	Pinhole Diam.(in)	f-stop	Time-Rel. to f/64	Focal Length(in)	Focal Length(ft)
10	0.1170	0.0046	85	1.8	0.39	0.03
20	0.1655	0.0065	121	3.6	0.79	0.07
30	0.2027	0.0080	148	5.3	1.18	0.10
40	0.2340	0.0092	171	7.1	1.57	0.13
50	0.2616	0.0103	191	8.9	1.97	0.16
60	0.2866	0.0113	209	10.7	2.36	0.20
70	0.3096	0.0122	226	12.5	2.76	0.23
80	0.3309	0.0130	242	14.3	3.15	0.26
90	0.3510	0.0138	256	16.0	3.54	0.30
100	0.3700	0.0146	270	17.8	3.94	0.33
110	0.3881	0.0153	283	19.6	4.33	0.36
120	0.4053	0.0160	296	21.4	4.72	0.39
130	0.4219	0.0166	308	23.2	5.12	0.43
140	0.4378	0.0172	320	25.0	5.51	0.46
150	0.4532	0.0178	331	26.7	5.91	0.49
160	0.4680	0.0184	342	28.6	6.30	0.52
170	0.4824	0.0190	352	30.3	6.69	0.56
180	0.4964	0.0195	363	32.2	7.09	0.59
190	0.5100	0.0201	373	34.0	7.48	0.62
200	0.5233	0.0206	382	35.6	7.87	0.66
210	0.5362	0.0211	392	37.5	8.27	0.69
220	0.5488	0.0216	401	39.3	8.66	0.72
230	0.5611	0.0221	410	41.0	9.06	0.75
240	0.5732	0.0226	419	42.9	9.45	0.79
250	0.5850	0.0230	427	44.5	9.84	0.82
260	0.5966	0.0235	436	46.4	10.24	0.85
270	0.6080	0.0239	444	48.1	10.63	0.89
280	0.6191	0.0244	452	49.9	11.02	0.92
290	0.6301	0.0248	460	51.7	11.42	0.95
300	0.6409	0.0252	468	53.5	11.81	0.98
310	0.6515	0.0256	476	55.3	12.20	1.02
320	0.6619	0.0261	483	57.0	12.60	1.05
330	0.6721	0.0265	491	58.9	12.99	1.08
340	0.6822	0.0269	498	60.5	13.39	1.12
350	0.6922	0.0273	506	62.5	13.78	1.15
360	0.7020	0.0276	513	64.3	14.17	1.18
370	0.7117	0.0280	520	66.0	14.57	1.21
380	0.7213	0.0284	527	67.8	14.96	1.25
390	0.7307	0.0288	534	69.6	15.35	1.28
400	0.7400	0.0291	541	71.5	15.75	1.31
410	0.7492	0.0295	547	73.0	16.14	1.35
420	0.7583	0.0299	554	74.9	16.54	1.38
430	0.7672	0.0302	560	76.6	16.93	1.41
440	0.7761	0.0306	567	78.5	17.32	1.44
450	0.7849	0.0309	573	80.2	17.72	1.48
460	0.7936	0.0312	580	82.1	18.11	1.51
470	0.8021	0.0316	586	83.8	18.50	1.54
480	0.8106	0.0319	592	85.6	18.90	1.57
490	0.8190	0.0322	598	87.3	19.29	1.61
500	0.8273	0.0326	604	89.1	19.69	1.64

Focal Length(mm)	Pinhole Diam.(mm)	Pinhole Diam.(in)	f-stop	Time-Rel. to f/64	Focal Length(in)	Focal Length(ft)
510	0.8356	0.0329	610	90.8	20.08	1.67
520	0.8437	0.0332	616	92.6	20.47	1.71
530	0.8518	0.0335	622	94.5	20.87	1.74
540	0.8598	0.0339	628	96.3	21.26	1.77
550	0.8677	0.0342	634	98.1	21.65	1.80
560	0.8756	0.0345	640	100.0	22.05	1.84
570	0.8834	0.0348	645	101.6	22.44	1.87
580	0.8911	0.0351	651	103.5	22.83	1.90
590	0.8987	0.0354	656	105.1	23.23	1.94
600	0.9063	0.0357	662	107.0	23.62	1.97
610	0.9138	0.0360	668	108.9	24.02	2.00
620	0.9213	0.0363	673	110.6	24.41	2.03
630	0.9287	0.0366	678	112.2	24.80	2.07
640	0.9360	0.0369	684	114.2	25.20	2.10
650	0.9433	0.0371	689	115.9	25.59	2.13
660	0.9505	0.0374	694	117.6	25.98	2.17
670	0.9577	0.0377	700	119.6	26.38	2.20
680	0.9648	0.0380	705	121.3	26.77	2.23
690	0.9719	0.0383	710	123.1	27.17	2.26
700	0.9789	0.0385	715	124.8	27.56	2.30
710	0.9859	0.0388	720	126.6	27.95	2.33
720	0.9928	0.0391	725	128.3	28.35	2.36
730	0.9997	0.0394	730	130.1	28.74	2.40
740	1.0065	0.0396	735	131.9	29.13	2.43
750	1.0133	0.0399	740	133.7	29.53	2.46
760	1.0200	0.0402	745	135.5	29.92	2.49
770	1.0267	0.0404	750	137.3	30.31	2.53
780	1.0334	0.0407	755	139.2	30.71	2.56
790	1.0400	0.0409	760	141.0	31.10	2.59
800	1.0465	0.0412	764	142.5	31.50	2.62
810	1.0530	0.0415	769	144.4	31.89	2.66
820	1.0595	0.0417	774	146.3	32.28	2.69
830	1.0660	0.0420	779	148.2	32.68	2.72
840	1.0724	0.0422	783	149.7	33.07	2.76
850	1.0787	0.0425	788	151.6	33.46	2.79
860	1.0851	0.0427	793	153.5	33.86	2.82
870	1.0913	0.0430	797	155.1	34.25	2.85
880	1.0976	0.0432	802	157.0	34.65	2.89
890	1.1038	0.0435	806	158.6	35.04	2.92
900	1.1100	0.0437	811	160.6	35.43	2.95
910	1.1161	0.0439	815	162.2	35.83	2.99
920	1.1223	0.0442	820	164.2	36.22	3.02
930	1.1283	0.0444	824	165.8	36.61	3.05
940	1.1344	0.0447	829	167.8	37.01	3.08
950	1.1404	0.0449	833	169.4	37.40	3.12
960	1.1464	0.0451	837	171.0	37.80	3.15
970	1.1524	0.0454	842	173.1	38.19	3.18
980	1.1583	0.0456	846	174.7	38.58	3.22
990	1.1642	0.0458	850	176.4	38.98	3.25
1000	1.1700	0.0461	855	178.5	39.37	3.28

Figure 5.18a © Robert Mikrut and Kenneth A. Connors, pinhole calculations from 10mm to 1,000mm focal lengths.

is too large for the focal length, the image will be blurry. If the pinhole is very, very small, the image also will be blurry. (It is possible, however, to photograph a very bright object, such as the sun, with an almost invisible pinhole—so small a pinhole that it would produce no image if it were used to photograph the landscape.)

A formula can be supplied for making pinholes. Any number of slightly different formulas have been calculated since Lord Rayleigh calculated his in the 1880s. The one suggested here is by Bob Dome, of Washington State:

$$A = \sqrt{55F}$$

where A equals the aperture diameter in thousandths of an inch, and F equals the focal length in inches. An example: You're converting an old box camera and want to use a focal length of 4 inches. The square root of 220 (55 x 4) is 14.8, so the optimal size pinhole diameter is 14.8 thousandths of an inch or .0148 inch.

For the curious, here is the evolution of the aperture diameter formula just presented. Most formulas I've seen for determining an optimum size pinhole are of the following general form:

$$R = \sqrt{WCF}$$

where

R = radius of the aperture,

W = wavelength of light,

C = a constant factor, usually a decimal fraction between $\frac{1}{2}$ and 1.

and

F = focal length

To be useful, the formula just given relies on one's choice of wavelength (ranging from about 15 to thirty millionths of an inch) and one's choice of the constant factor. After studying the work of many researchers, especially Ken Connors, I decided upon a wavelength as multiplied by a chosen constant and arrived at the following:

$$R = \sqrt{.00001375F}$$

where

R = Radius of the aperture in inches,

and

F = Focal length in inches

But most pinhole experimenters want to know the diameter of the aperture, not the radius, so I rewrote the formula again:

$$A = \sqrt{(.00001375)(4)F}$$

and then, of course:

$$A = \sqrt{.000055F}$$

Figure 5.18b Needle shaft diameters.

Needle #'s that Correspond to Pinhole Diameters Although it is rarely possible to find numbered needles, here is a chart in both inches and millimeters:

Needle Diameter (Inches)	Needle #
0.010	15
0.012	13
0.014	12
0.018	10
0.021	9
0.024	8
0.027	7
0.030	6
0.034	5
0.037	4
0.040	3
0.043	2
0.046	1

Needle Diameter (mm)	Needle #
0.25	15
0.30	13
0.36	12
0.46	10
0.53	9
0.61	8
0.69	7
0.76	6
0.86	5
0.94	4
1.02	3
1.09	2
1.17	1

where

$$A = \text{aperture diameter in inches.}$$

It now remained to do something about all those zeros because they can cause entry, processing, and data retrieval problems on some handheld calculators. So:

$$A = \sqrt{55F}$$

where

$$A = \text{aperture diameter in thousandths of an inch,}$$

and, as before,

$$F = \text{focal length in inches.}[4]$$

In the last one hundred twenty-five years of pinhole photography, at least fifty charts suggesting pinhole diameters have been devised. One of the most curious formulas came from M. Jules Combe, in France in 1899, whose pinhole photographs were very sharp. Combe's formula is as follows:

Multiply the diameter of the hole in thousandths of an inch by itself, then by four, and divide the result by one hundred and twenty-seven. This gives the camera extension in inches.

Example: I will take the case of the hole made by a No. 10 needle, which has a diameter of eighteen-thousandths of an inch.

$$18 \times 18 \times 4 = 1{,}296$$

$$1{,}296 \text{ divided by } 127 = 10.20$$

The distance is therefore 10.20 inches.[5]

When you need to calculate the f stop of your pinhole, simply divide your focal length by the pinhole diameter.

Optimal sharpness is seldom the first requirement for most pinhole photographers; most pinhole images are made with considerably less definition than an optimal pinhole would achieve. Some pinhole photographers choose to make an oversized or irregularly shaped pinhole in various materials such as aluminum foil, which is generally difficult to use anyway, for optimal pinholes. Thomas Kellner of Germany uses a very enlarged pinhole for his expressive portraits (Color Plate 5.19).

Building Plans for a Four-inch by Five-inch Superwide Pinhole Camera

It's easy to make pinhole cameras that hold single sheets of photographic paper or single pieces of film, but not nearly as easy to make pinhole cameras that take four-inch by five-inch commercial film holders and Polaroid backs. Standard double-sided film holders allow photographers twice as many images as they have film holders. Figure 5.20 shows how to make a four-inch by

Figure 5.20 *Superwide Pinhole Camera, 4" x 5", 1998, designed by the author. This camera can be easily made if you have access to a bench saw. Materials needed are $\frac{1}{2}$" birch plywood, $\frac{1}{8}$" tempered Masonite, a $\frac{1}{4}$" x $1\frac{3}{8}$" molding strip, $\frac{1}{8}$" thick x $\frac{1}{4}$" wide foam weather stripping, and wood glue.*

A SUPER-WIDE ANGLE 4" x 5" PINHOLE CAMERA

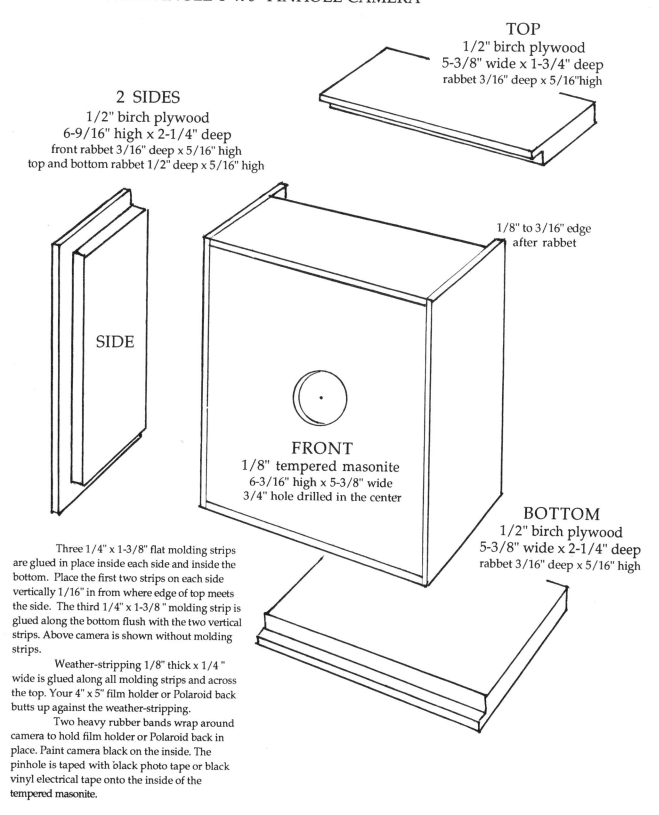

TOP
1/2" birch plywood
5-3/8" wide x 1-3/4" deep
rabbet 3/16" deep x 5/16"high

2 SIDES
1/2" birch plywood
6-9/16" high x 2-1/4" deep
front rabbet 3/16" deep x 5/16" high
top and bottom rabbet 1/2" deep x 5/16" high

1/8" to 3/16" edge
after rabbet

SIDE

FRONT
1/8" tempered masonite
6-3/16" high x 5-3/8" wide
3/4" hole drilled in the center

BOTTOM
1/2" birch plywood
5-3/8" wide x 2-1/4" deep
rabbet 3/16" deep x 5/16" high

Three 1/4" x 1-3/8" flat molding strips are glued in place inside each side and inside the bottom. Place the first two strips on each side vertically 1/16" in from where edge of top meets the side. The third 1/4" x 1-3/8 " molding strip is glued along the bottom flush with the two vertical strips. Above camera is shown without molding strips.

Weather-stripping 1/8" thick x 1/4 " wide is glued along all molding strips and across the top. Your 4" x 5" film holder or Polaroid back butts up against the weather-stripping.

Two heavy rubber bands wrap around camera to hold film holder or Polaroid back in place. Paint camera black on the inside. The pinhole is taped with black photo tape or black vinyl electrical tape onto the inside of the tempered masonite.

five-inch superwide pinhole camera for film holders. The angles of view on various sizes of four-inch by five-inch cameras are as follows:

$1\frac{1}{2}$ -inch (38mm) focal length 4-inch by 5-inch (superwide) = 118 degrees

3-inch (75mm) focal length 4-inch by 5-inch (wide) = 78 degrees

6-inch (150mm) focal length 4-inch by 5-inch (normal) = 45 degrees

A 545 or 545i Polaroid back also fits into this Leonardo design. Four inches by five inches is a good size. It's easy to enlarge four-inch by five-inch film, and used Omega D2 enlargers are readily available at a reasonable price. Exposure time for this one and a half–inch camera using Tri-X film in bright sun is about one second.

MAKING A PINHOLE TURRET

Using a pinhole turret is one of the best ways to produce a set of images showing varying degrees of definition, from blurry to sharp (Figures 5.21a–h). Jim Moninger of New York has made several turret designs and explained his procedure:

I tackled the problem of how to use a whole range of tiny drilled pinholes conveniently enough to vary and select the level of sharpness I want. For this I simply revived a feature not uncommon to some of the early commercially produced pinhole and other cameras; something still used on some enlargers and movie cameras: The Turret. By drilling my selection of pinholes on a single disc of .002" brass in a circular configuration, I can easily rig a device that will allow me to quickly "dial in" almost any number of different apertures. I've been using a Speed Graphic Press Camera for most of my pinhole work. One of the advantages of a press or field camera is that it enables the shooter to draw the bellows in and out for various focal lengths. Another is that pinhole devices can be fixed to removable lens boards. Instead of building a whole camera, it can be easier to adapt one for experimental photography. [Figure 5.22a] shows my Speed Graphic with a pinhole turret built into a lensboard. [Figure 5.22b] is a sketch of the design.

Figures 5.21a–h © *Jim Moninger*, Postmodern Saint: Our Lady of the Immaculate Confection, *1991. Eight degrees of sharpness are shown. Focal length is $2\frac{1}{4}$ inches. Pinholes are mounted in a Super Speed Graphic. From the collection of the photographer.*

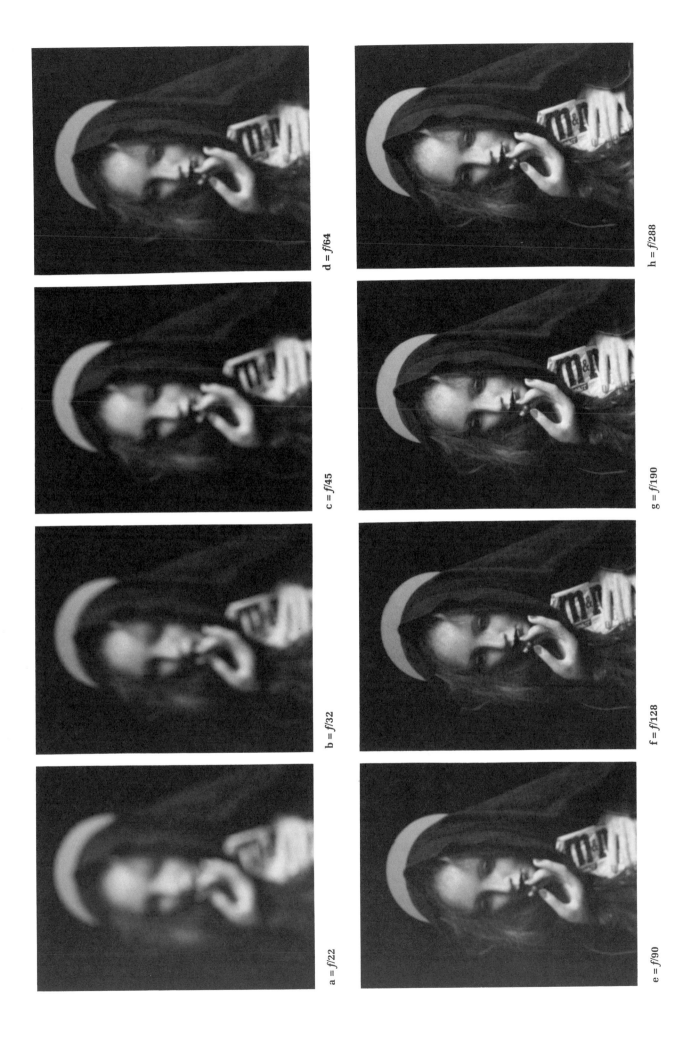

a = f/22 b = f/32 c = f/45 d = f/64

e = f/90 f = f/128 g = f/190 h = f/288

To make it I drew two circles on a sheet of .002" brass: one to mark the diameter of the disc and another inside to mark the circle on which to drill the pinholes. I then divided the disc so that eight evenly spaced pinholes could be drilled at marked locations. After selecting the sizes of the pinholes desired, I carefully drilled them. Next I drilled a plastic disc with eight holes which would line up with the pinholes. This was stuck to the brass disc with rubber cement. This plastic disc serves as a retainer to keep the brass disc flat and to provide a "dial" to change apertures. A lensboard was drilled in the center for the light path of the pinholes. Another hole was drilled off-center to secure the disc at its center. The holes are carefully placed so that the pinholes on the rotating disc will line up one at a time with the center hole on the lensboard. In order to avoid light leaking between the disc and the lensboard, I pressed discs of black self-stick flock paper (paper felt, available at art supply stores) to the back of the brass disc and to the face of the lensboard. The turret was fastened to the lens board with a small machine screw. The threads on this had to be filed down just below the head so that they wouldn't chew up the center hole in the turret. The nut was tightened enough to allow free rotation of the disc while holding a tight connection with the lensboard. Once adjusted, I permanently fixed its position with epoxy. For this project I was primarily interested in wide angle work in the field so I planned to use the minimum bellows draw for most of the pictures shot with this pinhole turret. The fixed focal length enabled me to calculate specific f/stop values for the holes. I was also able to adjust the pinhole sizes so that they were close to one f/stop apart and could be easily used

Figure 5.22a © *Jim Moninger,* Speed Graphic with Turret Attached, *lens photo from the collection of the photographer.*

Figure 5.22b © *Jim Moninger,* Sketch of Pinhole Turret. *From the collection of the photographer.*

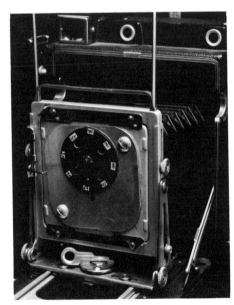

5.22a

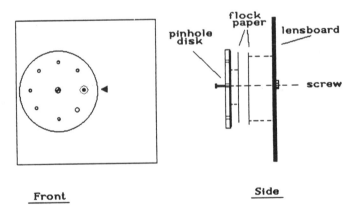

Front   Side

PINHOLE TURRET

for Press, Field and View Cameras

5.22b

with a light meter and adjusted for various conditions of light intensity and the desired level of softness. [6]

The Finney Field Pinhole Camera (Figure 5.23), designed by Kevin Finney of Englewood, Colorado, came with a turret that held four pinholes, three zone plates (see Chapter 6 for information on zone plates), and one viewing pinhole. This beautiful, versatile camera, reminiscent of the quality in an old Deardorff camera, first appeared in the marketplace in 1996 and was available until 1998. It featured an unusual scissors design for extending the bellows; therefore, the entire camera weighed only two and one-half pounds. One hundred and one Finney cameras were sold.

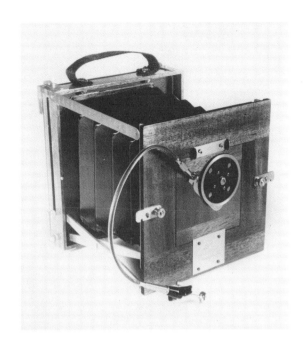

Figure 5.23 © *Kevin Finney*, Finney Field Pinhole Camera, *lens photo, 1998.*

PINHOLE CAMERA GEOMETRIES

Depth of Field

Pinhole images have infinite depth of field. Everything from the closest object to the most distant object is in the same relative focus (Figure 5.24). The only exception is one hundred or more yards away; these objects are less sharp because of particles in the atmosphere.

Photographing onto a Flat Film Plane

A pinhole casts a usable circular image of approximately one hundred twenty-five degrees onto a flat film plane. The image fades from the center outward because the focal distance increases toward the edges, resulting in a decrease in light intensity (Figure 5.25). Some pinhole photographers choose to show most of the image, including its fall-off toward the edge (see Color Plate 4.14). If the center of the image is overexposed, the image is cast at a greater angle than one hundred twenty-five degrees; likewise, if the center of the image is underexposed, the image is cast at less than a one hundred twenty-five degree angle.

Image size increases as the focal length increases. One example of how the image increases in size as focal distance increases can be seen in Figure 5.26a, b, c, which was made from a commercial Leonardo four-by-five pinhole camera with focal lengths of one and one-half inch (38mm), three inches (75mm), and six inches (150mm). All three cameras use four-by-five film holders. The one and one-half inch focal length acts as a superwide angle and the three-inch focal length as a wide angle. The six-inch length is normal, or 1:1, which is equal to the angle at which a person sees. Even though the image increases in size with distance, what is really happening in the three- or six-inch cameras is that most of the image is outside the film holder. In other words, most of the image is past the film edge and therefore not recorded. If each

Figure 5.24 *Marianne Neuber,* Hole in Wall, *16" x 20" pinhole photograph, 1992. From the collection of the photographer.*

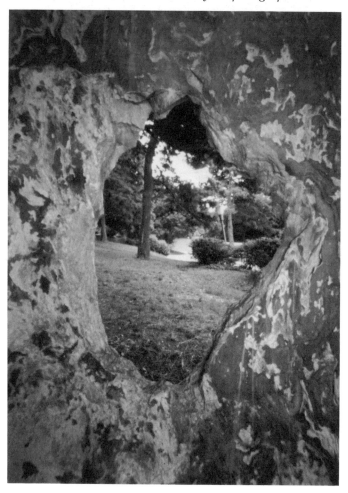

camera were to take a considerably larger film size as focal length increased, all three images would appear wide angle.

To know how to arrive at the focal length of a "normal" pinhole camera, you can simply use the age-old rule of diagonal measurement of the film size you intend to use. That measurement becomes the focal length for normal, as follows:

For four by five, the diagonal measure is 6 inches.

For eight by ten, the diagonal measure is $12\frac{1}{2}$ inches.

For undistorted full-frame portraits use a normal focal length pinhole camera.

You can make an image look panoramic simply by cropping it long and thin or by using a camera that takes a long strip of film (Color Plate 5.27).

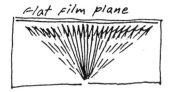

Figure 5.25 *Drawing illustrating how light intensity decreases as focal length increases. Drawing by author.*

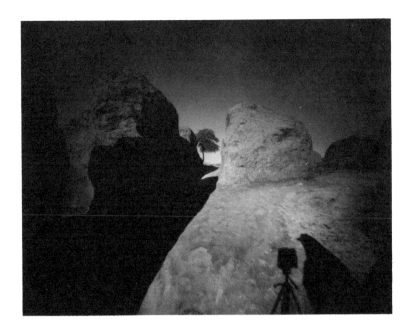

Figure 5.26a © *Nancy Spencer,* Image from $1\frac{1}{2}''$ Leonardo Pinhole Camera, *1998.*

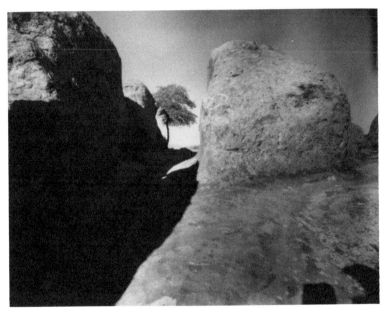

Figure 5.26b © *Nancy Spencer,* Image from $3''$ Leonardo Pinhole Camera, *1998.*

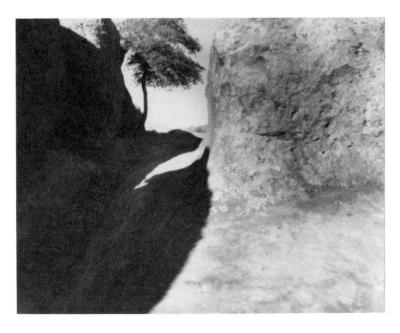

Figure 5.26c © *Nancy Spencer,* Image from $6''$ Leonardo Pinhole Camera, *1998.*

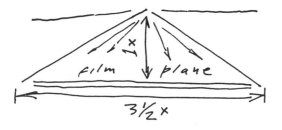

Figure 5.28 *Drawing illustrating image diameter–to–focal length ratio. Image diameter is approximately 3½ times the size of any given focal length. Drawing by the author.*

Image Size

A one-inch focal length (pinhole to film plane) produces approximately a three-and-one-half-inch diameter circular image. A two-inch focal length produces approximately a seven-inch diameter circular image. This becomes a useful ratio—image diameter is three and one half times the size of any given focal length (Figure 5.28). This ratio is valuable in making multiple-pinhole cameras, which may produce images that overlap slightly. The amount of overlap can vary according to each photographer's need (Figure 5.29, Color Plate 5.30a, Figure 5.30b, and Color Plate 5.31).

If the flat film plane is parallel to the object being photographed, there is no linear distortion in the image. The image may look distorted at its edges, however, simply because we are not accustomed to seeing as wide an angle as a pinhole can photograph (Color Plate 4.14). If we view only the center area of the image, it does not look distorted. Many pinhole photographs taken on a flat film plane show only the central part of the image, the rest of the circular image has been allowed to fall off the light-sensitive area (Figure 5.32, Color Plate 5.33).

Figure 5.29 *© Eric Renner,* Dale Gottlieb, *30-second exposure, 10" diameter pinhole photograph from a 19-pinhole camera, 1972.*

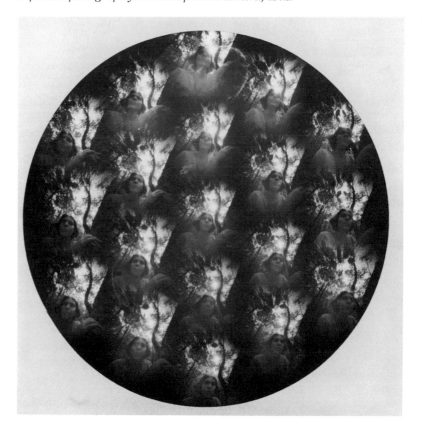

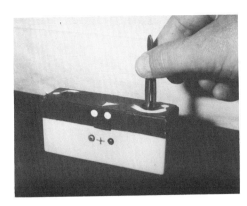

Figure 5.30b © *Paolo Gioli,*
Microcamera Stereostenopeica, *lens photo, 1986. This camera was used to photograph the stereo image in Color Plate 5.30a. From the collection at Pinhole Resource.*

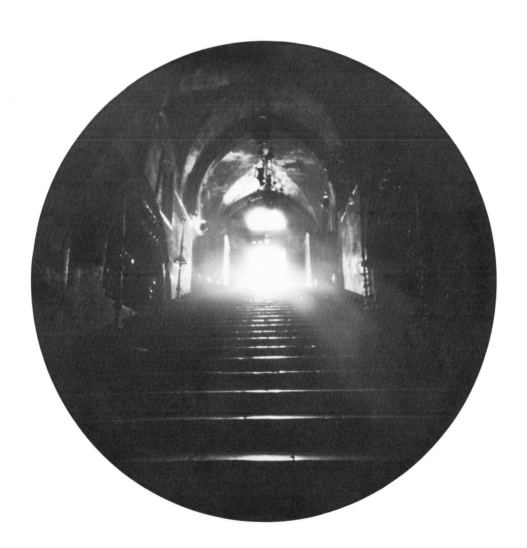

Figure 5.32 © *Marianne Engberg,* Staircase in Mary's Tomb (Jerusalem), *9" diameter pinhole photograph, 1984. From the collection at Pinhole Resource. The photographer commented, "Standing at the foot of the steps in Mary's Tomb, with the light pouring down from above, touching and caressing each step, I felt the mystery of the place and knew I wanted to photograph it. It was difficult to imagine the place without people, who kept coming down the steps, but I knew that they would not be visible in my shot. I wanted a shot that would capture the beauty and stillness of the place. This can only be achieved with a pinhole box."*[7]

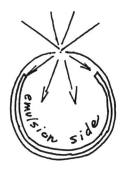

Figure 5.34 *Drawing illustrating photographic image reaching around inside grits box. Drawing by the author.*

Photographing onto a Curved Film Plane

A curved film plane produces a distorted image. Why? Because the image has been captured on a curved surface and is being viewed flat on a piece of photographic paper. If viewed curved, as it had been originally photographed, it would not be distorted. To make it perfectly undistorted, one would have to use only one eye and place it at the position of the pinhole. When a concave container is used, a pinhole casts an image approximately one hundred sixty degrees onto photographic paper that has been almost completely wrapped around the inside of the container, the paper and the image reaching almost to the pinhole (Figure 5.34). A pinhole will photograph this wide an angle inside a curved container simply because the photographic paper is being curved back toward the pinhole, where light intensity is strongest. However, image size near the pinhole is small; it increases as the paper curves toward the back of the container (Figure 5.35). This explains why a cylindrical container makes an elliptical image, if the paper or film is long enough. Ilan Wolff, of France, and Walter Crump, of Boston, use concave distortion in their images (Figures 5.36a, 5.36b).

Cutting a cylinder in half (Figure 5.37) produces a pinhole camera with even exposure across the negative, because the focal distance is constant. However, because this camera is curved, it produces a distorted image—one that covers almost one hundred eighty degrees when a very sharp pinhole in very thin material is used. Kurt Mottweiler's Curved Back 120 Roll Film Camera is an example of this kind of camera.

Photographing onto a convex surface forces the image to fade more quickly at the edge, because light intensity decreases rapidly around the curve (Figure 5.38). This fading can be advantageous, particularly when multiple pinholes are used and photographic film or paper is wrapped around an inner cylinder. A camera can be devised with six pinholes, each hole casting an image where sixty degrees is captured onto the cylinder. Each image fades proportionally into the one next to it, so that in the

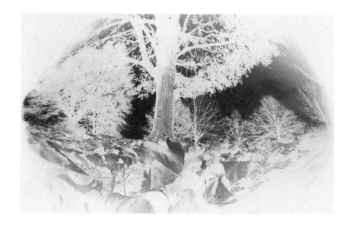

Figure 5.35 *Pinhole photograph (paper negative) illustrating image shape when paper is wrapped almost completely around inside a cylinder. Forty-five-second exposure in full sun. Photograph by author.*

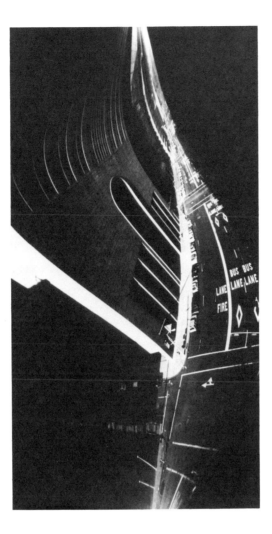

Figure 5.36a © *Ilan Wolff*, NYC, 6"
*x 11" pinhole photograph, 1987. From
the collection of the photographer.*

overall total image there is even exposure (Figure 5.39). When one image is coming in at seventy percent light intensity, the one overlapping it at that spot is coming in at thirty percent; eighty percent and twenty percent; ninety percent and ten percent; and so on. More or fewer than six pinholes can be used around an inner cylinder. When six pinholes are used, each one capturing sixty degrees of image, a ratio can be given for structuring any size camera: focal distance equals the radius of the inner cylinder (Color Plate 5.40; see Figures 3.5a, 3.5b, 3.5c).

Photographing onto an Anamorphic Flat Film Plane

In anamorphic photography, the film plane is radically angled to the pinhole (Figure 5.41). Images can be produced with the film plane almost perpendicular to the pinhole (Figure 5.42). However, light fall-off is severe. An everyday example of an anamorphic plane can be seen while driving through a school zone. The elongated letters SCHOOL are painted on the pavement. When viewed

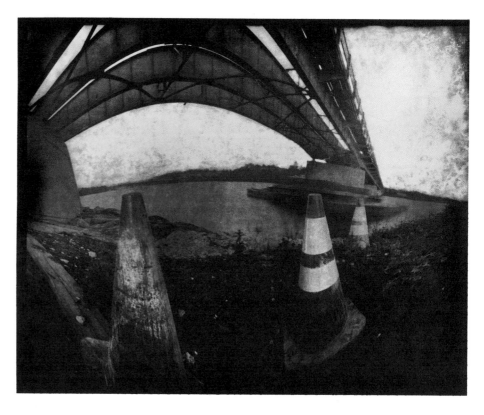

Figure 5.36b © *Walter Crump,* Abandoned Bridge, *16" x 20" pinhole photograph, 1998. From the collection of the photographer.*

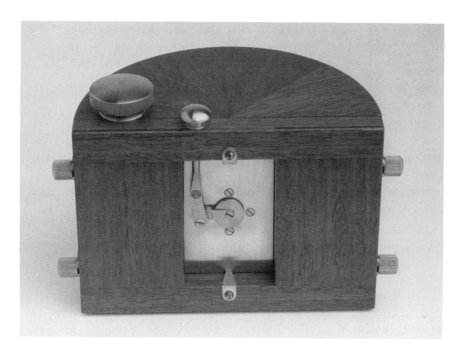

Figure 5.37 © *Kurt Mottweiler,* Curved Back 120 Roll Film Pinhole Camera, *lens photo, 1990. From the collection of the photographer.*

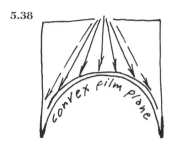

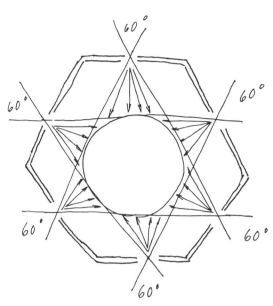

Figure 5.38 *Drawing illustrating a pinhole image going onto a convex film plane. Drawing by author.*

Figure 5.39 *Drawing illustrating a six-pinhole camera. Drawing by author.*

on approach, the letters are visibly foreshortened and therefore readable.

Anamorphic images with a radically angled film plane can be seen only in their original form with one eye where the pinhole would have been. Gillian Brown's painted image in Color Plate 6.13b is an anamorph, as is Leonardo's drawing in Figure 2.11. Working in anamorphs is an unexplored area of pinhole photography.

Making Room-size *Camerae Obscurae*

A room-size pinhole *camera obscura* is simply a larger version of the hand-sized pinhole camera with one wonderful difference—you can walk into a *camera obscura*. In the last ten years, *camerae obscurae* have renewed many photographers' sensory experience because the photographer can be *inside* a camera. You let your eyes adjust, then you see a *grand* image! All of a sudden you realize the huge width of a pinhole image. It's on the floor, the ceiling, the side walls, and the back wall! This is what anamorphs are all about. Hold Marja Pirilä's *Sarianna* in Color Plate 5.43 upside down and see the pinhole image inside Pirilä's *Sleeping Room* series. A ten-foot focal length requires a pinhole about three-eighths to three-fourths inch in diameter, depending on image sharpness versus image brightness. Many photographers make lens photographs of the projected pinhole image using a lens camera with a long exposure. Yet to be made is a *pinhole* image of the projected pinhole image. At the Pinhole Resource in New Mexico, we are fortunate to have a *camera obscura* shaped like a *nautilus* shell (Figure 5.44) built by Nilu Izadi of London. Thomas Kellner

Figure 5.41 *Drawing illustrating anamorphosis, in which photographic film or paper is severely angled away from pinhole. Drawing by author.*

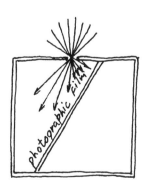

Figure 5.42 © *Eric Renner,* Stretching Marilyn, *11" x 14" anamorphic pinhole photograph, 1996. From the collection of the photographer. The 11" x 14" film was placed along the side of the camera with the pinhole in the front near the film edge. Using film in this way goes against all exposure-guide rules. The leading film edge is extremely over-exposed and the far edge is extremely underexposed, yet it is still possible to print the image by means of stepped dodging and burning. You can use a pinhole occluder (see Chapter 1) to return this anamorph to the original image of Marilyn. Hold the pinhole card directly over one eye and close or cover the second eye. View the image from about two inches away at an eighty-degree angle. The left side of the image should be closest to the eye.*

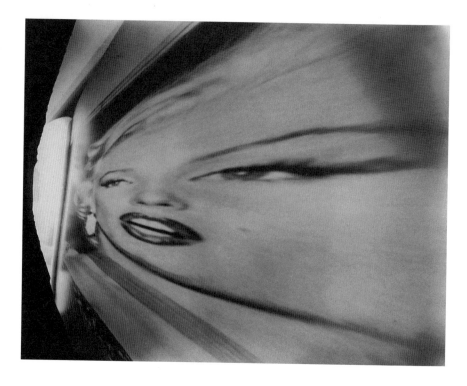

metaphorically conceptualized a country-sized *camera obscura.* He traveled around the perimeter of Germany photographing outward at every border crossing, as if Germany itself were a multiholed pinhole *camera obscura* and each border crossing were an entrance for light (Figure 5.45). Franz John, also from Germany, worked within military bunker remains near the Golden Gate Bridge in California to turn them into *camerae obscurae.* At Penland School of Crafts, in North Carolina, Pinky Bass built a pinhole *camera obscura* meditatively situated within a small grove of trees and facing toward the sunrise. As part of the 1996 Arctic Festival, in Luleå, Sweden, Marja Pirilä fascinated visitors with a walk-in, working snow *camera obscura.*

Photographing onto a Moving Film Plane or Rotating the Camera

Rotating the camera or moving the film plane creates panoramas. Robert Lang, of New York, has made several exceptional panoramic cameras. His first camera, from 1979, had a periscope structure made out of plumbing pipe rotated by means of a motor and belt drive system. The film and container were stationary and the pinhole periscope moved. Of this camera and its resulting image (Figures 5.46a, 5.46b), Lang said:

In my camera, which must be darkroom loaded, an entire roll of 120 film fits in a slot around the inside surface of the drum. The structure in the middle is a periscope with the pinhole mounted

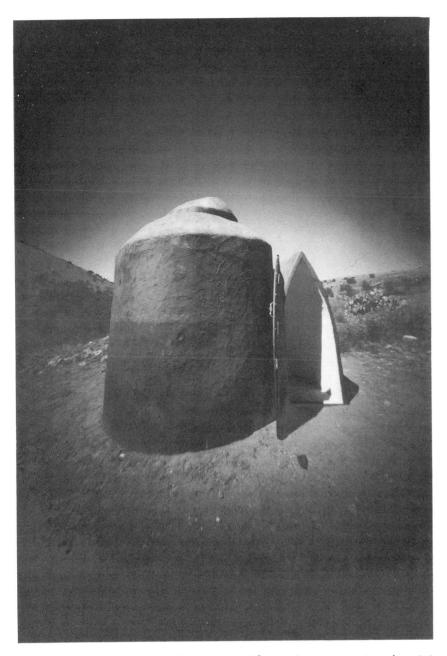

Figure 5.44 © *Nilu Izadi*, Nautilus Camera Obscura, *pinhole image, 10' diameter, 12' high ferrocement building, 1997.*

horizontally between the mirrors. The periscope structure is rotated by motor and belt drive system. The bottom section of the periscope is fitted with a slit which scans the film, producing the panoramic images. The mirrors are front-surfaced aluminized glass which I made myself since I have access to vacuum metalization equipment. The pinhole size was calculated using the criteria set forth by Sayanagi (*Journal of the Optical Society of America*, Vol. 57, No. 9, Sept. 1967). The camera produces images that are foreshortened in the horizontal direction since the distance from the pinhole to the mirror and then to the film plane is greater than the radius of the drum. The camera is remarkably free of banding (vertical stripes) which tends to plague continuous scanning panoramic cameras. [8]

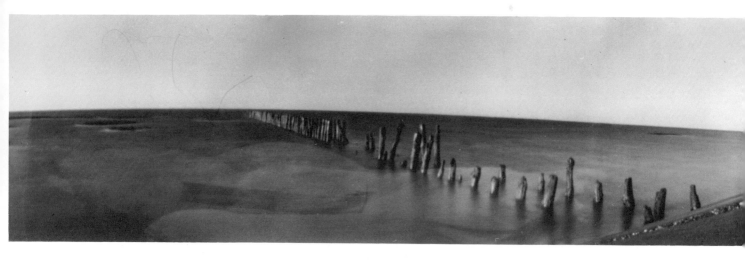

Figure 5.45 © *Thomas Kellner, Grenzgänge Series, 4½" x 18" pinhole photograph, 1996. From the collection at Pinhole Resource.*

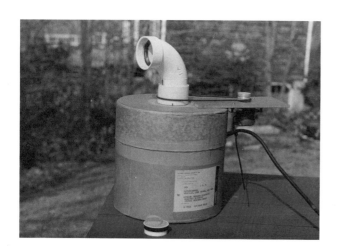

Figure 5.46a © *Robert Lang, Panoramic Camera, lens photo, 1979. From the collection at Pinhole Resource.*

Figure 5.46b © *Robert Lang, My Cars and I, 2" x 30" 330-degree panorama, 1979. From the collection at Pinhole Resource.*

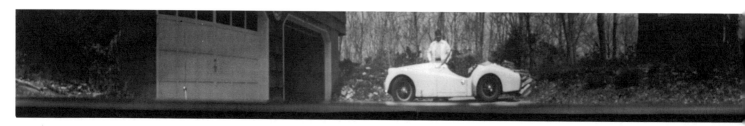

EXPOSURE TIMES

There are many ways to calculate exposure times. Whatever works for you is best. I am reminded of James Thurber's *Many Moons,* a story I often read to my children. In the story, the king asks the royal wizard, the royal mathematician, and the lord high chamberlain the distance to the moon and of what material it is made. Each of the three has a completely different answer. The king then asks the court jester which one has given the right answer. The court jester replies that each is a wise man; therefore all their answers must be correct! This philosophy applies to exposure times—however you go about it is best.

I use the trial-and-error intuitive method for exposure. After making a camera, I try it out and arrive at an exposure time. Because pinhole has a wide latitude, I can usually guess fairly well. I've done pinhole for a number of years, so most often my memory bank has enough in it to work. I've never used a light meter. The most difficult exposures to measure without a light meter, at least for me, are ones in low-light situations or in which light is fading rapidly, as at dusk.

Nancy Spencer explained her exposure method as follows:

I generally use Tri-X film which I rate at ISO 200. I use this rating because I think that if you over-expose Tri-X, the shadow detail is better. I use a Gossen Luna-Pro meter, set at ISO 200. I then point the meter at a Kodak 18 percent gray card placed as closely as possible and in the same light as my subject. I turn on the meter, turn the dial until the needle is on zero, and then read the exposure value (EV), sometimes also referred to as the exposure index. The EV is a chart, available on most handheld meters, which has numbers from 19 to −4. In bright sunlight in New Mexico in the summer, the EV is 16 or slightly higher. On the East Coast in bright sunlight in the summer, the EV is usually around 15. I have worked out a chart, which I have recorded on the back of my gray card. Through tests, I have decided that 2 seconds is a good exposure time for EV 16 with Tri-X film and a $1\frac{1}{2}$" *Leonardo* Camera. I have then worked out the other EV numbers from 16 to 11, with 11 being the darkest lighting situation attempted outdoors. For example, at EV 15, I expose for 4 seconds, at EV 14 for ten seconds, etc.

With this method, you don't have to know your f/stop, pinhole diameter, or focal length. You simply measure the amount of light

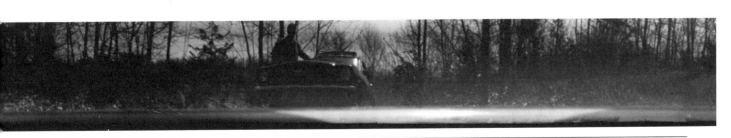

available and learn through trial and error how your film, camera, and developer will react to this lighting situation. In the normal range of lighting situations outdoors, I usually work in the EV 16 to EV 11 range, which amounts to six different exposure times. You will have to run new tests if you use a different size camera. I suggest you work out your own times, taking into consideration type of film, developer and developing times, and reciprocity. [9]

Nancy Spencer and I developed the following chart to supply times for the most commonly available film speeds and RC paper. We have selected the most normal light conditions, ignoring superbright and sunset dark. Because reciprocity is in effect with the longer exposure times on the chart, exposure time varies to a great degree with the reciprocity of each film. For instance, TMAX has less than half of the reciprocity of any other film. In deep shade with the f/470 pinhole, with TMAX 400, exposure time is less than 1 minute, 15 seconds, as suggested on the chart. In addition, people see light situations differently.

We have selected four of the most widely used f stops for the chart. These f stops can be related to specific camera lengths with optimal pinholes as follows:

Camera Focal Length	Pinhole Size (mm)	f Stop
75mm	0.32	f/230
150mm	0.45	f/335
300mm	0.64	f/470

Of course you don't have to have an optimal pinhole on your camera, so all you need to know to use the chart is your f stop. To calculate your f stop divide your camera's focal length by the pinhole diameter. Pinhole exposures do have a wide latitude; often an exposure time of ten seconds can be successfully shortened to seven seconds or increased to twenty seconds to produce a usable negative. A lot depends on the details you want in the image—details in the brightest areas and details in the darkest areas. A lot also depends on whether you prefer a thin or somewhat dense negative. If you prefer a denser negative, double the times. At best an exposure chart is only a starting point.

Light Condition	f Stop	Paper RC	ISO Film Speed		
			Speed 100	Speed 200	Speed 400
Full Sun					
Distinct Shadows, EV 16 at ISO 400					
	f/160	15	3	1.2	.5
	f/230	40	7	3	1.2
	f/335	3M	16	7	3
	f/470	8M	34	16	7
Hazy Sun					
Weak Shadows, EV 15 at ISO 400					
	f/160	40	7	3.1	1.5
	f/230	3M	16	7	3.1
	f/335	8M	34	16	7
	f/470	18M	1M 15	34	16
Cloudy					
No Shadows, EV 14 at ISO 400					
	f/160	3M	16	7	3.1
	f/230	8M	34	16	7
	f/335	18M	1M 15	34	16
	f/470	40M	3M	1M 15	34
Deep Shade					
Heavy Overcast, EV 13 at ISO 400					
	f/160	8M	34	16	7
	f/230	18M	1M 15	34	16
	f/335	40M	3M	1M 15	34
	f/470	90M	7M	3M	1M 15

All times in seconds unless indicated M (minutes). EV, Exposure value.

A final method would be to use the relatively inexpensive, dial-type Black Cat Exposure Guide. This guide is particularly useful for pinhole because it shows f stops up to 1024. To use it, you connect a wide variety of lighting situations to your film speed and f stop to obtain the correct exposure time. The times on the Black Cat generally are faster than those on our chart. Chapter 6 contains an exposure chart for use of zone plates with f stops of 65 to 90.

ADDITIONAL TECHNICAL INFORMATION

Filters

Adding a filter means increasing the exposure time. Many pinhole photographers who use outdoor color film in daylight do not use filters. Fuji Reala film seems to maintain the best color with reciprocity. Ilfochrome Classic paper used directly in the camera for photographing outdoors can be filtered with an 85B filter to change tungsten light to daylight; additional filters can be added to completely correct the color. Examples of filtered Ilfochrome Classic are shown in the images by Willie Anne Wright in Color Plate 4.14 and Howard E. Williams in Color Plate 5.47. Williams, of Florida, provided the following information on filtering Ilfochrome Classic (referred to in his statement as Cibachrome, its former name):

> Cibachrome paper is not designed to be exposed in sunlight. The "color temperature" of sunlight at noon is 5400 K. Converting daylight to tungsten by using an 85B filter in exposing Cibachrome in a pinhole camera is just the beginning. The inherent color balance of Cibachrome differs from batch to batch and box to box. Therefore it is possible that using an 85B filter might still result in a print which is a little too warm (yellow) or a little too cool (blue). This can be remedied with additional filters called light-balancing filters (filter series 81 and 82). These filters allow you to adjust the color temperature, cooler or warmer, in increments as little as 100 degrees K.
>
> The other critical element of pinhole Cibachrome is how long to expose the image. Compared to photographic films, Cibachrome paper is incredibly slow with an effective film speed of ISO 1. The focal length of the camera being used, the diameter of the pinhole, the number of filters added for color correction, and the time of day the exposure is being made all affect exposure time. When purchasing Cibachrome paper try and match, as closely as possible, the color code of one box to another. This will keep you from having to start over from scratch each time you test for exposure and color correction from one box of paper to another. To keep your color and exposure tests consistent, photograph during the middle of the day, in bright sun with little or no clouds. The color temperature of sunlight early in the morning and late in the afternoon is different from that of sunlight at midday. Cloud cover also affects color temperature.[10]

With Ilfochrome Classic placed directly in a pinhole camera, but unfiltered, the color balance can shift toward blue (Color Plate 4.5b), magenta (Color Plate 4.15), or green (Color Plate 6.8), or it can be fairly accurate if you photograph in extremely bright light, as at a beach. Generally it is best to slightly underexpose rather than slightly overexpose.

A simple way to add a filter holder and a snap-cap shutter (Figure 5.48) was designed by Joseph Jakusz, of Nevada. Some pinhole photographers find it useful to add filters to lengthen the exposure time when shooting in black and white or to change subject contrast. Jakusz explained:

> I bought a 58 to 62mm step-up adapter ring and ground off the 58mm male threads. This left a nice flat surface on the back of the ring, which I then glued to the front of the camera with a smear of 5 Minute Epoxy. For those times when you want a busy street to appear devoid of traffic, the 62mm female threads will accept several filters in a stack without vignetting. More often,

though, I'll just use a #25 Red to darken the blue sky on black and white film or a polarizer to kill a bothersome reflection. My Fast Cap is a 62mm W. A. (wide angle) hinged and spring-loaded lens cap. It threads onto the adapter ring or on top of whatever filter I'm using, pops open with the touch of a finger to begin an exposure, then securely snaps shut to end it.[11]

Possibly the filter-camera combination that gets the most laughs is the red-pepper natural safe light camera (Figure 5.49) for black-and-white paper. When finished for the day, the photographer can eat the camera. The darkest red pepper works the best.

Viewfinders

To help visualize the boundaries of an image, a simple sighting mechanism can be added to the top and both sides of the camera. This is particularly easy to do if your camera is rectangular or square. Draw straight lines on the outside of the camera that extend from the pinhole to the edge of the film plane (Figure 5.50). Everything within the triangle will image.

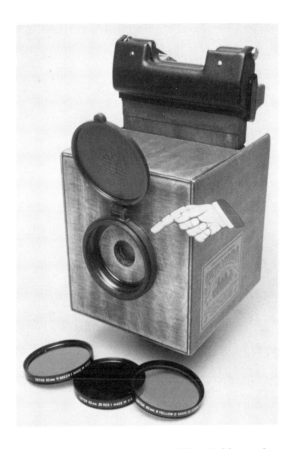

Figure 5.48 © *Joseph Jakusz*, Filter Holder and Snap Cap for a Santa Barbara Pinhole Camera, *lens photo, 1992. From the collection of the photographer.*

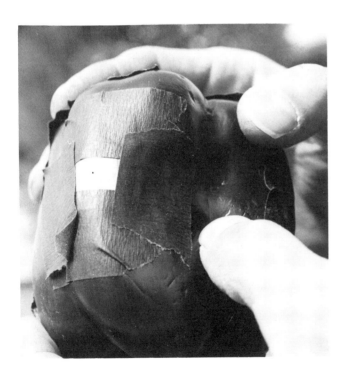

Figure 5.49 © *Eric Renner*, Red Pepper Natural Safe Light Camera *for use with black-and-white photographic paper, lens photo by Russ Young, 1987. From the collection at Pinhole Resource.*

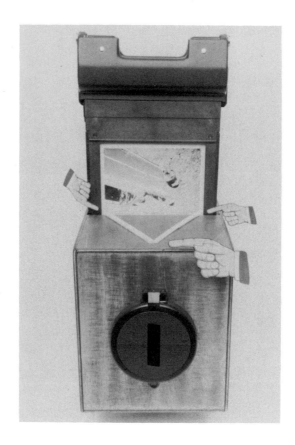

Figure 5.50 *© Joseph Jakusz,* Sight Lines on a Santa Barbara Pinhole Camera, *lens photo, 1992. From the collection of the photographer.*

Shutters

A variety of sliding shutters can be devised. One of the best examples comes from Sam Wang and the late Todd McKinney-Cull, both from Clemson, South Carolina. This shutter (Figure 5.51) is made from a bent brass plate, piano wire, a cable release, a paddle, and bolts. Multiple-ply model airplane plywood in one-eighth-inch thickness also is very useful for shutters and is available from woodworkers' supply houses. Thin, black urethane foam for backing the paddle is available from hobby stores.

Adapting Lens Cameras to Pinhole

Almost every lens camera, including a Polaroid, can be fitted with a pinhole. Even video cameras have been used for pinhole photography. For 35mm cameras with interchangeable lenses, simply use a body cap. A large hole must be drilled and a pinhole made in shim stock or aluminum. Commercial pinhole-fitted body caps are available from Pinhole Resource (address in *List of Suppliers* in the appendix). If fast film is used, the camera can be held by hand. Commercial pinhole mounts for Leica cameras are available from Dominique Stroobant (address in the *List of Suppliers* in the appendix). Even the classic plastic Diana and its recent update the Holga will work for pinhole photography if the lens is removed and a pinhole added.

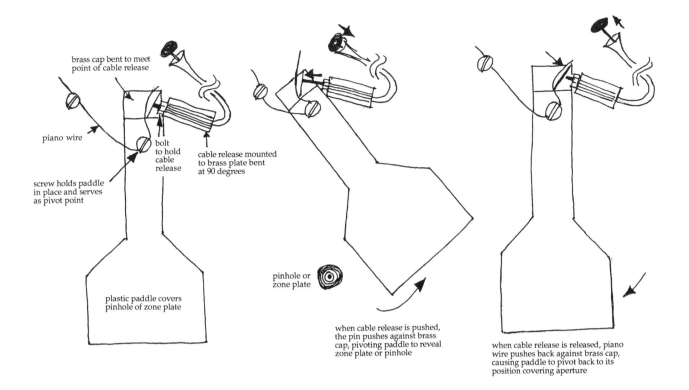

brass cap bent to meet point of cable release

piano wire

screw holds paddle in place and serves as pivot point

bolt to hold cable release

cable release mounted to brass plate bent at 90 degrees

plastic paddle covers pinhole of zone plate

pinhole or zone plate

when cable release is pushed, the pin pushes against brass cap, pivoting paddle to reveal zone plate or pinhole

when cable release is released, piano wire pushes back against brass cap, causing paddle to pivot back to its position covering aperture

Figure 5.51 © *Sam Wang and Todd McKinney-Cull,* Shutter Drawing, *1993.*

ADDITIONAL HINTS FOR BUILDING PINHOLE CAMERAS

Many pinhole cameras have been constructed of mat board, which works best when doubled. White glue can be used to hold two sheets together. While they are drying, weight these sheets with heavy books on a flat surface such as a tabletop. Very rigid corners can be made with doubled mat board according to the construction detail in Figure 5.52a. Light trap tops can be made according to the construction detail shown in Figure 5.52b.

Just about anything can be made into a light-tight camera; even vehicles have been made into portable cameras and dark-rooms. Peggy Ann Jones made her Dasher station wagon into the "Auto-Focus." Many have turned vans into touring cameras or have used truck bodies for even larger images.

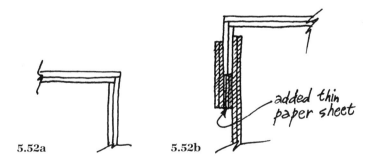

added thin paper sheet

5.52a

5.52b

Figure 5.52a *Construction detail of overlapping mat board corners. Drawing by author.*

Figure 5.52b *Construction detail of a mat board light trap. Drawing by author.*

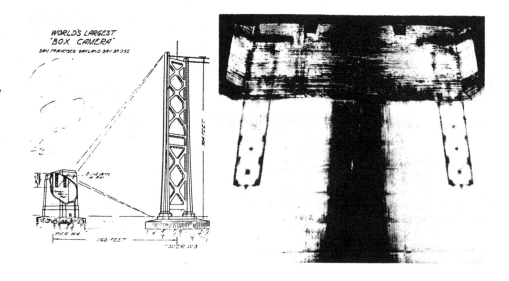

Figure 5.53 *© Gabriel Moulin Studios,* World's Largest Pinhole Camera, *lens photograph of the two pinhole images inside the Bay Bridge anchor tower, circa 1930. From the collection of Gayle Smalley.*

What was once known as the World's Largest Pinhole Camera (Figure 5.53) was nothing less than a huge concrete room with two rectangular air vents. Each vent acted as an elongated pinhole aperture. Measured separately, each vent was one foot wide by two feet long and cast a fifty-foot-long image of one of the Bay Bridge's suspension towers during construction in 1930. These two images were completely accidental. Fortunately, someone was observant enough to see them. The one-hundred-fifteen-foot-square room where these images were projected was designed to be an anchor tower, not a camera. After the bridge was completed, this tower room was removed. So much for the World's Largest Pinhole Camera. It, too, was disposable. A hole as large as one foot by two feet will make an image as long as the focal length is correct.

NOTES

1. Tom Fuller, letter to the author, 5 December 1991.
2. Ibid.
3. Jay Bender, *The Pinhole Photography Kit: The Complete Guide to Lensless Photography* (self-published, 1990), 16.
4. Bob Dome, letter to the author, 5 November 1991, 5–6.
5. M. Jules Combe, "Pinhole Photography," *Photography* 12(20 December 1900):842.
6. Jim Moninger, "Variable Aperture Pinhole Photography," *Pinhole Journal,* 7(1991):5–6.
7. Marianne Engberg, "Artist's Statement," *Pinhole Journal* 1(1985):24.
8. Robert Lang, "Artist's Statement," *Pinhole Journal* 2(1986):23.
9. Nancy Spencer, "Making a Simple Pinhole Camera," *Pinhole Journal* 8(1992):16.
10. Howard E. Williams, "In-Camera Pinhole Cibachromes," *Pinhole Journal* 8(1992):18–19.
11. Joseph Jakusz, "Filters," *Pinhole Journal* 1(1992):20.

All the fifty years of conscious brooding have brought me no closer to the answer to the question, "What are light quanta?" Of course today every rascal thinks he knows the answer, but he is deluding himself.

ALBERT EINSTEIN, 1951

Only a weak light glimmers, like a tiny point in an enormous circle of blackness. This weak light is no more than an intimation which the soul scarcely has the courage to perceive, doubtful whether the light might not itself be a dream, and the circle of blackness, reality.

VASILY KANDINSKY

6

Zone Plates, Slits, and Other Apertures

ZONE PLATES

A zone plate diffracts light; consequently zone plates are closely related to pinhole. Zone plates render soft-focus imagery, yet they are not like soft-focus lens imagery, and their look is not at all like pinhole imagery. The beauty within a zone plate image is the recognizable halo or glow that surrounds any strong-contrast edge, such as the edge of the moon's path on a dark night in Nancy Spencer's *Moonrise over Pinhole Resource* (Figure 6.1). This glow occurs because light rays from the bright moon are considerably bent (diffracted) when hitting the edges of the opaque rings within the zone plate. Foliage such as grasses and leaves under certain lighting conditions may resemble infrared imagery (see Figure 6.5).

Matt Young, a physicist who has written widely on zone plates and pinholes since the early 1970s stated:

> The zone plate consists of a series of concentric rings, alternating clear and opaque. It works by blocking diffracted rays that would have caused destructive interference at the image point.[1]

> The zone plate, like the pinhole camera, exhibits no linear distortion. . . . Zone plates have resolution limits comparable to lenses with the same F-number, and they may be overlapped to form multiple images spaced by less than the diameter of the zone plates themselves. Unfortunately, the zone plate has low efficiency and suffers from veiling glare because most of the light incident on the zone plate passes through it undiffracted and falls onto the image plane.[2]

Because zone plates involve *constructive interference*, exposure times for zone plate images are drastically reduced to

151

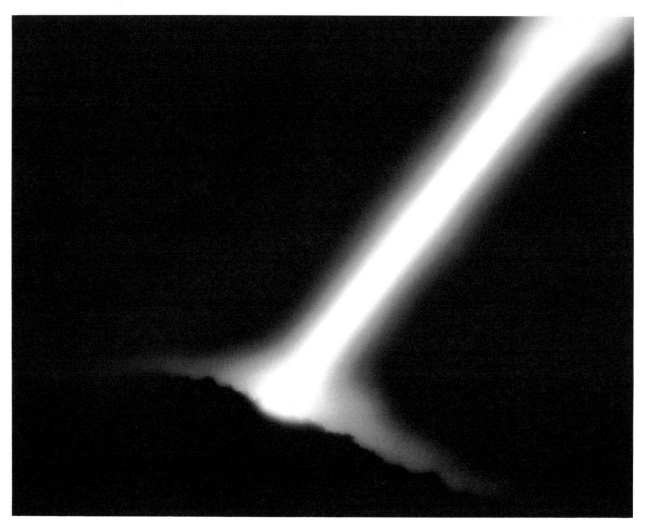

Figure 6.1 *Nancy Spencer,* Moonrise over Pinhole Resource, *$10\frac{1}{2}$" x $12\frac{1}{2}$" zone plate photograph, 1995. Collection of the photographer.*

approximately one-seventh those for pinhole images. Pinholes are examples of *destructive interference,* because many of the light rays going into a pinhole are destroyed by one another. Pinhole f stops begin at about f/120 and go to f/1,000 or more. Zone plate f stops start at about f/65 and usually end at about f/120, unless you make a very long focal-length camera to match the zone plate. Zone plates focus to a point, as lenses do, so you need a zone plate of a specific diameter and focal length to match the focal length of your camera.

Lord Rayleigh was the first to design a zone plate. The entry in his research diary for April 11, 1871, reads as follows:

> The experiment of blocking out the odd Hughens' zones so as to increase light at centre succeeded very well and could be shown

in quite a short space. The negatives should not be varnished. I have little doubt that the number of zones blocked might be advantageously increased much beyond what I used (15). No great accuracy is required in filling in the odd zones with black. [3]

In 1888 Lord Rayleigh suggested a phase-reversal zone plate, which increased light intensity fourfold rather than blocking out alternative zones.[4] In 1898, the well-known American physicist Robert Wood drew a two hundred thirty zone phase-reversal zone plate and was the first to use zone plates for landscape photography. This zone plate can be found in Wood's 1934 classic, *Physical Optics*, which reintroduced zone plates to a wider scientific audience.

In the 1970s Kenneth A. Connors researched zone plates and again they were reintroduced, this time by Connors in his publication *Interest*.[5] However, few art photographers were aware of *Interest*. It was not until 1988, when Connors wrote about zone plates for *Pinhole Journal* and made them commercially available, that a growing number of art photographers became fascinated with zone plates. Connors gave the following explanation:

> Fresnel half-wave diffraction zones have been rendered opaque, so that destructive interference of waves from adjacent zones does not take place; instead, the waves passing through the remaining transparent zones constructively interfere, with a consequent large increase in amplitude of the optical disturbance.[6]

Connors explained as follows the preliminary drawing of an enlarged zone plate (Figure 6.2) and photographic reduction onto 35mm film:

> The classical preparation of a zone plate begins with the drawing of concentric rings having radii proportional to the square roots of the integers; alternate zones are blackened, and a photographic reduction is made on high-contrast film. This film negative serves as a zone plate.
>
> The degree of photographic reduction required to produce a zone plate with desired focal length is readily calculated. For the copy camera set-up the following equations are applicable,

$$F = f(1 + 1/M)$$

$$U = f(1 + M)$$

$$M = U/F$$

where M is the ratio object-to-image size as recorded on the negative, f is the focal length of the copy lens, F is the lens-to-film distance, and U is the object-to-lens distance. It may be necessary to carry out the reduction in two steps.[7]

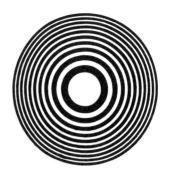

Figure 6.2 *© Kenneth A. Connors, Zone Plate Drawing, 1988, used to make a zone plate. Reproduced from Pinhole Journal, vol. 4, no. 1.*

Figure 6.3 © *Kenneth A. Connors, Surf at Salmon Creek, CA, 9" x 11$\frac{3}{4}$" zone plate photograph, 1986. From the collection at Pinhole Resource.*

ZONE PLATE CAMERAS, IMAGES, AND METHODS

Connors's zone plate photograph *Surf at Salmon Creek, CA* (Figure 6.3) is a perfect example of the evocative qualities available to a photographer using a zone plate. Through a subtle yet surprising use of shifting gray values, the viewer can almost feel the ocean's shimmering movement.

Zone plate exposures usually fall within the one-fourth-second to several-second range. Sam Wang, professor of photography at Clemson University, suggests the use of a commercial shutter, as follows:

> The resulting short exposures ($\frac{1}{30}$ to $\frac{1}{4}$ second in normal outdoor situations) make it fairly awkward to use without a fairly precise shutter—one that's more precise than a lens cap or the proverbial photographer's hat. Unfortunately spare shutters are not readily available, and not inexpensive when they are available. Consequently, it is desirable to convert a cheap existing camera (Figure 6.4) or a really beat-up one to zone plate than to build it from the ground up.[8]

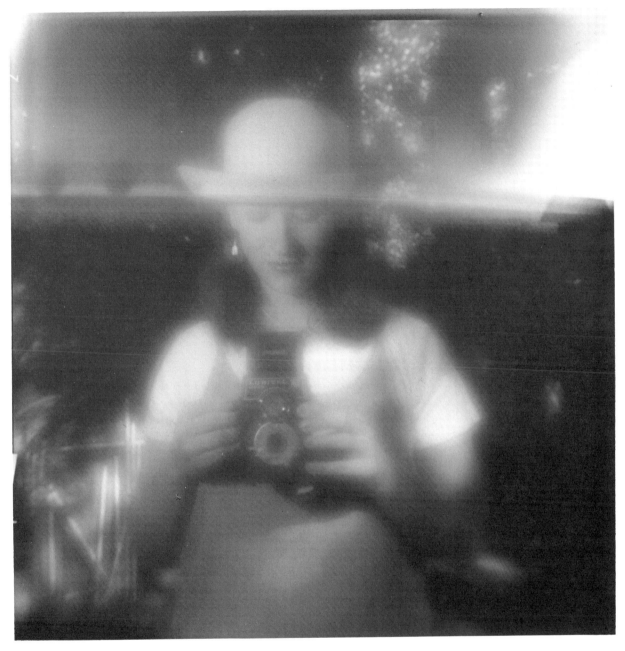

Figure 6.4 © *Sam Wang*, Teresa with Her Zone Plate, $6\frac{1}{2}$" x $6\frac{1}{2}$" *zone plate photograph, 1996. Collection of the photographer.*

Wang continues his article suggesting use of a Russian Lubitel TLR camera with a 75mm zone plate to replace the lens. However, the Lubitel camera seems to come and go from the marketplace. If the Lubitel is available, it is a perfect choice for use with a 75mm zone plate.

Most often a zone plate is simply attached to an extra lens board and used on a large-format (four-by-five or eight-by-ten) camera with focal lengths of 75mm and more. Another option is to convert an existing 35mm lens camera by removing the lens and adding extension tubes to bringing the total length out to 75mm. The zone plate is mounted on a body cap that fits in the end of the tubes.

Mounting a Zone Plate

Commercially available zone plates from Pinhole Resource are on 35mm film. Their sizes and corresponding f stops are as follows:

75mm zone plate	f/65
90mm zone plate	f/70
120mm zone plate	f/80
150mm zone plate	f/90
180mm zone plate	f/95
210mm zone plate	f/100
240mm zone plate	f/110
300mm zone plate	f/120

A zone plate should be mounted with the emulsion side toward the inside of the camera. A two-inch square piece of shim stock or pie-pan aluminum should have a hole in it slightly larger than the outermost zone plate ring. The zone plate is mounted behind the shim. Black photographic tape (Scotch no. 235) can be used to attach the shim and zone plate to the inside of the camera opening. The black photo tape should be affixed to the emulsion side of the film near the zone plate. The tape decreases light reflection from the slightly reflective surface, much the same way as does darkening the back side of the metal around a pinhole. This offers protection for the zone plate. A scratch will destroy the usefulness of the zone plate, so care must be taken. Dust can be cleaned with canned air or a very soft brush, although generally the zone plate should not be left open to the air to catch dust. Never use black photographic tape as a shutter over a zone plate; this works over a pinhole but will destroy a zone plate.

Exposing

The following exposure chart can be used for zone plate photography. The advice about exposure charts given in Chapter 5 applies to this chart. If you prefer a denser negative, double the times.

Light Condition	Focal Length	f Stop	Paper RC	ISO Film Speed Speed 100	Speed 200	Speed 400
Full Sun Distinct Shadows, EV 16 at ISO 400						
	75mm	f/65	4	1	.4	.2
	150mm	f/90	10	2.2	1	.4
Hazy Sun Weak Shadows, EV 15 at ISO 400						
	75mm	f/65	10	2.2	1	.4
	150mm	f/90	22	4.8	2.2	1
Cloudy No Shadows, EV 14 at ISO 400						
	75mm	f/65	22	4.8	2.2	1
	150mm	f/90	48	10.7	4.8	2.2
Deep Shade Heavy Overcast, EV 13 at ISO 400						
	75mm	f/65	48	10.7	4.8	2.2
	150mm	f/90	1M 40	25	10.7	4.8

All times in seconds unless indicated M (minutes). EV, exposure value.

Increasing Contrast on Zone Plate Negatives

Zone plate negatives generally suffer from lack of contrast unless a procedure is used to heighten contrast. Several choices are available beyond the usual procedure of developing negatives thirty percent longer (Figure 6.5). To heighten contrast you can add a lens hood to the outside of a camera. An interior light-trapping configuration (which is what a bellows is) between the zone plate and film also is useful. Black flocked paper can be placed inside the camera to trap extraneous light that would normally go beyond the film area (see Edmund Scientific in the *List of Suppliers*). There is a marked difference between images obtained without light-trapping configurations as opposed to with light-trapping configurations.

Robert N. Nelson of Colorado uses Tec-Pan film (Figure 6.6) to solve low contrast. Nelson specifically photographs in low light or shady situations because of the high contrast of this specialized film. Tec-Pan should never be used in normal, bright sunlight. Nelson explained:

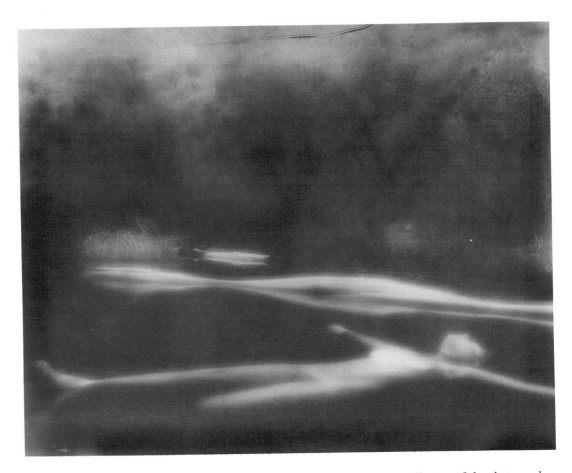

Figure 6.5 © *Nancy Spencer,* Beth, *11" x 14" zone plate photograph, 1996. Collection of the photographer. Film developing time was increased by one third to increase contrast.*

One of the problems of using zone plates is getting enough contrast in soft lighting situations (i.e. portraits). Here is a trick I have learned using Tec Pan Film which will supply all the contrast needed—and then some! For a subject showing a 2–3 stop Subject Brightness Range (SBR), set meter ISO at 64. Place the brightest value of the subject on Zone V and process in HC-110 diluted 1:63 for approximately 8 minutes at 70 degrees. For a subject showing a 1–2 stop SBR, use ISO 100, place brightest value on Zone V and process in TMAX-RS 1:9 for approximately 10 minutes at 75 degrees. The results of this film/developer combination can be stunning. The telltale "glow" of zone plate photographs is enhanced as well as shadow detail even when printed on grade 2 paper. If you love zone plates, you will love this method, but be warned—don't use this method in harsh light. If your SBR is greater than 3 stops, use standard plus development methods.[9]

Russ Young, of Santa Fe, has worked with zone plates for almost ten years. He gave the following advice on films, developing, and focusing:

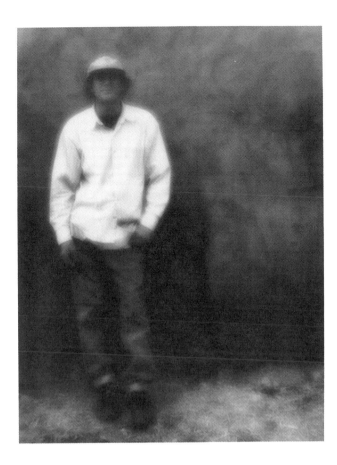

Figure 6.6 © *Robert N. Nelson, Eric Renner, $10\frac{1}{4}$" x $13\frac{1}{2}$" zone plate photograph made from a Tec-Pan film negative, 1996. From the collection at Pinhole Resource.*

Films

A substantial problem for both pinhole and zone plate photographers is reciprocity failure. Most black-and-white films begin to experience serious reciprocity effects at exposure times of one second or more, quite common in non-lens photography. The only way to compensate for reciprocity is to increase the already lengthy exposure time. The moral: use films with improved reciprocity characteristics. The only two I can recommend are Kodak's TMAX 100 and TMAX 400. A bonus is that they are fine grained and also more pan-chromatic than other black-and-white films. TMAX 400 can readily be pushed to higher exposure indexes, too, but this will produce shorter tonal range images.

For color film, the low contrast nature of zone plates acts to mute the colors. If you wish to retain a reasonably normal color saturation, you need to use a contrasty film. Fuji's Reala print film answers this need admirably. Part of the lack of color saturation is also due to the marked chromatic aberration in zone plates with more than five zones (like the ones sold through Pinhole Resource).

Print film has a much broader exposure latitude than transparency (or slide) film; I would never recommend slide film for lensless photography. Print films are standardly available in speeds up to

ISO 3200. The rule of thumb is that the higher the speed, the less saturated the color, which exacerbates the inherent low-contrast nature of zone plates. If you desire saturated colors, keep to ISO 400 or less films.

In the Darkroom

The contrast in black-and-white films can be increased easily by increasing development time. This is the simplest remedy for the inherently low-contrast images. You can also use a more contrasty grade of printing paper (say #4 or #5), but the effect is different.

Most developers in general use today are at least partially solvent developers. These types of developer (Microdol, D-76, ID-11) yield the finest grain, but that is normally not a consideration with our techniques, since preservation of fine details is impossible. Furthermore, fine grain developers create a "mushy" grain structure that makes an already "soft" image appear even less sharp. Instead, try a high acutance developer such as Acufine or any of the pyrogallol formulas; the negative will have larger grain but the image will appear "crisper." If you are using sheet film, grain size is probably of no consequence anyway.

When you first look at a negative made using a zone plate, it will seem hopelessly "soft" and unfocused. Don't despair—it will make a far better print (Figure 6.7) than the negative suggests. Definitely make contact prints rather than trying to assess the negative itself. You'll be pleasantly surprised at the outcome!

Focusing

What? Focus? Yes, you should focus a zone plate. Zone plates operate at around f/65 to f/128 and as such, they have less depth of field than a pinhole. Hence, you should focus particularly if the subject is fairly close. Because zone plates pass so much more light than pinholes, focusing usually is not difficult. After letting my pupil dilate for a few seconds, I have no problems seeing the image through a single lens reflex camera (using a rubber eye cup around the viewfinder really helps). If you are using a view camera with a ground glass, a Fresnel lens on the ground glass will brighten the image considerably; be sure your dark cloth is both large enough and opaque enough to exclude all unwanted light.[10]

PINHEAD MIRRORS AND PINSPECK

In the mid 1980s Thomy Nilsson, of Prince Edward Island, discovered pinhead mirrors, in which a pinhole image is formed by a practically microscopic mirror, approximately 0.5mm in diameter. Of tests made with a 0.3mm diameter pinhead mirror Nilsson stated:

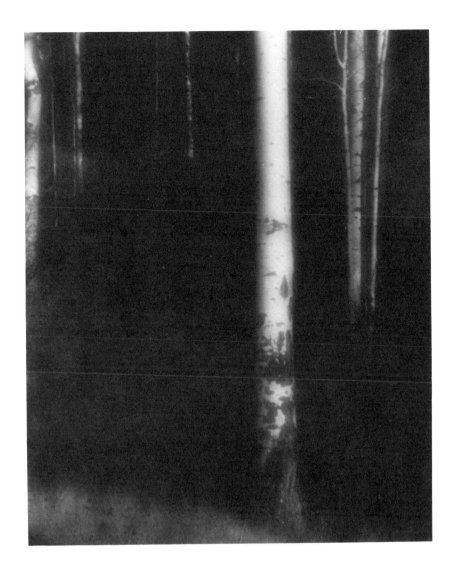

Figure 6.7 © *Russ Young*, Aspen Stand, *5" x 7" zone plate photograph, 120mm zone plate, 1991. From the collection at Pinhole Resource.*

Results obtained with the 0.3mm mirror clearly demonstrated that a small flat mirror could be used to form an image. Furthermore the object and image distances are exactly what is predicted by the pinhole lens equation for a 0.3mm pinhole. Evidently pinhead mirrors have imaging characteristics that are similar to those of pinhole lenses. . . . In addition to the pinhole lens, convex mirror and convex lens, it appeared I had discovered a fourth, basic imaging device—a device for which the name "pinhead mirror" seemed most appropriate.[11]

In the late 1970s Adam Lloyd Cohen, of Chicago, and scientists at Texas Instruments somewhat simultaneously discovered pinspeck imaging,[12] otherwise known as antipinhole imaging, whereby a contrast reversed image is formed by a pinhole-sized opaque object or *pinspeck*. Because pinhead-mirror imaging and pinspeck imaging are of little practical value to pinhole photographers, they are not discussed further.

SLIT APERTURES

Useful to pinhole photographers is slit imaging, whereby a pinhole is stretched to become a slit, allowing an image to be formed. This apparently crude aperture still produces an image of reasonable quality. If the image is too blurred, the slit may be too large for the focal length. In many of my cameras, I have consciously preferred to see a crude aperture, even an aperture that looks like a gash, produce a degraded image rather than have a clean aperture produce a sharp image. For example, in one portrait camera, I used a slit in a rose petal as an aperture. To do this, I taped the petal over a large hole and loaded the camera. When ready to photograph, I slit the petal and made the image (Color Plate 6.8). Each image required a new petal, and each petal had a very different slit, which seemed to correspond to the veins within the petal. I am always surprised such an unsophisticated aperture works so well.

A series of single slit images can be seen in Color Plate 6.9. In this long-hallway slit *camera obscura,* Harry Littell of New York covered a row of windows except for horizontal slits, which acted as apertures for each window. The images from these apertures were rear-projected onto a long translucent screen and viewed from the front. Color Plate 6.9 is actually a series of upside-down images. Sky, street, and moving cars are easy to see if you turn the figure upside down.

Slit photography, which dates back to the late 1800s, seems to be first mentioned by William H. Pickering, as follows:

> The pinhole principle may also be used for another purpose, more amusing, perhaps, than artistic, which was first suggested to me by Mr. J. R. Edmands. Let us substitute for the lens a narrow vertical slit, about three inches long by one-fiftieth of an inch wide, made by pasting two strips of black paper side by side. About two inches behind this arrange a horizontal slit of the same dimensions. Two inches behind this place the sensitive plate. The apparatus is analogous to two cylindrical lenses of different foci placed at right angles, but is more readily adjusted. If an exposure is now made we shall find everything distorted to twice the size horizontally than it is vertically. By turning the camera on its side we get a vertical distortion. By inclining the slits at different angles variously distorted pictures may be obtained.[13]

Pickering's dimensions are perfectly useful today. A combination of two slits, one placed vertically and one placed horizontally (as Pickering suggests), will produce distorted images, such as those made by Doris Markley, of Philadelphia (Figures 6.10a, b, c).

Hans Knuchel, author of *Camera Obscura* (Lars Müller Publishers, Baden, Switzerland, 1992), Jürgen Königs and Simon Puschmann from Germany, and Marnie Cardozo from Boston, are among a handful of practicing slit photographers. Slit photography is one of the least explored areas in art photography. Marnie Cardozo explained how to make a slit as follows:

Making Slits

An ideal material for making slits is exposed litho film. Lay sheets of litho film in a sunny place for several days, and develop them in full strength paper developer. Fix and wash the film normally. When the film is dry, use a Sharpie pen to draw the slit you want to make on the emulsion side of the film. Use sharp, clean scissors to cut the film in half along the line.

Cut pieces of black-on-black matboard the same size as the lens board of the camera you'll be using. Center a piece of cut film on the matboard, and trace around the cut side to transfer the shape of the slit to the matboard. With a knife, make a $\frac{1}{4}$" cutout around the tracing. The cutout should be centered on both axes of the lensboard. For a 4 x 5 camera, it should be approximately 3" long on the vertical axis, and $2\frac{1}{2}$" long on the horizontal axis.

Use slow drying water-soluble contact cement or other glue to glue the film to the matboard. Spread glue on the matboard on the top, or the right, side of the cutout; leave an unglued $\frac{1}{8}$" border around the cutout. While the glue still is wet, glue the appropriate piece of the film to the matboard so the cut edge of the film covers half of the cutout and is centered over it. Glue the other piece of film to the matboard. The second piece must line up with the first and make a slit approximately 0.5 mm wide. A strip of double-weight photo paper should slide

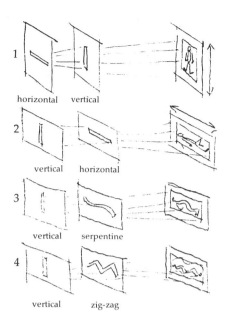

Figure 6.10a © *Doris Markley*, Slit Drawings, *1987. From the collection at Pinhole Resource.*

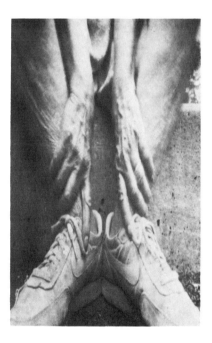

Figure 6.10c © *Doris Markley*, Untitled, *4" x 5" slit photograph (horizontal front slit, vertical back slit) 1987. From the collection at Pinhole Resource.*

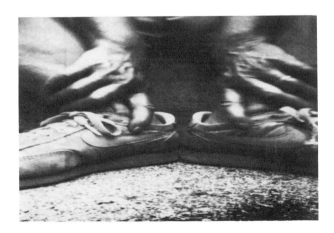

Figure 6.10b © *Doris Markley, Untitled, 4" x 5" slit photograph (vertical front slit, horizontal back slit), 1987. From the collection at Pinhole Resource.*

through the slit with ease. To define the length of the slit, cover both ends with light-proof tape. Tape the outer edges of the film to the matboard.

Inspect the slit with a comparator or loupe; make sure the edges are clean. If the edges are ragged or dirty, remove the first pieces of film from the matboard and make a new slit.

Put the lensboard-with-slit between two pieces of waxed paper, lay it on a flat surface, weight it, and let the glue dry. Repeat this process with all your slits.

Straight-line slits don't need to be trimmed to keep the width of the slit consistent from one end to the other. Curved slits may need to be trimmed to keep the same width at the ends of the curve as in the center. Trim the slits before you glue them to the lensboard.

Shooting through Two Linear Slits

The image in a slit camera is exposed at *two different focal lengths*. . . . Thus a slit image is recorded at two different scales [Figures 6.11a, 6.11b, 6.11c]. The image also passes through slits of *two different shapes* and is bent by both of them. It follows, then, that the image will be doubly distorted *in the camera*. If nothing else, slit images are studies in distortion.[14]

OTHER APERTURE ALTERATIONS

Using a variety of techniques, many photographers are altering the pinhole image. Sam Wang scans pinhole (actually nail hole) images into a computer. The dot matrix in the printed image further breaks the continuous tone (Color Plate 6.12).

Gillian Brown, of Maryland, creates anamorphic installations. With her seated figure (a painting of Professor Jeff Weiss, of the Rochester Institute of Technology), Brown forces the viewer first to see Weiss by looking through a hole placed at eye level in the door to his faculty office (Color Plate 6.13a). In this view, he looks as if he were really there. Upon entering the office, it becomes apparent Weiss is nothing more than a life-size anamorph painted onto the chair, lamp, desk, and floor (Color Plate 6.13b). Of this piece, Brown said:

I covered the window in this office with black mat board with a hole at eye level the size of a 35mm contact print. Through this hole one could see the painted installation. Or the hole could be blocked with a 35mm contact print of the scene within. Both the life-size installation and the small contact print in some sense filled the same space. The faculty member was painted ever-present at an ever-vacant desk. Many students worked on the painting and also executed art works which could be found upon opening drawers or flipping the blinds.[15]

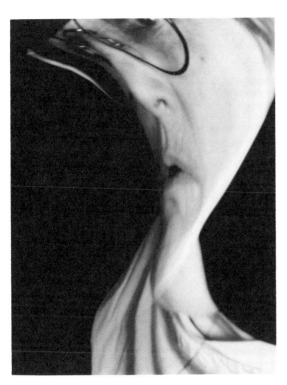

Figure 6.11a © *Marnie Cardozo*, Self Portrait, Vase, *1998. From the collection of the photographer.*

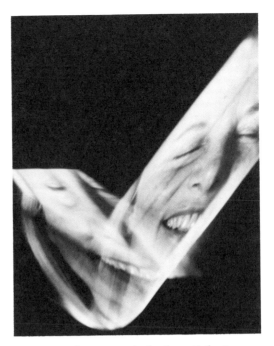

Figure 6.11b © *Marnie Cardozo,* Catherine Checking Out, *1998. Interesting to note is that when Cardozo makes portraits she requests each person choose the two slits they would like used for the photograph. From the collection of the photographer.*

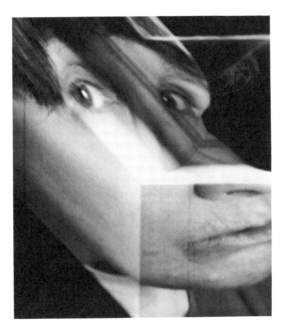

Figure 6.11c © *Marnie Cardozo*, Self Portrait, Fox Face, *1998. From the collection of the photographer.*

NOTES

1. Matt Young, "Zone plates and their aberrations," *Journal of the Optical Society of America* 62 (1972):972.

2. Matt Young, "The Pinhole Camera," *The Physics Teacher* (December 1989):654.

3. Lord Rayleigh (John William Strutt), research notebook entry on 11 April 1871, in R. J. Strutt, *Life of John William Strutt, Third Baron Rayleigh* (Madison, WI: University of Wisconsin Press, 1968), 88.

4. Kenneth A. Connors, "Zone Plate Photography," *Pinhole Journal* 4(1988):26.

5. Kenneth A. Connors, "Pinhole Photography. VI: Studies on Zone Plates Having One or Two Clear Zones," *Interest* 16(1979):41–51.

6. Connors, "Zone Plate Photography," *Pinhole Journal* 1(1988):26–27.

7. Ibid.

8. Sam Wang, "Lubitel ZP Customizing to Zone Plate," *Pinhole Journal* 12(1996):27.

9. Bob Nelson, personal letter to the author, August 18, 1988.

10. Russ Young, "Some Practical Hints for Zone Plate Photographers," *Pinhole Journal* 8(1992):28–30.

11. Thomy Nilsson, "Pinhead Mirrors: Imaging, Computing and the Nature of Light," *Pinhole Journal* 4(1988):2–3.

12. Adam Lloyd Cohen, "Pinspeck," *Pinhole Journal* 4(1988):6–7.

13. William H. Pickering, "The Pinhole Camera," *Anthony's Photographic Bulletin* 18(11 February 1888):71–72.

14. Marnie Cardozo, *Through The Eye of a Pinhole* (unpublished manuscript, 1988), 26–28.

15. Gillian Brown, "Artist's Statement," *Pinhole Journal* 7(1991):21.

Brunelleschi, looking through a hole at a street in Florence, makes a depiction of it from a fixed viewpoint. . . . The photographic process is simply the invention in the 19th century of a chemical substance that could "freeze" the image projected from the hole in the wall, as it were, onto a surface. It was the invention of the chemicals that was new, not the particular way of seeing. . . . So the photograph is, in a sense, the end of something old, not the beginning of something new.

DAVID HOCKNEY
That's the Way I See It, 1993

Seeing light is a metaphor for seeing the invisible in the visible, for detecting the fragile imaginal garment that holds our planet and all existence together. Once we have learned to see the light, surely everything else will follow.

ARTHUR ZAJONC
Catching the Light, 1993

Eye, Image, Camera, Mind: The 1990s

THE SHIFTING IMAGE OF REALITY?

The painter-photographer David Hockney is expressing the mechanistic viewpoint toward the perspective produced by a camera, whether it be a pinhole camera or a lens camera. Hockney is correct; the photograph, with its built-in perception of the way we visualize one-point perspective, is indeed the end product of the early Italian Renaissance, even though we are beginning another millennium. Our present-day pinhole camera may well be representative of a five-hundred-fifty-year-old Renaissance tool, whereas the slightly more than one-hundred-fifty-year-old chemical process known as photography is living proof that a permanent one-point perspective image can be archivally retained.

David Hockney is asking for more. He wants a new way of defining space. Cubism was the first art form to attempt to alter one-point perspective, yet even Picasso abandoned it to return to one-point perspective. Hockney challenges us to find "the beginning of something new"—to reinvestigate the altering, destruction, or natural evolvement of one-point perspective and create another visual structure. This, of course, is a grand request. Hockney is well aware of the staying power involved in Filippo Brunelleschi's pinhole perspective device. It's not so easy to remove the vanishing point, which is central to much of our visual acuity.

In *The Day the Universe Changed*, in the mid-1990s on PBS television, Samuel Y. Edgerton, Jr., explained the monumental significance of the vanishing-point continuum of pinhole, a continuum that began on the day Brunelleschi made his pinhole device.

Edgerton chronologically traced important historical events that connect the vanishing point of a pinhole—to Paolo Toscanelli's advising Columbus to sail west to find the east, to present-day airplanes' departing toward distant landing points, and to "smart" missiles' being fired at distant targets.

Before this documentary, Edgerton had grasped immense implications that confirm an unusual aspect of the sociologic contribution of pinhole. Edgerton's insights are profound. In the epilogue of his book *The Heritage of Giotto's Geometry* (Cornell Univ. Press, 1991), Edgerton stated:

> Geometric linear perspective was quickly accepted in western Europe after the fifteenth century because Christians wanted to believe that when they beheld such an image in art, they were perceiving a replica of the same essential, underlying structure of reality that God had conceived at the moment of Creation. By the seventeenth century, as "natural philosophers" (such as Kepler, Galileo, Descartes, and Newton) came more and more to realize that linear perspective does in fact conform to the actual optical and physiological process of human vision, not only was perspective's Christian imprimatur upheld, but it now served to reinforce Western science's increasingly optimistic and democratic belief that God's conceptual process had at last been penetrated, and that knowledge (and control) of nature lay potentially within the grasp of any living human being. [1]

Simply put, Edgerton is saying Christian institutions realized one-point perspective; that is, the one-point perspective of pinhole made the Christian miracles look completely real and therefore believable. One-point perspective consequently was worth promoting! Taking Edgerton's theory to completion, I can only conclude that the invention of photography is Christianity's child, born from the marriage of reality with the miraculous. I have come to realize how much of the history of photography, even up to the present, falls under this umbrella—particularly any image that has mysterious connotations.

David Hockney's and Samuel Edgerton's theories together express how the camera's one-point perspective combined with the camera's miraculous reality remains a sociologic structure that holds the Western-Christian visual world together. To change this structure would be sociologically monumental. Possibly the only places where Brunelleschi's centuries-evolved structured reality falls apart are our dreams and a painter's canvas. Here space is not always so necessarily rational or so all-conforming to the "actual optical and physiological process of human vision" described by Edgerton.

Pinhole photography and other alternative processes in the last decades have brought a somewhat changed visual sensibility into acceptance, although not one that breaks with one-point perspective. Reliance on the hard-edged, sharply focused lens image that pervaded much of the imagery of the twentieth century has receded. Certainly the 1990s have seen an increase in art photographers' use of pinhole. Why? On the surface it would seem that many who are new to pinhole simply want to try something different. Computers are one way, pinhole another. Yet in a deeper vein, the mysterious qualities of pinhole, which readily portray something of the dark side, an altered reality so to speak, are part of the reason. Within this dark side resonates the combined interaction of a global community of pinhole photographers. Many of the images within this chapter seem entwined. I believe artists through their intuitions share a collective unconsciousness.

1990s IMAGES

Continuation of the Camera and Image as One

Pinhole photographers, some of whom had worked for many years—Peter Olpe, Julie Schachter, Jo Babcock, Ilan Wolff, Jochen Dietrich, Peggy Jones, Thomas Bachler, Paolo Gioli, Marja Pirilä, and I—continued in the 1990s to make camera and image as one interconnected artwork.

In 1994 and onward Ilan Wolff's pinhole cameras became photographs-cameras (Color Plate 7.1) when he painted liquid emulsion onto metal containers. In 1996 Wolff continued the idea using plywood constructions that could be assembled into cameras. After images were obtained, the cameras were deconstructed into images that could be exhibited. Of his work Wolff stated simply:

> The camera becomes part of the image and the image is part of the camera.[2]

Bethany DeForest, of the Netherlands, builds miniature environments, places as diverse as palaces constructed from sugar cubes and ocean floors with ruins and real fish embedded in the transparent polyester sides, in which to photograph. Several pinhole cameras are placed within each environment and most times a camera is camouflaged into the image.

Jochen Dietrich, of Germany, created a set of cameras in search of global photographers when he built one hundred twenty pinhole cameras inside waterproof boxes. Each camera carried an instruction manual written in seven languages asking the finder to make an image and return the camera to him. The cameras were thrown into the Atlantic Ocean off the coast of Portugal to be returned days, months, even years later. There is a deeper meaning to this project than just throwing one hundred twenty pinhole cameras into the sea. Here is a unique way to connect different cultures of the world even at different times. Who knows how long his cameras will travel?

In 1993 Thomas Bachler of Germany wrote:

I "opened" a (still closed) pinhole camera with a pistol shot [Figure 7.2]. The picture of me has been made through the entry hole of the bullet. The bullet went through the pinhole camera and left through a hole at the back side. That is why there is a hole exactly where my eye is supposed to be. The photograph has thus been made with the help of the bullet, which at the same time destroys the most important part of the picture, my eye. [3]

This, of course, is not so much a metaphor for self-destruction as a metaphor for opening one's eyes as widely as possible to create a perfectly clear vision in artistic terms. Thomas Bachler's bullet hole camera is an intellectual achievement, not a violent act.

In my *Homage to Vincent,* made in 1996 while in Arles, France, I cut the ear out of a silk-screened Van Gogh portrait that had been printed on a tourist sweatshirt. Behind and through this ear hole in the sweatshirt, I photographed various places where Van Gogh had been, slightly more than one hundred years before. In another series titled *Couples,* my suitcase camera acted as a place where two eleven-inch by fourteen-inch pieces of film would be squeezed next to one another, as were the couples I photographed. The middle edge in the two photographs gave important physical definition to the wide-angled imagery (Figure 7.3).

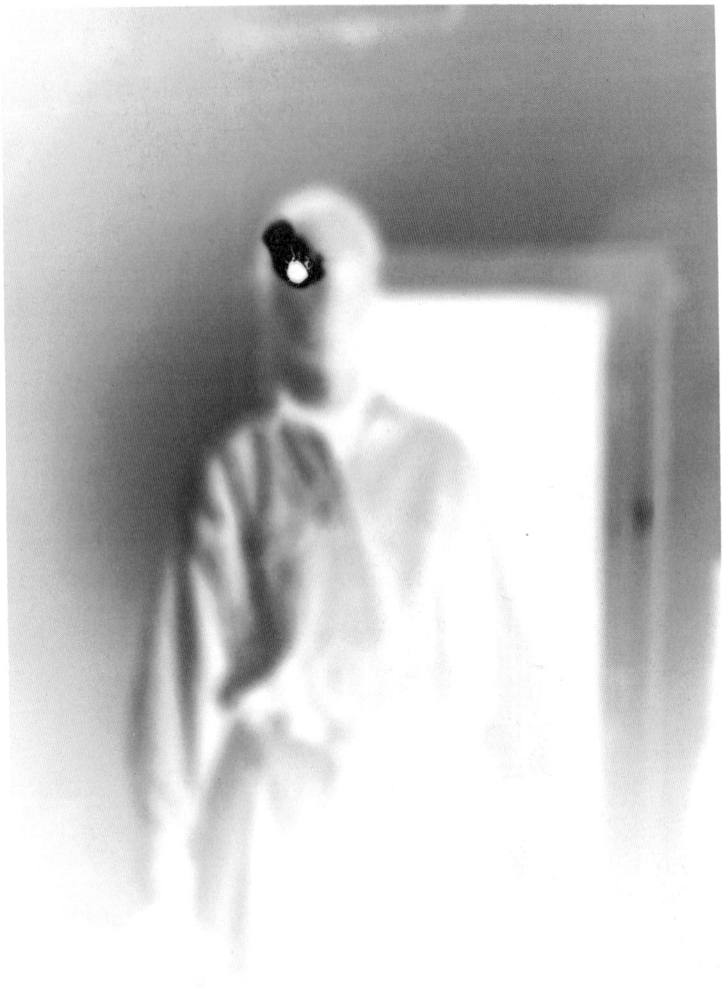

Personal Images

Leah Stubbs combines metaphorical purity with the realities of life (Figure 7.4). Of her pinhole photographs, she wrote:

The subject of my work is the restructured female. I make collages from magazine images, and place the collages in any location I choose to photograph. Most often, the women in my photographs are not complete: they are missing their eyes, or the face, and in some cases, the entire head. They represent my continued exploration of my identity. I disembody and reassemble the women to express what I believe has been the fragmentation and restructuring of my own identity due to messages I have received from the media, our society, and my past. The finished photographs possess certain surreal, dreamlike qualities. I often

Figure 7.2 © *Thomas Bachler,* Shot in a Head, *6" x 8" pistol bullet hole photograph, 1994. From the collection at Pinhole Resource.*

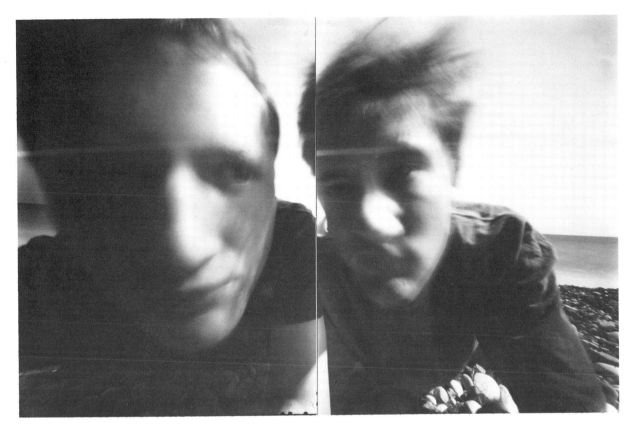

Figure 7.3 © *Eric Renner,* Yarian and Zephyr, *two 11" x 14" pinhole photographs as one photograph, 1998. From the collection of the photographer.*

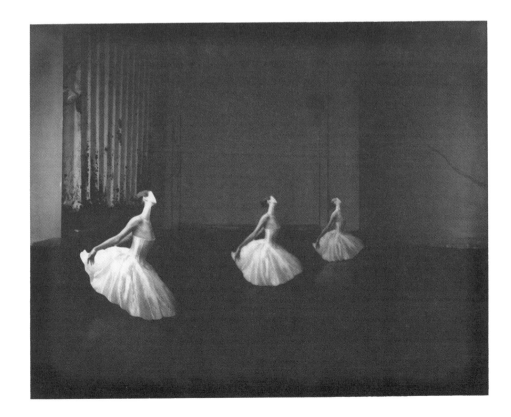

Figure 7.4 © *Leah V. Stubbs,* The Dancers, *16" x 20" pinhole photograph, 1996. From the collection of the photographer.*

think of them as "stills" of dreams—"beautiful" in a spooky way, and only part of a whole story that feels difficult to explain. They are glimpses into my private reality and perhaps my subconscious mind. [4]

Of his series of pinhole photographs titled *Murder Sites* (Figure 7.5), Harlan Wallach wrote:

In Chicago there has been a tremendous escalation of the murder rate. You hear about it and it's pretty insignificant to you. An unbelievably grisly murder took place in an alley near where I lived, and in fact, I knew people who lived in the building that this murder occurred right behind. It hit home with me. I got this idea that there are two levels to the murders—the way it's reported and intellectually perceived, and then there's the actual reality of it. These are places where people actually live and are not necessarily bad neighborhoods. So I went to the site and documented it with pinhole, and I processed the images and looked at them and it wasn't enough just to say that they were murder sites. I felt that I needed to incorporate another element. So I went back to the actual description in the city column of the newspaper. I clipped out that section, [photocopied] it, and printed it with a contact print, so that the actual article would appear on the final print. . . . I would collect the city columns for about a week. I didn't want to go back to the site too soon. I didn't want to be there that day or even the next day. I wanted a period of time to go by, either a week or longer. . . . 922 murders took place in Chicago last year, that's 3 a day. . . . I have photographed about 60. . . . When I combined pinhole photography with murder sites, the result seemed perfect. [5]

Most of us have a mental picture of the Holocaust and the Nazi extermination camps, yet few of us know, unless we've visited the sites, what they really looked like and what is left. We should thank the person who made the decision to leave hundreds to thousands of shoes intact, for here is a true, absolutely horrid reminder of what happened here. We are transported to a dream state by Patrick Poels's manipulation of the image edges, isolating us in the center with the shoes (Figure 7.6). We know only too well where the people are who wore them. The dream is a nightmare never to be forgotten. Poels's image reinforces our image of the unforgettable. Poels, from Belgium, stated:

This documentary series was made in several Nazi extermination camps in Poland. During trips in 1992 and 1993, I visited Auschwitz, Birkenau, Chelmno, Majdanek, Beizec, Treblinka and Sobibor. The entire series contains about 40 pictures made with a

Figure 7.5 © *Harlan Wallach,* Zdziarski Died Early . . . , *from the series* Chicago Murder Sites: Works in Progress, *11" x 14" pinhole photograph, 1992. From the collection of the photographer.*

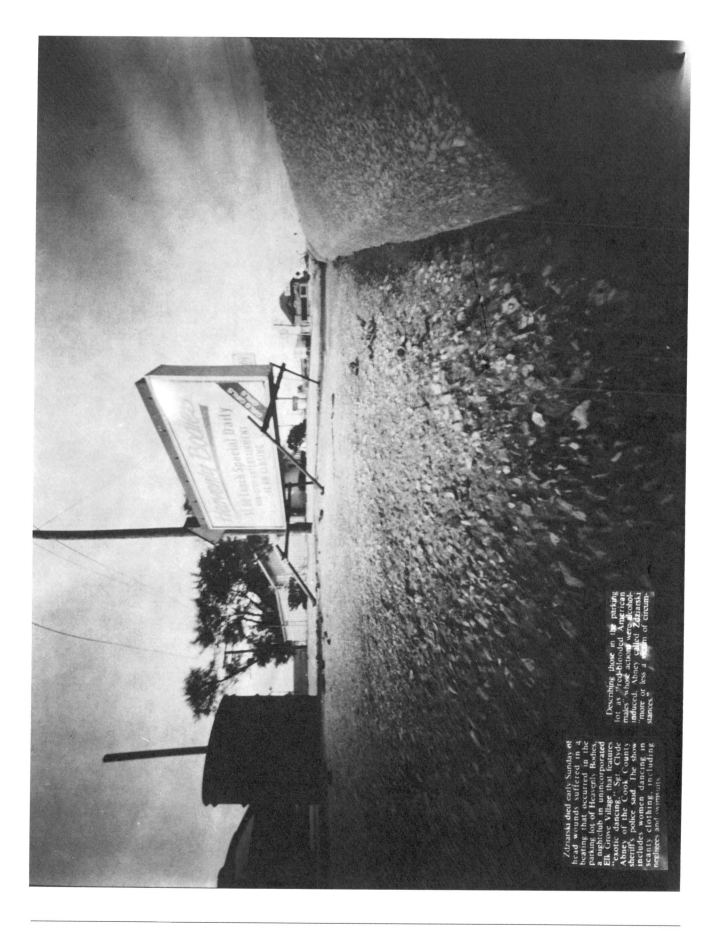

Zdzurski died early Sunday of head wounds suffered in a beating that occurred in the parking lot of Heavenly Bodies, a nightclub in unincorporated Elk Grove Village, that features "exotic dancing," Sgt. Clyde Abney of the Cook County sheriff's police said. The show includes women dancing in scanty clothing, including negligees and swimsuits.

Describing those in the parking lot as "red-blooded American males" whose actions were alcohol-induced, Abney called Zdzianski "more or less a victim of circumstances."

173

cardboard pinhole camera on Polaroid 665 film. The focal length of the camera is 25mm and the diameter of the hole is 0.2mm.

Before starting this series I dug into the necessary literature and watched many photographs and documentaries. I thought this the best way to have an idea of what I might find once I got to Poland. However, when one actually visits a camp or a former campsite, one becomes aware that 50 years after the facts, one is entering a museum. It is quiet and desolate (I even thought I could hear more birds sing outside the camp than inside). You can smell the mowed grass and the humid dark pinewoods in the area. So it is like archeology: you only have a few fragments or details from which you have to reconstruct the awful things that have happened here. You can only say that words are not enough for this. I could only "hang onto" a few details that moved me in a big way and served as *pars pro toto:* in Majdanek

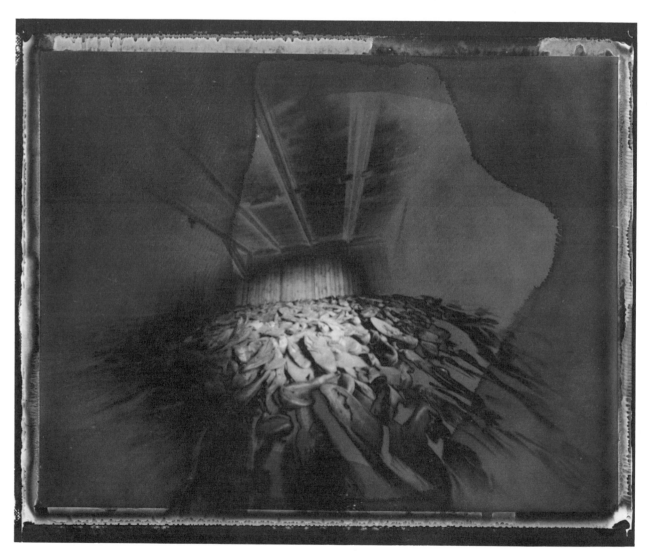

Figure 7.6 *Patrick Poëls,* Shoes, Majdanek Nazi Extermination Camp, *6" x 7½" pinhole photograph taken in Poland, 1993. From the collection of the photographer.*

I found a child's shoe in a large heap of tens of thousands of men's and women's shoes. In Birkenau and Sobibor, I dug a couple of inches in the soil and found ashes and fragments of human bones, even a tooth. In Auschwitz I saw a photograph of a newborn, literally thrown in the corner of a room, the navel string still there. Sometimes I was relieved that, as some sort of protection, I could place my pinhole camera between these horrible places and myself.[6]

Jesseca Ferguson, of Massachusetts, uses partial exposure to add a sense of life and movement to her otherwise still-life imagery. The figure is surrounded by objects, which speak mysteriously, seeming to fill her world with the surreal. As viewers we are left to ponder. I see symbols and gestures, and I am reminded of paintings by Vermeer. Of the image in Figure 7.7 Ferguson said:

> Working alone in my studio, I set up objects deeply encoded (for me) with personal associations, my private mythology. The (scary) fairy tale that was my childhood continues to haunt me as I dip into and drink from what novelist Michael Ondaatje has termed "the well of memory." I am witnessing myself being photographed, as if in a dream. The existence of this particular visual (and psychological) situation is possible only through pinhole photography.[7]

Nancy Spencer in her series *Millennia* manipulates the viewer's sense of space and time by juxtaposing focused or unfocused zone plate images and sharp or blurred pinhole images together as one grouping. In the darkroom during film development, Spencer technically reorders the photographer's sense of imaging by slightly soaking her film in photographic fixer before development. How the fixer alters the film's silver is fairly accidental. This leaves each image stained with a deeper meaning, an introspection, that produces new portraits of the Mediterranean. Present, past, and future seem to be one; a crumbling ruin darkly resonates, as does the ridiculous expression (!?) shown by Larry of the Three Stooges on a T-shirt worn by the author. Psychological and environmental questions are being asked: Who are the demons of yesterday and today? What is real and what is not? What of the Acropolis (Figure 7.8); does it represent democracy or a vast city-state built by slaves? And what of the natural elements surrounding humanity, so exemplified in Greece—water, air, earth, and most of all, light?

During the 1990s the wide acceptance of pinhole was echoed in many books, innumerable exhibitions, and the much greater availability of commercial pinhole cameras. Important monographs were published on Ruth Thorne-Thomsen (*Within This Garden*, Aperture, 1993) and Paolo Gioli (*Paolo Gioli*, Art&, 1996). The Smithsonian Institution Press, in their *Photographers at Work* series, published Abelardo Morell's *A Camera in a Room* (1995),

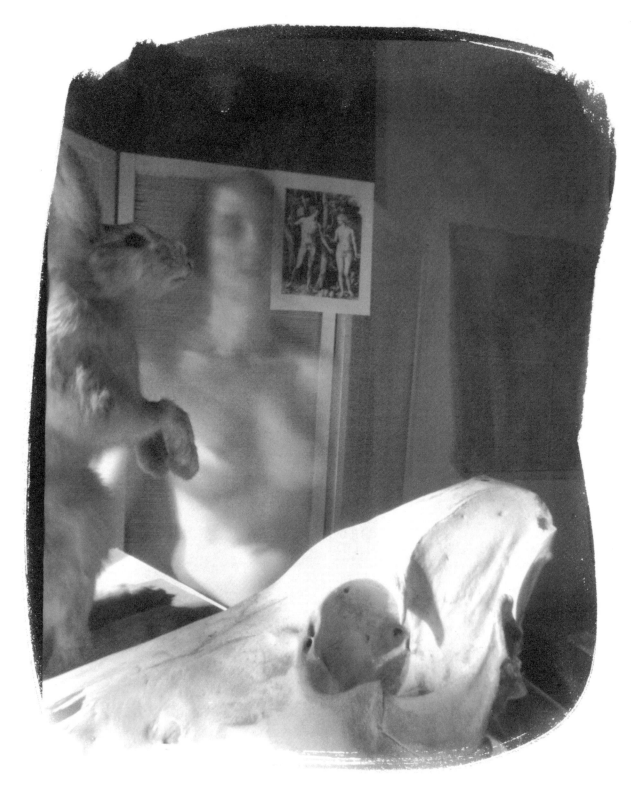

Figure 7.7 © *Jesseca Ferguson*, In My Studio (Self/Pig Skull/Rabbit), *8" x 10" Van Dyck pinhole photograph, 1993. From the collection of the photographer.*

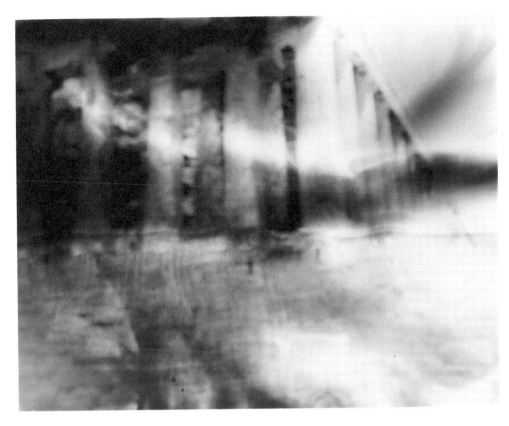

Figure 7.8 © *Nancy Spencer*, Parthenon, *11" x 14" pinhole photograph, 1998. From the collection of the photographer.*

which is a fine example of camera and image as one, and Adam Füss's *Pinhole Photographs* (1996). Pinhole photographers published their own works: Jurgen Konigs (*Triviale Objekte,* 1995), Marja Pirilä (*The Eyes of the Fingertips are Opening,* 1993), Scott McMahon (*Suspended Passages,* 1995), Peter Olpe (*Die Lochkamera von Peter Olpe,* 1993; *Die Lochkamera, Funktion und Selbstbau,* 1995), William Eakin (*Monuments,* 1998), Ilan Wolff (*Ilan Wolff, Camera Obscura at Work 1982–1997,* 1998), Jochen Dietrich (*Cine-teatros de Portugal,* 1998), and Thomas Kellner (*Deutschland Blick nach Draussen,* 1988). Hans Knuchel's slit and pinhole images with cameras were beautifully documented in *Hans Knuchel: Camera Obscura* (Lars Müller Publishers, 1991). Renée O'Brien through New York University published her doctoral dissertation *The Post-Romantic Vision of Contemporary Pinhole Photographers* (1998).

By 1999 *Pinhole Journal* was publishing in its fifteenth year. International pinhole group exhibitions were presented in the United States (The Gleaning Light, Austin), Canada (Lonsdale Gallery, Toronto), and New Zealand (The World Through a Pinhole, Wellington). The British Broadcasting Company produced and broadcast a documentary on the Welsh pinhole photographer David Gepp (1996), a photograph from his *Venice* series is shown in Color Plate 7.9. Commercial large-format four-inch by five-inch cameras were widely available. Along with the Lenseless Camera of Santa Barbara were the Robert Rigby camera (1995), the Leonardo camera (1995) designed by the author, the Finney Pinhole Field Camera (1996), and the Finney UltraWide (1998) designed by Kevin Finney. In Europe the 503 (Lochkamera) using 120 roll film (1998) was commercially produced by Lorelei Grazier (Peter Olpe acted as project coordinator) at the Basel School of Design. A pinhole mailing list was begun on the Internet by James Kellar at http://www.eGroups.com/list/pinhole. During the 1990s the number of pinhole gallery Web sites expanded daily, visibly documenting pinhole interest on the Internet. One of the best is Gregg Kemp's pinhole.com. Kemp, who has worked in pinhole since the 1970s, has created an international gallery and information Web site.

The Primal Experience

The sensibilities inherent in the soft focus of pinhole images have been widely accepted by Madison Avenue (just look in any magazine for advertisements that are in soft focus; the number you find is a reflection of the acceptance of pinhole imagery). It is not surprising therefore that in the early 1990s, *Art in America* and *Artforum* published pinhole photographs on their covers, made by the New York–based pinhole photographer Barbara Ess. The context of photography is now so broad that all means of photographic expression are viable. Whether the image is produced by means of computer, lens camera, television, video, or pinhole camera is no longer an issue. Altered imagery is a perfectly reasonable starting place—plenty of people are using pinhole cameras. What is important is the aesthetic context. In the 1990s the primal experience is one of the primary aesthetic contexts. The dark (Scott McMahon, Figure 7.10), the bizarre (Robert Oehl, Color Plate 7.11), the earthly life-force states (including death), the demonic (Laura Carton, Figure 7.12) are all in the forefront. Therefore, the "look" of Ess's image was of utmost importance. It had to be primal. That she used a pinhole camera only accentuated the novelty of her image-making process. In an interview conducted by P. C. Smith for the *Art in America* article, Barbara Ess stated:

> That my work is done with a pinhole is the least interesting part. At first I felt like a scientist; now it's just a tool that I use. But I use primal imagery, so maybe it's fitting that I use the most primitive of cameras. Since there's no viewfinder, the image is much more of a surprise—as if some outsider came and looked at earth for the first time. . . .
>
> I do drawings before I photograph; it's like being a painter. I'm looking for something in the world that will speak. I try to photo-

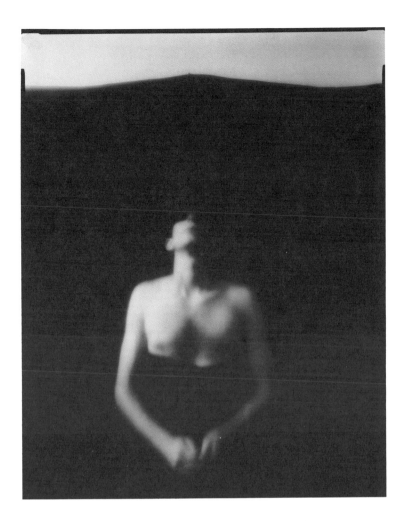

Figure 7.10 © *Scott McMahon*, Set for the Rise, *8" x 10" zone plate photograph printed in gum bichromate, 1997. From the collection of the photographer.*

graph what can't be photographed—psychological or subjective reality, which seems more real than physical or consensual reality. It's a different idea of vision.[8]

The Primal Performance

In December 1993 the Museum of Modern Art in New York mounted an exhibition of pinhole cameras and photographic pieces by London photographer Steven Pippin. Pippin's washing machine pinhole camera is mentioned earlier in the preface to this book. All Pippin's cameras as performance pieces are perfect examples of the primal experience. Pippin's toilet camera received the most notoriety. As an icon, everyone loves a toilet. Immediately, a toilet suggests an artistic assault on conventional sensibilities. That Pippin's toilet was a complete pinhole camera, with light-tight porcelain body and light-sensitive material curved underwater accentuated the novelty of his image-making process. The look of Pippin's image was of utmost importance. It had to be primal. Had he held a Nikonos (Nikon's underwater lens camera)

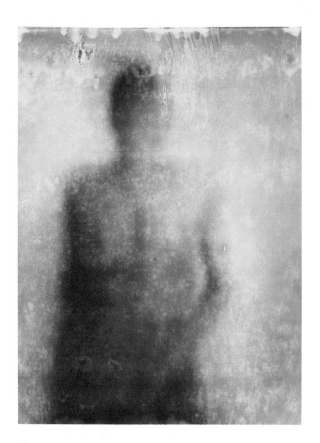

Figure 7.12 © *Laura Carton, Untitled, 9½" x 12½" zone plate photograph, 1996. From the collection at Pinhole Resource.*

under the water in a toilet bowl pointing it upward, his image would have never answered the aesthetic. The exhibition was intended to titillate and at the same time create wonder. Robert Evrén, curatorial assistant in the department of drawings at MOMA wrote the catalog. Evrén observed:

> In each case Pippin's instruments of choice have been the pinhole camera and paper negative, the same ones used by the inventors of photography in the early nineteenth century. In recent times, this method has been favored only by obsessive antiquarians and occasionally snoopers. [9]

By "snoopers" Evrén is referring to a newspaper photograph he saw on a trip to London of the late Diana, Princess of Wales, working out at a gym. Purportedly, a pinhole camera had been installed in the ceiling to secretly take her photograph. It is open to question whether pinhole photographers are "obsessive antiquarians."

Pippin wrote the following for the catalogue of his exhibit:

> The future of photography seems to rely on the progress of the camera and its ability to be continually refined, to a point whereby images will be indistinguishable from reality. Working in the opposite direction to this mentality I have become fascinated with the idea of constructing a camera whose viewpoint is not some external subject, but instead one having the capability of looking back in on itself toward its own darkness.

Pippin described his pinhole toilet camera as follows:

> Using a large black cloak to prevent fogging, a semi-circular piece of photographic paper was formed into a cone and pushed into a toilet bowl. An attachment made from wood, rubber, and fabric was then fitted onto the toilet and inflated. A small aperture in the top of the cover projected an image of the room down into the toilet. After the exposure (approximately 40 minutes), developer was added to the cistern and heated using a small portable electric element wired to the light fitting. Once the water reached 20 degrees C the toilet was flushed, processing the image in the bowl. [10]

Joseph Jakusz, of Nevada, makes motion photographs that involve a tunnel vortex. In Color Plate 7.13a the tunnel is clear light, suggesting through metaphor that we have made it to the other side. In Color Plate 7.13b the tunnel remains dark, suggesting we are still traveling. That we are!

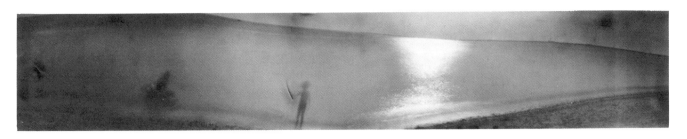

Figure 7.14 © *Marian Roth*, Child at the Beach, $2\frac{1}{2}$" x $13\frac{1}{2}$" *pinhole photograph from a cookie tin pinhole camera, 1998. From the collection of the photographer.*

In this book we have traversed more than a century and a half of photographic history and almost six thousand years of pinhole technique, from Mo Ti's first written account observing the formation of a pinhole image to the present day. We still find the pinhole camera a means to expressive response (Figures 7.14 and 7.15). This book is not meant to suggest that everything possible has been done with pinhole. Quite the opposite is true. There is much, much more to explore in the twenty-first century.

NOTES

1. Samuel Y. Edgerton Jr., *The Heritage of Giotto's Geometry: Art and Science on the Eve of the Scientific Revolution* (Ithaca, NY: Cornell University Press, 1993), 289.
2. Ilan Wolff, personal communication with the author, 15 June 1988.
3. Thomas Bachler, personal communication with the author, 10 February 1994.
4. Leah V. Stubbs, personal communication with the author, 6 January 1999.
5. Harlan Wallach, "Chicago Murder Sites: Works in Progress," *Pinhole Journal* 8(1992):9.
6. Patrick Poels, personal communication with the author, 6 August 1993.
7. Jesseca Ferguson, personal communication with the author, 23 February 1994.
8. P. C. Smith, "Complex Vision," *Art in America* (March 1993):69.
9. Robert Evrén, catalogue notes from *Projects 44*, Sarah Lucas, Steven Pippin (New York: The Museum of Modern Art, 1993), unpaginated.
10. Steven Pippin, *The Rigmarole of Photography* (London: Institute for Contemporary Arts, 1993), 52.

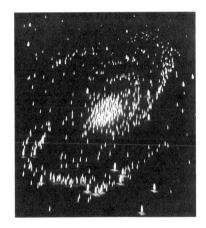

Figure 7.15 © *Dianne Bos*, Galaxy M 81 by Candle Light, *1999. 11" x 14" pinhole photograph. To make this image Bos created an aperture plate drilled with hundreds of differing sized pinholes that conformed to the look of Galaxy M 81—then one candle was photographed. From the collection of the photographer.*

List of Suppliers

Nonprofit Organizations

Pinhole Resource
Star Route 15, Box 1355
San Lorenzo, NM 88041
(505) 536-9942
E-mail: pinhole@gilanet.com
Web site: pinholeresource.com
(*Pinhole Journal*—published three times a year; pinhole photo archive, pinhole cameras, pinhole body caps, pinholes, zone plates, books on pinhole, and other pinhole products.)

Private Individuals Selling Pinhole Products

W. Joseph Christiansen
7586 County H
Maplewood, WI 54226
(414) 856-6842
(Pinholes, viewing pinholes, drills, pin vises.)

Dominique Stroobant
11 Via Fantiscritti
1.54033 Miseglia di Carrara
Italy
(Lensless Leica pinhole mounts.)

Kurt Mottweiler
2 Bonito Court
Santa Fe, NM 87505
(120 roll film pinhole cameras.)

Robert Rigby
Store Street
Bollington, Macclesfield
Cheshire SK10 5PN
England
01625-575591
(Pinhole cameras.)

Lenseless Camera of Santa Barbara
P.O. Box 20163
Santa Barbara, CA 93120
(805) 966-1181
(Pinhole cameras.)

Jay Bender
19619 Highway 209
Leavenworth, WA 98826
(Bender View cameras—can be ordered with pinholes.)

Black Cat Photo Products
3410 Harney Street
Vancouver, WA 98660
(888) 272-4708
(*Black Cat Exposure Guide*, useful for pinhole.)

Photo Mail Order Corporations Selling Pinhole Products

Calumet Photographic
890 Supreme Drive
Bensenville, IL 60106
(888) 367-2781
(Pinhole cameras, pinholes, pinhole body caps.)

Beseler
1600 Lower Road
Linden, NJ 07036
(800) 237-3537
(Pinhole cameras.)

Freestyle Sales
5124 Sunset Boulevard
Los Angeles, CA 90027
(800) 292-6137
(Pinhole cameras.)

High-tech Suppliers

Below are the addresses of several companies dealing in products of possible interest to the pinhole photographer. (List compiled by Tom Fuller.)

Edmund Scientific Company
101 East Gloucester Pike
Barrington, NJ 08007-1380
(609) 573-6260
(Tools, optics, black flocking, and general scientific equipment. Ask for their *Annual Reference Catalog.*)

Ealing Electro-Optics, Inc.
New Englander Industrial Park
Holliston, MA 01746
(800) 343-4912
(Manufacturers of advanced optical equipment for research and industry; they carry precision zinc, copper, and stainless steel pinhole discs.)

Melles Griot
1770 Kettering Street
Irvine, CA 92714
(800) 835-2626
(Same general product line as Ealing.)

Index